D1622678

109 Walks
in British Columbia's
Lower Mainland

Woodstock Public Library

Woodstock Public Library

JOHN HALLIDAY • ALICE PURDEY
MARY & DAVID MACAREE

109
WALKS

in British Columbia's
Lower Mainland

Revised and updated eighth edition

WOODSTOCK PUBLIC LIBRARY WITHDRAWN

GREYSTONE BOOKS
Vancouver/Berkeley

Copyright © 1976, 1982, 1990, 1997, 2002, 2009 by Mary and David Macaree
Copyright © 2014, 2019 by John Halliday and Alice Purdey

19 20 21 22 23   5 4 3 2 1

All rights reserved. No part of this book may be reproduced, stored in a retrieval system or transmitted, in any form or by any means, without the prior written consent of the publisher or a licence from The Canadian Copyright Licensing Agency (Access Copyright). For a copyright licence, visit www.accesscopyright.ca or call toll free to 1-800-893-5777.

Greystone Books Ltd.
greystonebooks.com

Cataloguing data available from Library and Archives Canada
ISBN 978-177164-431-0 (pbk.)
ISBN 978-1-77164-432-7 (epub)

Editing by Lucy Kenward (eighth edition)
Copy editing by Alison Jacques
Proofreading by Alison Strobel
Cover and interior design by Nayeli Jimenez
Cover photograph of Whyte Islet, West Vancouver, by Wan Ru Chen/ Getty Images
Interior photographs by John Halliday, except as noted
Maps by Mary Macaree and Gray Mouse Graphics

Printed and bound in Canada on ancient-forest-friendly paper by Friesens

Greystone gratefully acknowledges the Musqueam, Squamish and Tsleil-Waututh peoples on whose land our offices are located.

We gratefully acknowledge the financial support of the Canada Council for the Arts, the British Columbia Arts Council, the Province of British Columbia through the Book Publishing Tax Credit and the Government of Canada through the Canada Book Fund for our publishing activities.

Greystone Books is committed to reducing the consumption of old-growth forests in the books it publishes. This book is one step towards that goal.

Canada

BRITISH COLUMBIA   BRITISH COLUMBIA ARTS COUNCIL
An agency of the Province of British Columbia

Canada Council   Conseil des arts
for the Arts   du Canada

CONTENTS

INTRODUCTION

WELCOME! WE INVITE you to explore, on foot, the outstanding urban walks and forest trails of the Lower Mainland. The abundant natural beauty and the joy of walking will surely elevate your personal happiness. Most of the walks in this book are on the traditional territories of Indigenous peoples: the Musqueam, Squamish, Tsleil-Waututh, Katzie, Kwikwetlem, Chilliwack, Kwantlen, Tsawwassen, Semiahmoo, Matsqui, Sumas and Sts'ailes. Their long stewardship of land and water resources and traditions is an essential element of what makes the Lower Mainland unique.

This eighth edition of *109 Walks* walking guide continues the pattern set by the original authors, Mary and David Macaree, by describing walks that are generally less than 4 hours long with, for the most part, modest elevation gains, if any, over well-marked, easy to moderate terrain.

We have added twenty-five new walks, including five old-timers, in this edition. All of the walks retained from the seventh edition have been walked recently and the descriptions and maps updated accordingly. Time and change stand still for no one, and alterations to trail conditions continue to occur, including disruptions and improvements wrought by municipal works and natural devastation. Perhaps the most common change is the growth of trees that obscure once-fine views!

WHAT IS A WALK?

What is a walk compared to a hike? Is it smoothness of path? Elevation gain? Distance? Length of time taken? Given the nature of the terrain in the Lower Mainland, the terms are often used interchangeably. However, to distinguish these walks from the outings described in the book *105 Hikes In and Around Southwestern British Columbia*, the characteristics for inclusion here are:

4 hours or less, elevation gain of 400 m (1300 ft) or less and clearly established, well-marked routes. The elevation gains are not cumulative; they're a simple measure of the difference between your starting point and the high point of the walk. How much time a walk will take depends on the state of the trail and its ups and downs, as well as your walking pace. We provide liberal time estimates, assuming a consistent pace.

RATINGS

The walks are rated subjectively by difficulty and quality to help you select a walk that you will enjoy.

Difficulty

● *Easy:* little or no elevation gain, mainly even surface, distance no more than 10 km (6.2 mi)

■ *Moderate:* some elevation gain, includes uneven trail or stairs, distance of 10 km (6.2 mi) or more

◆ *Challenging:* over 300 m (984 ft) elevation gain, mainly rough trail

Quality

★ *Urban:* predominantly streets and paved greenway; traffic noise intrudes.

★★ *Urban/Natural:* predominantly streets and paved greenway with some trail through natural area; some traffic noise intrudes.

★★★ *Natural/Multi-user:* More trail through natural area than streets, may be shared with bicycles; reasonably quiet, some traffic noise may intrude.

★★★★ *Natural/Quiet:* A remarkable outdoor experience; predominantly trail, though not necessarily wild; quiet, very little traffic noise intrudes; may be shared with bicycles.

★★★★★ *Wilderness:* A preserved natural habitat for plants, wildlife and humans who need recharging; quiet, no traffic noise intrudes.

SHINRIN-YOKU 森林浴

Shinrin-yoku, a Japanese term that translates as forest bathing, means to immerse oneself in the forest atmosphere, absorbing the forest through the senses. A forest bath disconnects you from technology and allows you to de-stress and relax. Scientists have proven that shinrin-yoku has many health benefits, including lowering blood pressure, lifting depression and elevating the immune system.

Briefly, to practise shinrin-yoku, you find a spot, leave your phone behind and walk slowly while allowing your senses to guide you. Listen, look, smell, taste and touch the environment. In this book, we have suggested several excellent places to practise shinrin-yoku.

TERRAIN

Metro Vancouver sits atop once-forested rolling hills, creeks now buried in drains and estuaries now altered beyond recognition. However, visionary community planners have preserved for us urban oases of nature both large and small. And they continue to do so with the ongoing construction of picturesque intra- and interurban greenways and pathways that are shared by walkers and cyclists.

The walks in this book offer a wide range of terrain. In or near the urban settlement, there are walks through protected forest and ravines surrounded by busy city activities. Farther afield, there are gentle trails adjacent to rivers, dyked marshes and ocean shores and trails through farmlands abandoned or active. Many are on multi-use paths. Dykes and greenways are shared with bicycles and horses; mountainside trails may be shared with mountain bikers. Beyond the urban boundaries, mainly north of Burrard Inlet, there are trails on mountainsides, in valleys and through wild forests.

As well, part of the pleasure of walking is in combining it with other pursuits: watching birds, observing plant life and geological features, practising shinrin-yoku, observing the variety of activity on rivers and waterways and thinking about the local history.

USING THIS BOOK

We have arranged the book in sections that run from north to south and west to east. Each walk is presented with quick facts, a trail map, a walk description with, where applicable, a longer or shorter option, and access directions. The quick facts give you at-a-glance information about the walk, such as round-trip time, length of walk and difficulty. The trail map illustrates the route in relation to local natural and human-built features. Familiarize yourself with the Key to Map Symbols on page 7 to better understand the symbols used on the maps. The walk description presents a guided tour of the trail by describing important junctions and landmarks and by pointing out natural and historical items of interest. And an accompanying photo provides a tantalizing visual clue to the nature of the walk. Some walks can accommodate all-terrain strollers and we've indicated these with the symbol ⚲. We have not identified walks accessible by wheelchair; these are designated as such in park brochures, on websites or on a sign at the trailhead. Distances and elevations are given in both metric and imperial units, except for distances of less than one kilometre; these are given in metres. The access directions provide detailed travel instructions to the trailhead by transit, where available, and by vehicle. We have included key intersection coordinates for people who use a car GPS (but if you don't, paper maps still work!) and trailhead latitude-longitude coordinates for hand-held devices.

SAFETY

Personal safety may be of concern on the non-urban walks where there are fewer people. Accidents—a twisted ankle, a serious medical problem—can happen unexpectedly. Would anyone know if you did not return home? Leave a note with someone as to your destination and expected time of return. It's always a good idea to carry a small first-aid packet, some water, snacks, a jacket and hat, a whistle and a lightweight flashlight. And of course, sturdy footwear is essential. Toes stubbed or feet cut by unseen hazards can ruin an outing.

Be aware that you cannot rely entirely on your cellphone in case of trouble on the more remote walks, as batteries may fail and reception may be patchy or nil. Be prepared for the unforeseen. People do occasionally get lost, so a map and compass (know how to use them!) would provide a good back-up.

During the late spring and summer months you may see a bear alert sign posted at a trailhead. Should you choose to continue, know what to do if you see a bear. To learn more, see www.bearsmart.com/play/bear-encounters.

OUTDOOR ETIQUETTE

Unpaved trails are subject to damage with the passage of many feet. Mud holes can develop in soggy areas and these grow ever larger when walkers try to go around them. Shortcutting on mountain slopes leads to erosion and rapid deterioration of the footbed. Please be aware of these issues and do your part to maintain the integrity of a trail. Another way to help is to carry an extra bag in which to pack out your garbage and the trash carelessly left behind by others.

What if you get the urge "to go"? The locations of toilets are noted on the maps where these exist, but if they don't? In the forest, please be considerate of others and bury your waste and carry out your toilet paper to avoid unsightliness.

DOGS

The human's best friend loves to go on walks with you, but please respect other trail users and wildlife. Use common sense and keep your dog under control at all times and out of wetlands and like habitat, the home to tiny living creatures. And, of course, scoop the poop and take it away with you. Many of the walks pass through parks that have designated off-leash areas within their boundaries.

PUBLIC TRANSPORTATION AND VEHICLE ACCESS

Walks accessible by public transportation are so noted in the *Getting There* section, with information about transit routes and stops provided. To plan your own transit route to a walk, visit the transit website for that area. For a list of websites, see the *Websites* section at the end of the book.

Vehicle access is described from the nearest major highway, though alternative approaches to a trailhead are possible. If you are unfamiliar with an area, you'll need to consult a map for directions or use the car GPS-entry street coordinates provided. These will take you to the nearest intersection or address from which you can follow directions in the walk's *Getting There* description.

Major, ongoing construction on the roads and highways may result in detours or delays. Please check road reports at www.drivebc.ca.

REFERENCES

A list of walking clubs and online references may be found at the end of this book. It is a good idea to check for the latest trail information, such as temporary closures, on a related website before setting out, especially during spring runoff or after heavy rains.

KEY TO MAP SYMBOLS

═════	highway	•—•	gate	✻	viewpoint
────	paved road	▭	parking lot	★	point of interest
==========	unpaved road	Ⓟ	parking	♠	old-growth tree
++++++	railroad	🚌	bus, SkyTrain, SeaBus stop	△	campground
------------	described trail	Ⓣ	toilets	⛩	picnic area
▬▬▬▬	trail is parallel to road	⚓	navigational light	⚘ ⚘	marsh
▬▬▬▬	walk on road or sidewalk	🗼	tower, water tower, lookout		tide flat
------------	other trail				
··········	route	⌂	school		river or stream
‖‖‖‖	stairway	⛪	church		waterfall
→	direction of travel	🏠	building, cabin or shelter		direction of river flow
][	bridge, boardwalk, trestle	▭	reservoir		body of water
▬ ▬ ▬	park boundary or other boundary		sports field (tennis court, soccer field, track)		
Λ Λ Λ	power line				
✕ ✕ ✕ ✕	fence				
•—•—•	ski lift				

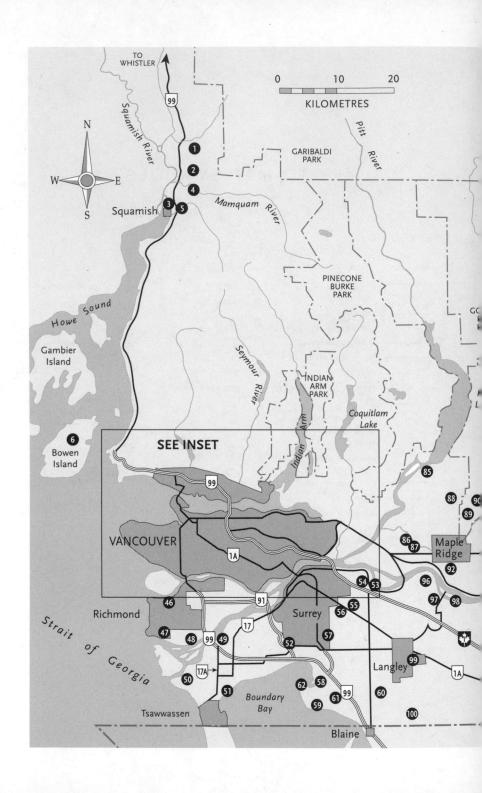

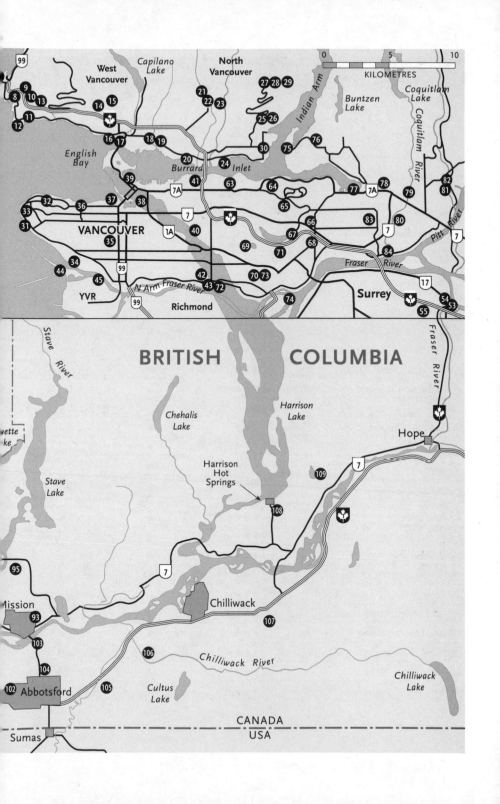

Walk	Quality	Difficulty	Distance
1 Four Lakes Trail	★★★★	●	7 km (4.3 mi)
2 Coho Park Loop	★★★★	■	4.8 km (3 mi)
3 Squamish Estuary Trail	★★★★	●	6 km (3.7 mi)
4 Mamquam Spawning Channels	★★★★	●	6 km (3.7 mi)
5 Smoke Bluffs Loop	★★★	■	3.5 km (2.2 mi)
6 Killarney Lake	★★★★★	●	8 km (5 mi)
7 Whytecliff	★★	●	4 km (2.5 mi)
8 Seaview/Larson Bay	★★★	●	6.7 km (4.2 mi)
9 Whyte Lake Loop	★★★★	◆	6 km (3.7 mi)
10 TCT/Nelson Creek Loop	★★★	◆	8.5 km (5.3 mi)
11 Caulfeild Trail/Klootchman Park	★★★	■	6.5 km (4 mi)
12 Lighthouse Park	★★★★★	■	6 km (3.7 mi)
13 Cypress Falls Park	★★★★	■	3 km (1.9 mi)
14 Hollyburn Heritage Trails	★★★★	◆	6.7 km (4.2 mi)
15 Brothers Creek Trails	★★★★	◆	11 km (6.8 mi)
16 Ambleside to Dundarave Seawalk	★★★	●	8.5 km (5.3 mi)
17 Bowser Trail Plus	★★	●	7.9 km (4.9 mi)
18 Mosquito Creek	★★★	■	8 km (5 mi)
19 Mahon Park	★★★★	●	5 km (3.1 mi)
20 Spirit Trail	★★★	●	8 km (5 mi)
21 Lynn Headwaters Loop	★★★ ★★★★	● ■	5.2 km (3.2 mi) 9 km (5.6 mi)
22 Rice Lake	★★★★	●	6 km (3.7 mi)
23 Fisherman's Trail	★★★★	■	13.6 km (8.5 mi)
24 Maplewood Flats	★★★	●	3.3 km (2 mi)
25 Historic Mushroom Loop	★★★	■	6.4 km (4 mi)
26 Three Chop/Old Buck Loop	★★★★	◆	7.7 km (4.8 mi)
27 Goldie and Flower Lakes	★★★★	●	4 km (2.5 mi)
28 Dog Mountain and Dinkey Peak	★★★	■	6 km (3.7 mi)
29 Mystery Lake and Peak	★★★	■	4.2 km (2.6 mi)
30 Indian Arm Parks	★★	■	10.5 km (6.5 mi)
31 Point Grey/Wreck Beach	★★★	■	10 km (6.2 mi)

Time	Elevation Gain	Shorter (S)/ Longer (L) Option	Stroller-Friendly	✓
2.5 hours				
2 hours	80 m (262 ft)			
2.5 hours				
1.5 hours		L	x	
1.5 hours	200 m (656 ft)			
3 hours		L		
1.5 hours				
2.5 hours				
3 hours	215 m (705 ft)			
3.5 hours	320 m (1050 ft)			
3 hours	100 m (328 ft)			
2 hours				
1.5 hours	152 m (500 ft)			
3.5 hours	315 m (1033 ft)			
4.5 hours	450 m (1475 ft)			
2.5 hours			x	
3 hours				
2.5 hours	210 m (689 ft)			
1.5 hours				
3 hours			x	
1.5 hours 3 hours	200 m (656 ft)	L		
2 hours		S	x	
4 hours	140 m (460 ft)			
1 hour			x	
2.5 hours	275 m (902 ft)	L		
3 hours	545 m (1788 ft)			
1.5 hours		L		
3 hours		S		
2 hours	200 m (656 ft)			
3 hours		S		
3.5 hours				

Walk	Quality	Difficulty	Distance
32 Chancellor Woods	★★★	●	6 km (3.7 mi)
33 UBC Gardens Tour	★★	●	5 km (3.1 mi)
34 Musqueam/Fraser River	★★★	●	8 km (5 mi)
35 Arbutus Greenway	★	■	12 km (7.5 mi)
36 Hastings Mill to Spanish Banks	★★	●	6 km (3.7 mi)
37 Kitsilano/False Creek	★★	●	7 km (4.3 mi)
38 False Creek	★★	●	8 km (5 mi)
39 Canada Place to Brockton Point	★★	■	12 km (7.5 mi)
40 Renfrew Neighbourhood	★★	●	5 km (3.1 mi)
41 New Brighton Park/Hastings Park	★★	●	6.5 km (4 mi)
42 The 3-C Circuit	★★★	●	5.5 km (3.4 mi)
43 Vancouver Fraser Foreshore	★★★	●	8 km (5 mi)
44 Iona Island Duo	★★★ ★★★	● ●	8 km (5 mi) 6 km (3.7 mi)
45 McDonald Beach Park/Pirates Cove	★★★	●	6.5 km (4 mi)
46 Lulu Island Dykes	★★★	■	18 km (11.2 mi)
47 Steveston Greenway	★★	●	8 km (5 mi)
48 South Dyke Trail	★★★	●	8.5 km (5.3 mi)
49 Deas Island Regional Park	★★★	●	4.4 km (2.7 mi)
50 Brunswick Point	★★★★	●	10 km (6.2 mi)
51 Boundary Bay Duo	★★★ ★★★	● ●	8.5 km (5.3 mi) 4.5 km (2.8 mi)
52 Watershed Park to Mud Bay	★★	■	14 km (8.7 mi)
53 Barnston Island	★★	●	10 km (6.2 mi)
54 Surrey Bend	★★★★	●	5 km (3.1 mi)
55 Tynehead Regional Park	★★★	●	5.5 km (3.4 mi)
56 Green Timbers Urban Forest	★★★ ★★★	● ●	3 km (1.9 mi) 5 km (3.1 mi)
57 Surrey Lake/Fleetwood Park	★★★★	●	7 km (4.3 mi)
58 Elgin Heritage Trail	★★★	●	7 km (4.3 mi)
59 South Surrey Urban Forests	★★★	●	3 km (1.9 mi)
60 Redwood Park	★★★★	●	4.5 km (2.8 mi)
61 Semiahmoo Trail	★★★	●	8 km (5 mi)

Time	Elevation Gain	Shorter (S)/ Longer (L) Option	Stroller-Friendly	✓
2 hours		S		
2 hours				
2.5 hours				
3.5 hours		S & L	X	
2 hours			X	
2.5 hours			X	
2.5 hours			X	
3.5 hours			X	
2 hours			X	
2.5 hours			X	
1.5 hours			X	
2.5 hours			X	
2.5 hours 2 hours			X	
2 hours		S		
5 hours		S	X	
2.5 hours			X	
2.5 hours			X	
1.5 hours			X	
2.5 hours			X	
3 hours 1.5 hours			X X	
4 hours			X	
2.5 hours			X	
2 hours				
2 hours		L	X	
1 hour 1.5 hours				
2.5 hours			X	
2 hours		S	X	
1.5 hours				
1.5 hours				
3 hours	110 m (361 ft)		X	

Walk	Quality	Difficulty	Distance
62 Blackie Spit/Crescent Beach	★★★	●	5.5 km (3.4 mi)
63 Confederation Park/Capitol Hill	★★★	■	6.2 km (3.9 mi)
64 Burnaby Mountain/SFU	★★★	■	8.5 km (5.3 mi)
65 Burnaby Mountain South	★★★	●	6.8 km (4.2 mi)
66 Stoney Creek/SFU	★★★	◆	8 km (5 mi)
67 Burnaby Lake	★★★	●	10 km (6.2 mi)
68 Brunette River	★★★	●	6 km (3.7 mi)
69 Deer Lake Park	★★★	●	7 km (4.3 mi)
70 Byrne Creek Ravine Park	★★★	●	3.5 km (2.2 mi)
71 Robert Burnaby Park	★★★	●	5.7 km (3.5 mi)
72 Burnaby Fraser Foreshore Park	★★★	●	8 km (5 mi)
73 Edmonds/New Westminster Quay	★	●	7 km (4.3 mi)
74 Queensborough Riverfront	★★	●	4 km (2.5 mi)
75 Belcarra Regional Park Duo	★★★★★ ★★★★★	● ■	5.2 km (3.2 mi) 5.5 km (3.4 mi)
76 Sasamat Lake/Woodhaven Swamp	★★★	●	8 km (5 mi)
77 Shoreline Trail	★★★★	●	6 km (3.7 mi)
78 Coquitlam Crunch Plus	★★★	■	5.7 km (3.5 mi)
79 Coquitlam River/Town Centre Park	★★★	●	9 km (5.6 mi)
80 Traboulay PoCo Trail/ Coquitlam River	★★★	●	10.5 km (6.5 mi)
81 DeBoville Slough/Pitt River	★★★	■	12 km (7.5 mi)
82 DeBoville Slough/Addington Marsh	★★★★	●	8.2 km (5.1 mi)
83 Mundy Park	★★★★	●	6 km (3.7 mi)
84 Colony Farm Regional Park	★★★	●	8 km (5 mi)
85 Grant Narrows	★★★★	■	12 km (7.5 mi)
86 Chatham Reach	★★★	■	11 km (6.8 mi)
87 Alouette River Dykes	★★★	■	14.8 km (9.2 mi)
88 UBC Research Forest	★★★★	◆	8 km (5 mi)
89 Mike Lake	★★★★	■	8 km (5 mi)
90 Alouette Nature Loop	★★★★	■	6 km (3.7 mi)
91 Gold Creek Lower Falls Trail	★★★★	●	5.4 km (3.4 mi)

Time	Elevation Gain	Shorter (S)/ Longer (L) Option	Stroller-Friendly	✓
1.5 hours		L		
2.5 hours	150 m (492 ft)	S		
3 hours	180 m (590 ft)	S		
2 hours				
3 hours	330 m (1082 ft)			
2.5 hours		S	X	
2 hours			X	
2.5 hours			X	
1.5 hours				
2 hours			X	
2.5 hours			X	
2.5 hours		L	X	
1.5 hours			X	
2 hours 2 hours				
3 hours		S		
2 hours			X	
2 hours	242 m (794 ft)			
3 hours			X	
3 hours				
3.5 hours			X	
2.5 hours		L	X	
2.5 hours			X	
2.5 hours			X	
4.5 hours		S		
3 hours		S	X	
4 hours			X	
3.5 hours	300 m (984 ft)	S		
2.5 hours	180 m (590 ft)	S		
2.5 hours	170 m (558 ft)			
2 hours			X	

Walk	Quality	Difficulty	Distance
92 Kanaka Creek Trails	★★★ ★★★★	● ●	3 km (1.9 mi) 3.3 km (2 mi)
93 Mission Trail	★★★	■	6.4 km (4 mi)
94 Hayward Lake: Railway Trail	★★★	■	12 km (7.5 mi)
95 Hayward Lake: Reservoir Trail	★★★★	●	8 km (5 mi)
96 Derby Reach Regional Park	★★★	●	8.5 km (5.3 mi)
97 Fort to Fort Trail	★★★	●	8 km (5 mi)
98 Brae Island	★★★★	●	4.2 km (2.6 mi)
99 Nicomekl Floodplain Trail	★★	●	6 km (3.7 mi)
100 Campbell Valley Regional Park	★★★★	■	11 km (6.8 mi)
101 Aldergrove Regional Park	★★★★	●	7 km (4.3 mi)
102 Discovery Trail/Fishtrap Creek	★★★	●	7.2 km (4.5 mi)
103 Matsqui Duo	★★★	■	14 km (8.7 mi)
104 Willband Creek Park	★★★	●	2.5 km (1.6 mi)
105 Arnold Dyke Trail	★★★	■	12 km (7.5 mi)
106 Heron Nature Reserve/Rotary Trail	★★★	■	14 km (8.7 mi)
107 Chilliwack Community Forest	★★★★	■	5 km (3.1 mi)
108 East Sector Lands	★★★★★	●	4.5 km (2.8 mi)
109 Hicks Lake/Sasquatch Park	★★★★	●	6.5 km (4 mi)

Time	Elevation Gain	Shorter (S)/ Longer (L) Option	Stroller-Friendly	✓
1 hour 1.5 hours			X	
2.5 hours	150 m (492 ft)			
3.5 hours		L		
3 hours		L		
2.5 hours		S	X	
2.5 hours		L	X	
1.5 hours			X	
2 hours			X	
4 hours		S		
2 hours		S	X	
3 hours		S	X	
4 hours			X	
1 hour			X	
3.5 hours		S	X	
4 hours		S	X	
2 hours	120 m (394 ft)			
2 hours				
2.5 hours		L		

FOUR LAKES TRAIL

Distance: 7 km (4.3 mi)
Time: 2.5 hours
Surface: trail
Quality: ★★★★
Difficulty: ●

Season: April to November
Car GPS entry: Alice Lake Rd & Sea-to-Sky Hwy Squamish, BC
Trailhead: 49°47'1" N 123°7'16" W

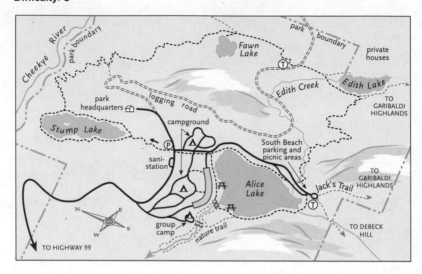

ALICE LAKE Provincial Park, a popular destination for families and campers, has a network of hiking trails. The longer Four Lakes Trail, as its name implies, links four lakes via a circuit through the forest, and two of these lakes, Stump and Alice, are encircled by their own trails, making shorter walks. Both Alice and Fawn Lakes are particularly nice for swimming.

On foot, backtrack a few paces from the parking lot to the information kiosk and the trailhead to Stump Lake. Your walk begins in thick bush, which thins out when you reach the fork where the arms of the Stump Lake circuit separate and you must choose your direction. The right branch gives glimpses over DeBeck Hill and towards the Tantalus Range; the left, of Mount Garibaldi and Alice Ridge. Gaps in the trees along the undulating trail provide peek-a-boo views of the lake and its sphagnum moss islets. The trails meet at the north end of the lake, where you turn left into lush understory.

Now you become aware of the increasing sound of rushing water; this is the Cheekye River to your left, flowing down from Mount Garibaldi. Plants such as skunk cabbage (swamp lantern) grow along this moisture-rich stretch.

View of Alpha Mountain from the Cheekye River. *Photo: Mary Halliday*

Next, you climb eastwards into a different environment, passing an escape route back to Alice Lake on the right, then rising to the trail's high point as you near Fawn Lake. Surrounded by young forest, Fawn Lake is a little off the trail to the right; where the spur road goes off to it, the foot trail you have been on becomes a firm road that takes you directly to Edith Lake.

On the way, you come to a major intersection, your route crossing the main approach to Alice (Cheekye) Ridge, an approach that predates creation of the park. Stay right at a fork just before the lake to go along the lake's west side until you come to a signposted junction. The route straight ahead leads to Thunderbird Ridge in Garibaldi Highlands, but you go right and uphill before descending to the South Beach of Alice Lake. From here, you may follow either shore to complete your outing. The east side is shorter and perhaps prettier, having views of DeBeck Hill across the water. However, if you choose the longer west and north sides, you may add a little nature walk on the Swamp Lantern Interpretive Trail at the lake's northwest corner.

Finally, at the lake's northeast corner, you walk up through the campsites to the park headquarters road and your starting point.

GETTING THERE

Transit: Better Environmentally Sound Transportation's Parkbus offers coach service on select summer weekends to Alice Lake Provincial Park from downtown Vancouver.

Vehicle: Drive Highway 99 (Sea-to-Sky Highway) north through Brackendale and watch for the Alice Lake Provincial Park turnoff. At the park entrance, keep left and drive uphill to a small parking area just beyond the sani-station instead of heading for the lake.

COHO PARK LOOP

Distance: 4.8 km (3 mi)
Time: 2 hours
Surface: trail, stairs
Elevation: 80 m (262 ft)
Quality: ★★★★
Difficulty: ■

Season: all year except when snow
Car GPS entry: BC-99 & Garibaldi Way
Squamish, BC
Trailhead: 49°44'32" N 123°07'31" W

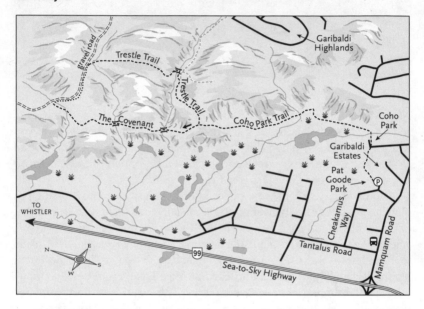

SQUAMISH IS world-renowned for its many challenging mountain biking trails. This outing in Squamish Nation territory takes you for a walk in the area around some of them.

To begin, walk through Pat Goode Park and along the residential street (Park Crescent) to the entrance to Coho Park. Cross the bridge and turn left to follow Coho Park Trail as it meanders through the forest along the creek to a signed junction. Take the left branch to stay on the Coho Park Trail as it bridges several creeks and skirts imposing blocks of Squamish granite. At the next junction, do not be alarmed at a sign stating "End of Coho Park Trail," for now you enter the realm of the mountain bikers and its quirky trail names. Note the trail to your right as your return path. However, take the left branch, named The Covenant, with its rougher path and gnarly bridges, to begin your loop.

The Covenant trail winding through the rainforest.

The trail traverses to the north before ascending to a junction with a gravel road. Go right and walk the road for about 350 m to a junction with a wide, unsigned trail on your right. Follow this trail, named Trestle, over flat terrain through an old cutblock, ignoring trails on your left and right. Drop into a ravine and cross a bridge before ascending to a junction. Go right to continue on Trestle, which parallels the ravine and then descends to the junction with Coho Park where you began the loop. Go left to follow your outbound route to the trailhead.

GETTING THERE

Transit: Take Squamish Transit Bus 2, 4, or 9 to Garibaldi Way and Tantalus Road. Walk east along Garibaldi Way for 250 m to Cheakamus Way. Continue on Cheakamus Way to the street on your right that leads to Pat Goode Park.

Vehicle: From Highway 99 (Sea-to-Sky Highway) and Cleveland Avenue, drive 4.5 km (2.8 mi) north and turn right at Garibaldi Way. Drive three blocks and turn left onto Cheakamus Way. Turn right to park at Pat Goode Park.

SQUAMISH ESTUARY TRAIL

Distance: 6 km (3.7 mi)
Time: 2.5 hours
Surface: gravel, trail
Quality: ★★★★
Difficulty: ●

Season: all year
Car GPS entry: Vancouver St & Cleveland Ave Squamish, BC
Trailhead: 49°44'02" N 123°06'58" W

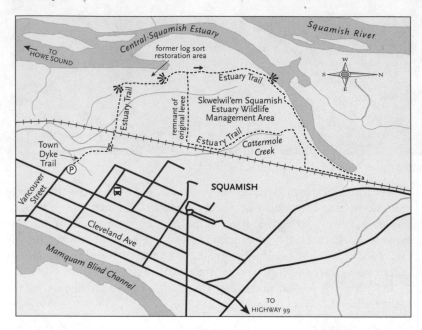

THE ESTUARY at the mouth of the Squamish River, in Squamish Nation territory, is successfully being reclaimed after decades of industrial activity. Originally, the Squamish people depended on the abundant fish and game of the estuary and had a village, Skwelwil'em, nearby. But an early farmer, George Magee, built levees with Chinese labour and drained the wetlands to provide hay for the oxen and horses used in logging from 1890 to 1910. Later, forestry work used the estuary for booming and shipping. Sawmills, a chemical plant and rail repair yards were situated on the flat land of the estuary. Today, the area around the estuary is popular with paddlers, kiteboarders, hikers and birders. The trails on this walk lie in the Skwelwil'em Squamish Estuary Wildlife Management Area (WMA) and take you through tidal mud flats, marshes and wetlands that now support abundant birdlife, salmon and mammals.

Mamquam Mountain with Smoke Bluffs in front.

To begin, take the gravel path—the Town Dyke Trail—that passes between a condo complex and a slough to the junction where you turn left and pass through a corridor in the trees to a railway crossing and a WMA information sign. Here you enter the estuary and, where the trail turns 90 degrees, you pass the log sort area currently undergoing restoration. Behind you, the imposing Stawamus Chief Mountain is in full view, and to its left you may see Mamquam Mountain in the distance behind Smoke Bluffs.

The trail, as it continues alongside the slough, is lined with cottonwood, alder, spruce and hemlock trees. Farther on, pop out to the edge of the slough for a view of Mount Garibaldi and Atwell Peak. At the railway tracks, turn right and follow the rough road to a crossing with a gravel road. Here you turn right and walk the gravel road while keeping a sharp eye out for the signed Estuary Trail on your left.

Follow this trail as it meanders beside Cattermole Creek until you, once again, encounter the railway tracks. And, once again, walk the road beside the tracks while keeping a sharp eye out for the signed Estuary Trail, this time on your right. This portion of the trail, which follows one of the original levees, is very rooty but also offers incredible views over the estuary to the Chief and Shannon Falls. At the T-junction, join your outbound route and go left past the log sort to return to the Town Dyke Trail and your starting point.

GETTING THERE

Transit: Take Squamish Transit Bus 1, 2, 3, 4 or 9 to Second Avenue at Main Street. Walk south on Second to Vancouver Street, turn right and follow to the end of the road.

Vehicle: From Highway 99 (Sea-to-Sky Highway), turn at Cleveland Avenue into downtown Squamish and follow to Vancouver Street. Turn right, drive to the end and park at yellow gate.

MAMQUAM SPAWNING CHANNELS

Distance: 6 km (3.7 mi)
Time: 1.5 hours
Surface: gravel
Quality: ★★★★
Difficulty: ●

Season: all year
Car GPS entry: Mamquam Rd & High-
lands Way S Squamish, BC
Trailhead: 49°44'2" N 123°6'58" W

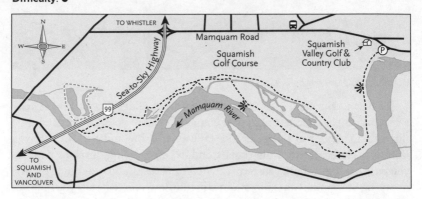

THE SPAWNING channels that lie between the Squamish Valley golf course and the Mamquam River are a fine example of a community caring for and restoring fish habitat. This pleasant and quiet area in Squamish Nation territory combines access to the fast-flowing Mamquam River, trails shaded by cottonwoods and alder, birdsong and, from November to January, the spawning runs of chum and coho salmon. Occasionally, a black bear passes through, to feed on nature's smorgasbord of berries and salmon.

Soon after you leave the parking lot, the trail emerges beside the golf course and a tee box. Please heed the warning signs and proceed only when it is safe to do so. As you pass the golf course, notice the original old-growth tree stumps on the fairway and the view to the mountains. Soon thereafter you reach a junction with an information sign that describes the life cycles of chum and coho salmon and, on the opposite side, presents a trail map. Here begin the spawning channels and a network of trails amongst them. Start by taking the left trail for a forest walk between the Mamquam River and the channels. Look for a trail on your left where you can pop out to the river for a downstream view to the mountains. Keep left at forks and reach a bridge over the spawning channel. At the T-junction, go left again and, keeping the river on your left, continue west, passing under power lines and arriving at the bridge that takes Highway 99 over the Mamquam River. This is your turnaround spot.

The fast-flowing Mamquam River.

On your return, follow the trail parallel to the highway, cross the Mashiter spawning channel and follow the trail along the north side of it. Just beyond where you rejoin your outbound route, you'll reach a junction. Go left on the trail along the edge of the golf course. Trails to your right may capture your curiosity and entice you to wander as you make your way east and return to your starting point.

LONGER OPTION

For an extended walk of another 2 km (1.2 mi), you may continue on the trail under the highway bridge to explore more spawning channels and, perhaps, reach the confluence of the Mamquam and Squamish Rivers.

GETTING THERE

Transit: Take Squamish Transit Bus 9 (Quest University/Downtown) to Mamquam Road and Highlands Way South. Walk east along Mamquam Road for 500 m, staying right at the fork with Paco Road, to the trailhead.

Vehicle: From Highway 99 (Sea-to-Sky Highway) and Cleveland Avenue, drive 4.5 km (2.8 mi) north and turn right at Mamquam Road. Continue past the golf course and park at the trailhead parking, about 100 m beyond the Squamish Valley Golf & Country Club parking lot.

SMOKE BLUFFS LOOP

Distance: 3.5 km (2.2 mi)
Time: 1.5 hours
Surface: path, stairs
Elevation: 200 m (656 ft)
Quality: ★★★
Difficulty: ■

Season: all year except when snow
Car GPS entry: BC-99 & Cleveland Ave
Squamish, BC
Trailhead: 49°42'34" N 123°08'32" W

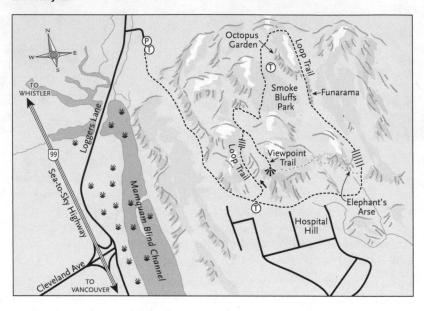

ALONG WITH its challenging mountain biking trails, Squamish is known as one of Canada's most important rock-climbing centres. Smoke Bluffs Park, established in 2006, protects a rock-climbing area with several hundred short, single-pitch routes on crystalline granite crags that offer smooth-face climbs and cracks of all sizes. This outing in Squamish Nation territory takes you past many of these crags with their quirky names, where, on dry days, they are festooned with ropes as people of all abilities can be seen working their way up the routes. A bluff-top viewpoint adds to your enjoyment with a panoramic view of the Squamish area.

Start at the information board at the end of the parking lot and follow the uphill trail that curves past the first of the crags. Ignore tracks on the left, which lead to the base of the climbs. At the next main junction, go left and continue as the trail surface changes to smooth granite slabs before entering a playground area.

Stawamus Chief Mountain from the Viewpoint Trail.

At the junction behind the composting toilet, go left and ascend on Loop Trail. At the junction with Viewpoint Trail, you may choose to take a short side trip to a bench on a bluff with a scenic view of Howe Sound, Squamish and the sheer walls of the Stawamus Chief. If you do, be sure to retrace your steps to Loop Trail. On Loop Trail, stay left and climb stairs and switchbacks always staying on Loop Trail/Upper Loop Trail at the signed junctions. Eventually you arrive at the Octopus Garden crag and, nearby, an outhouse toilet.

Soon after, the trail levels as you reach its highest point and begin your descent, on which you pass Funarama crag and, lower down, Elephant's Arse crag. At the junction at the bottom of steep steps, go left and descend a wooden staircase to an open area where you go right on level ground as you head back past houses to arrive at the playground to complete the loop. From here, follow your outbound path back to the parking lot.

GETTING THERE

Vehicle: At the intersection of Highway 99 (Sea-to-Sky Highway) and Cleveland Avenue, turn right onto Loggers Lane and follow it north past the Squamish Adventure Centre. Turn right at the parking lot for Smoke Bluffs Park.

KILLARNEY LAKE

Distance: 8 km (5 mi)

Time: 3 hours

Surface: paved roads, trails

Quality: ★★★★★

Difficulty: ●

Season: most of the year

Car GPS entry: Horseshoe Bay West Vancouver, BC

Trailhead (Cardena Road): 49°22'50" N 123°20'02" W

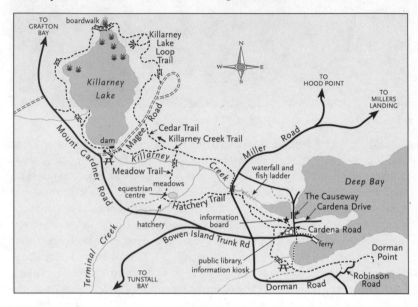

THIS EXCURSION begins with a delightful 20-minute ferry ride across Howe Sound from Horseshoe Bay to Bowen Island in Squamish Nation territory, with panoramic sights of mountains, forest and water. On disembarking at Snug Cove, walk one block north on Bowen Island Trunk Road and turn right on Cardena Road, the first intersection above the ferry terminal. The Secrets of Bowen Island brochure, which includes trail maps, may be available at the tourist centre or the trailhead.

Your route, along a well-signed trail system, begins about 100 m along Cardena Road at an information kiosk. Follow Aldergrove Trail, but divert briefly through the peacefully situated Memorial Garden with its view over Deep Bay to the mountains above Howe Sound. Continuing, you pass above a little stream, complete with fish ladders and viewing access, and arrive at Miller Road, which you cross onto Hatchery Trail. This leads you through mixed forest to a wide meadow and an intersection, with the hatchery to the

Looking east across Deep Bay to the mountains above Howe Sound. *Photo: Alice Purdey*

left. Go right, however, past the equestrian centre and cross the meadows to meet a major trail, where you proceed left for a short distance to another fork, this time going right on Cedar Trail to eventually come out on a country lane, Magee Road. On this lane, walk a few metres to the left before turning right onto Killarney Lake Loop Trail to begin your circuit of the lake.

The ground drops away to the left, giving glimpses of the lake through the trees and of the Mount Gardner massif behind. Then, finally, after a detour to a viewpoint, you reach marshy ground at the north end of the lake—a good place for bird watching. Boardwalks traverse this and another marsh on the west side as you stay on the Killarney Lake Loop, ignoring branches to the right. At the lake's south end, your track lies close to Mount Gardner Road; however, you soon turn left towards a picnic area by the lake's dam. Back at Magee Road, go left and cross the outlet; then, after a few metres, go right on a track that starts up the roadside bank and eventually rejoins the Killarney Creek Trail back to Miller Road. Here, you turn right to find your outward trail on the left just after crossing the bridge over Killarney Creek.

LONGER OPTION

If you have time before catching your ferry home, you might walk south across the picnic area near the ferry terminal and ascend the track on the wooded slope to Dorman Point, with more views of Howe Sound. The round trip is about 2 km (1.2 mi), but the steepness of the last part of the climb suggests that you should allow at least 45 minutes return.

GETTING THERE

Transit: Take TransLink Bus 250 (Horseshoe Bay/Dundarave/Vancouver) or 257 (Horseshoe Bay/Vancouver Express) to Horseshoe Bay Ferry Terminal.
Vehicle: Drive to Horseshoe Bay on Highway 1/99 (Upper Levels Highway) and follow signs to the village. There is paid parking near the ferry terminal. (Note: parking may be crowded seasonally and on long weekends.)

WHYTECLIFF

Distance: 4 km (2.5 mi)
Time: 1.5 hours
Surface: trail, paved
Quality: ★★
Difficulty: ●

Season: all year
Car GPS entry: Marine Dr & Dufferin Ave
West Vancouver, BC
Trailhead: 49°22'23" N 123°17'22" W

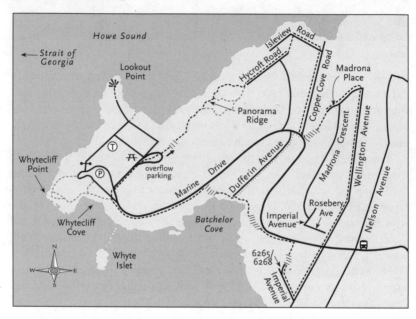

WHYTECLIFF PARK and Batchelor Cove are two worthwhile destinations at the westernmost end of West Vancouver. This outing links the two via a route along a natural ridge and along streets through attractive residential areas where you may follow your own inclinations.

On foot in Whytecliff Park, head towards the far end of the overflow parking lot to find the start of a steepish trail to Panorama Ridge, built over a waterline and, interestingly, through a not insignificant rock cut. What were once undoubtedly impressive views are now obstructed by tall trees, except for a snapshot north to Brunswick Mountain and Mount Harvey, with its nearby junior summit known as Harvey's Pup. Choosing left forks as you proceed brings you to the northern margin of the park. (If you wish to take only a short outing, turn back right, then left, re-joining your outward route for a return to the busier regions of the park. Now, you may drop down to the shore at Whytecliff Cove and then, if the tide is favourable, cross the causeway to Whyte Islet.)

For a longer circuit, mainly on streets, descend Hycroft Road at the park's northern extremity and go left at its bend to find a track connecting with Isleview Road. Walk down Isleview to its junction with Copper Cove Road, where you turn right. As you walk,

View across Whytecliff Cove to Whytecliff Point.

look for a few houses that appear to date from the early cottage days. Once at Marine Drive, you have a choice: a jog right then left onto Dufferin Avenue takes you to Batchelor Cove, a secluded little beach enclosed by rocky cliffs; alternatively, a jog left then quickly left again puts you onto an inconspicuous track with stairs up to Madrona Place. At Madrona Crescent, go left to Wellington Avenue.

Now it's an easy stride down Wellington, with an occasional backwards glance to the distant mountains, until you cross Rosebery Avenue and Marine Drive in quick succession. Then, just when you think you are approaching a dead end, you go right on Imperial Avenue, another cul-de-sac! But look to your right for the stone stairs between house numbers 6265 and 6268, which, despite first impressions, are public and lead to Marine Drive. Now, go left and, a few metres past house number 6678, you escape the busy road down another set of steps to Batchelor Cove.

Finally, to complete your outing, cross the beach to the western end of the cove where stairs ascend to Marine Drive and a picturesque 5-minute walk back to your starting point.

GETTING THERE

Transit: Take TransLink Bus 250 (Horseshoe Bay/Dundarave/Vancouver) to Marine Drive at Nelson and join the route at Wellington, one block west.

Vehicle: Travelling west on Highway 1/99 (Upper Levels Highway), take Exit 2 (Marine Drive–Eagleridge), veer left to cross the overpass, then stay with Marine Drive to Whytecliff Park.

8 WEST VANCOUVER
SEAVIEW/LARSON BAY

Distance: 6.7 km (4.2 mi)
Time: 2.5 hours
Surface: paved roads, trail
Quality: ★★★
Difficulty: ●

Season: all year
Car GPS entry: 5743 Cranley Dr West
Vancouver, BC
Trailhead: 49°21'37" N 123°15'47" W

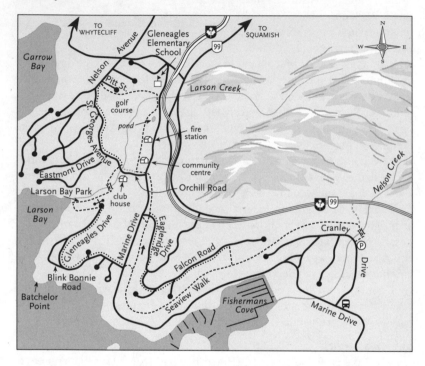

THIS WALK follows an abandoned railway right-of-way (Seaview Walk) and residential streets to its highlight, the secluded little Larson Bay.

You begin on a path beside Nelson Creek, almost beneath the towering Nelson Creek Bridge. Ascend for about 2 minutes to a junction where to the right is the tunnel entrance for the railway that once occupied the roadbed on which you now proceed west. The marine views and the plants, notably arbutus, bigleaf maples and mosses, provide the main attractions along this flat stretch.

Eventually you come to Eagleridge Drive, which you cross and continue beside Marine Drive to the crosswalk inscribed with Spirit Trail swirls, where you cross to Orchill Road. Follow the sign to Horseshoe Bay onto the gravel

The peeling bark of the arbutus tree is a familiar sight along Seaview Walk.

path that goes behind the Gleneagles Community Centre and the fire station and over the deck of a building to a small pond and footbridge. Continue alongside the golf course to its end, where you turn left immediately through a gap in the fence and, using the golf course fence as your guide, go through the parking lot and school playground, then up a slope on a rough trail and a left curve. Stay close to the fence until you exit onto St. Georges Avenue, near the junction with Nelson. Continue around the golf course on St. Georges until you come to a golfers' crossing, where you take the path that descends beside the fairway. Just beyond the tee box, a narrow track drops you into a different world, a little glen by a creek. Ignoring all trails on your left, keep descending until you emerge at Larson Bay and its enjoyable little beach.

From this peaceful spot, you may return to St. Georges, which curves into Orchill Road and meets Marine Drive opposite the western end of Seaview Walk, on which you return to your transportation. Alternatively, ascend the steep service road, which begins near the benches, to Gleneagles Drive; follow it right as it winds through this pleasant residential area to meet Marine Drive beside a bus stop. Directly across is a steep track, which you ascend on a rocky switchbacked trail for about 2 minutes until you reach Seaview Walk. Go right and you'll arrive back at your starting place in about 20 minutes.

GETTING THERE
Transit: Take TransLink Bus 250 (Horseshoe Bay/Dundarave/Vancouver) to Marine Drive at Cranley Drive or various stops to join the route midway.
Vehicle: Travelling west on Highway 1/99 (Upper Levels Highway), take Exit 4 (Caulfeild Road) and then left to Westport Road. Descend to Marine Drive and turn right; then, in the 5700 block, turn right again onto Cranley Drive. Park by the side of the road at Nelson Creek. If approaching from the north, access Marine Drive at Horseshoe Bay and follow it to Cranley Drive.

WHYTE LAKE LOOP

Distance: 6 km (3.7 mi)
Time: 3 hours
Surface: trail
Elevation gain: 215 m (705 ft)
High point: 335 m (1100 ft)

Quality: ★★★★
Difficulty: ◆
Season: most of the year
Car GPS entry: 5608 Westport Pl West
Vancouver, BC
Trailhead: 49°21'39" N 123°15'32" W

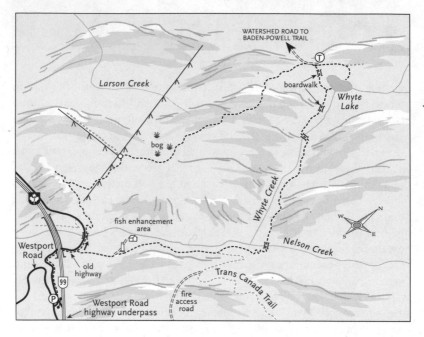

THE TRAIL to Whyte Lake, and beyond to Eagle Bluff, is attractive and popular; somewhat less travelled is the western side of the loop, which is more strenuous and passes near a fine grove of arbutus trees.

From the parking area, pass an information kiosk and a yellow gate on the old highway, then pass under the current highway to reach the original 1956 Nelson Creek Bridge. Your trail exits on the near side of the bridge, but your route, beginning with the more demanding part of the circuit, plunges into the bush at the bridge's west end.

You immediately begin to climb, zigzagging upwards and trending generally westwards before coming to a fork, at which you may take a detour left for about 5 minutes, your destination being a lovely mossy area with a grove of young arbutus trees. Back at the fork, you head up over rocks, many bare of soil but with enough sustenance to encourage a few flowers in spring— delightful white camas and tiny yellow mimulus. After you cross the power line and ascend a short distance in the forest beside it, you again emerge into the open, where a helipad invites you to rest. From the helipad, watch for a trail leading off to the right.

Next comes a very pleasant stretch, meandering and undulating past a boggy area with decaying bigleaf maple, mosses and ferns and through mixed woods with remnants of a fire that swept from Hollyburn Mountain to Eagle Harbour in 1884. Within about 15 minutes, at a junction, bear left on the more heav-

Whyte Lake is a peaceful spot amid first- and second-growth trees. *Photo: Buck Halliday*

ily used trail and descend to meet the old watershed road to Whyte Lake. Going left here takes you down to connect with the Baden-Powell Trail, but staying right you descend for a few minutes to a wider path, then to another fork. Note here the attractive outhouse with Dutch doors. Turn right to follow a sturdy boardwalk on what was an old logging road. Also note that dogs must be leashed in the Whyte Lake watershed.

Follow the boardwalk to the south end of the lake, then follow a short side trail to the left that leads to a new dock, where you can rest and enjoy the view and perhaps take a quick dip.

The time will come when you must continue. Your homebound route takes you down the left bank of the lake's outlet, Whyte Creek; through a stretch of magnificent old-growth forest; across Nelson Creek, which you stay alongside for a short distance; and uphill to join the Trans Canada Trail (TCT), which you descend to a service road, exiting at the 1956 bridge, thus completing the loop. (This walk connects to Walk 10 via the TCT, a convenient link should you wish to extend your ramblings in the area.)

GETTING THERE

Vehicle: From Highway 1/99 (Upper Levels Highway) take Exit 4 (Caulfeild Road–Woodgreen Drive), drive west past Headland Drive on Westport Road and, immediately after passing under Highway 1, go right into a parking lot.

TCT/NELSON CREEK LOOP

Distance: 8.5 km (5.3 mi)
Time: 3.5 hours
Surface: trail
Elevation gain: 320 m (1050 ft)
High point: 450 m (1475 ft)

Quality: ★★★
Difficulty: ◆
Season: most of the year
Car GPS entry: 5608 Westport Pl West
Vancouver, BC
Trailhead: 49°21'39" N 123°15'32" W

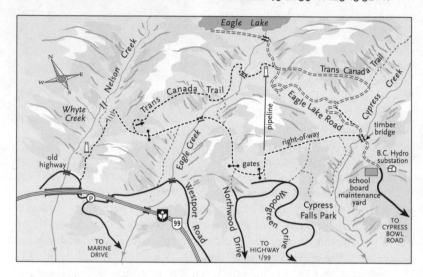

THIS TRAIL follows an undulating loop across the lower slopes of Black Mountain, with views over Burrard Inlet on a clear day. It is part of the Trans Canada Trail (TCT), which stretches 24,000 km (15,000 mi) and links the Pacific, Atlantic and Arctic Oceans.

From the information kiosk, walk along the old road and under the highway to a trail sign for Whyte Lake and TCT, just before a bridge over Nelson Creek. Ascend towards a water tower, to the right of which you embark on a delightful trail above the Nelson Creek canyon. Continue straight at a fork that goes to Whyte Lake (Walk 9). A sturdy set of stairs leads to the end of an abandoned road, which you follow briefly to a signed, significant trail leading left. This trail zigzags at first to gain elevation and often uses old forest roads amongst quite large second-growth trees. After about 15 minutes, you descend to a damp section near the small Eagle Creek. This you approach, then swing away left to arrive at a wooden bridge and a TCT sign pointing your way left at a junction. (Turning right offers you a shorter circuit.) Your track now rises, crosses the creek on a bridge, then emerges on the grassy waterline right-of-way, just below another water tower. It might surprise you to see a fire hydrant nearby; this and others are kept operational.

Next, you go right twice, skirting protected watershed lands and following the old Eagle Lake Road to meet the new, on which you go right again to a significant fork. Follow an old road to your right, signed Old Cypress Bowl Road. Take an immediate right again at a power line and, a few metres farther, watch for a path heading into the woods on your right. This leads to a mossy, rocky knoll with a good view of the entrance to Burrard Inlet and Vancouver, the perfect place for a break. Next, continue downhill as the trail becomes a gravel road and meets

Snow dusting the trail in winter. *Photo: Buck Halliday*

an actively used paved road. Just before a timber bridge over Cypress Creek, turn right onto a fire access road and follow it to another T-junction, where this time you drop left at another pipeline and hydrant. Above a residential area, go right through a gated fence with a sign disclaiming liability, erected by British Properties.

Now, homeward bound and some 10 minutes after passing through a second fence, note a road forking back on an angle then a trail angling in from another—your exit point if you had bailed out earlier. Continue westwards across Eagle Creek, encounter a third gated fence, pass your earlier TCT junction and continue downhill to your vehicle.

GETTING THERE
Vehicle: From Highway 1/99 (Upper Levels Highway), take Exit 4 (Caulfeild Road–Woodgreen Drive), drive west past Headland Drive on Westport Road and, immediately after passing under Highway 1, go right into a parking lot.

CAULFEILD TRAIL/ KLOOTCHMAN PARK

Distance: 6.5 km (4 mi)
Time: 3 hours
Surface: paved roads, trails, rocky bluffs, stairs
Elevation gain: 100 m (328 ft)

Quality: ★★★
Difficulty: ■
Season: all year
Car GPS entry: Marine Dr & Stearman Ave West Vancouver, BC
Trailhead: 49°20'24" N 123°14'34" W

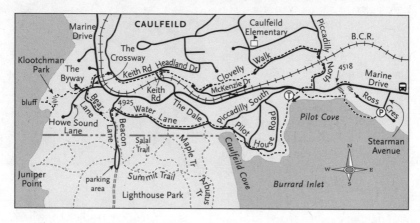

THIS EXCURSION highlights an oceanside and forested trail, water views, mature trees and rocky shores.

If the tide is out, you may start your walk along the beach accessed from the parking lot, then clamber up a low rocky buttress 200 m west onto the Caulfeild Trail, which is not immediately obvious as it passes in front of a house. Alternatively, walk west along Ross Crescent to its end, climb steps to Marine Drive, then, a few paces along, descend again just before house number 4518 to join the trail. Now your route undulates along the foreshore, out over rocky promontories and back amongst mature trees, until, moments beyond another access from Marine Drive, a side track descends to a sandy beach. After continuing along rocky bluffs overlooking the ocean, the trail emerges in a clearing, the site of an anchor embedded in a rock with a commemorative plaque to Francis Caulfeild, the visionary pioneer who designated the shoreline park. Exiting Caulfeild Trail, continue west on Pilot House Road and Piccadilly South, noting snug little Caulfeild Cove and, across The Green, the attractive church of St. Francis in the Woods, before you come to the junction with Water Lane and The Dale.

A bridge along Clovelly Walk.

Follow the ups and downs of Water Lane to the intersection with Beacon Lane, where you go left and, beside house number 4925, find a short track connecting with Bear Lane. Follow Bear Lane, go left on Howe Sound Lane and within 15 paces beyond The Byway, find the entrance to Klootchman Park. A narrow path and more than 100 steps descend to the pleasant, rocky shores—a must for arbutus-lovers.

Back at Howe Sound Lane, go left on The Crossway, which crosses the railway tracks to Keith Road. Turn right. Just past The Dale, go right into the Keith Road cul-de-sac; Clovelly Walk trail begins at its end. When you emerge onto pavement, go left at the next intersection onto Clovelly Walk. Continue on to the trail at the end of the street and re-emerge onto the paved street—Clovelly Walk again. Note the many mature, possibly original-growth cedars and Douglas-firs until you swing right to join Piccadilly North, descending over the tracks to Marine Drive. Turn right briefly to reach Caulfeild Trail, then left for the last lap of your outing.

GETTING THERE

Transit: Take TransLink Bus 250 (Horseshoe Bay/Dundarave/Vancouver) to Cypress Park Shopping Centre, walk west 100 m to Stearman Avenue and then south on Stearman to Ross Crescent. Go right for 45 m on Ross to the beach access road and trail.
Vehicle: Make your way to Marine Drive and Stearman Avenue. Drive south on Stearman, turn right onto Ross Crescent and then quickly left to park.

LIGHTHOUSE PARK

Distance: 6 km (3.7 mi)

Time: 2 hours

Surface: trails, granite slabs, stairs

Quality: ★★★★★

Difficulty: ■

Season: all year

Car GPS entry: Marine Dr & Beacon Ln
West Vancouver, BC

Trailhead: 49°20'17" N 123°15'48" W

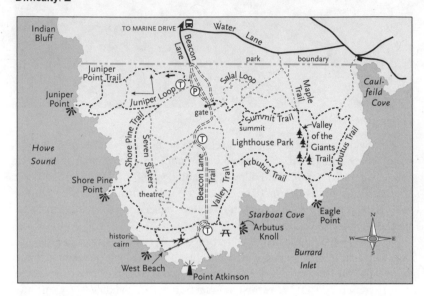

LIGHTHOUSE PARK, a preserve of first-growth forest, rocky shorelines and hidden coves since 1881, is an adventure destination for those who want a light stroll, a vigorous walk or a quiet oceanside view. The lighthouse itself sits prominently on rocky Point Atkinson, where it has been flashing its light and sounding its foghorn since 1874, marking the spot where Burrard Inlet meets Howe Sound.

Pick up a trail pamphlet from one of the information kiosks, then walk to the entrance end of the parking lot, to the trailhead of the northern Juniper Loop. This outing proceeds in a counter-clockwise direction around the park's perimeter and leaves the intersecting trails for your own discovery.

Beginning on the northern Juniper Loop arm, you soon come to a wetland with an information board; keep right on Juniper Point Trail at the next junction and descend, crossing a boardwalk and stairs, to a rocky promontory. Instead of returning up the stairs, bear right, then right again at a signed junction, ascending to meet the southern arm of the Juniper Loop Trail. Watch for

Howe Sound from Juniper Point, with Bowen Island beyond.

the stretched red cedar root in mid-air that resulted when its nurse log disintegrated long ago. Now go right onto Shore Pine Trail, which leads to another promontory with views of Howe Sound. Farther along, your next diversion lies a couple of minutes down a rocky track to West Beach, where you can get close to the water to look for little marine critters and traverse the rock slabs to have your first view of the lighthouse. A closer view of the 1912 tower is gained from a knoll near facilities used by the navy during World War II, now the Phyl Munday Nature House. You may now return up the road to your transportation or continue to the eastern side of the park.

Valley Trail climbs steadily, with diversions to views of Burrard Inlet at Arbutus Knoll and Starboat Cove. Go right on Arbutus Trail, which ascends and then descends to the signed intersection with the gentle Valley of the Giants Trail. Go left to walk amongst the towering first-growth Douglas-fir, as well as hemlock and Western red cedar, where you can practise shinrin-yoku. Or continue to the next intersection where the trail straight ahead leads to Eagle Point lookout, which is rich with lilies in the spring, and left takes you on the steep Arbutus Trail. Valley of the Giants and Arbutus meet at the Summit Trail, from which any of the short tracks that are now before you lead back to the parking lot.

GETTING THERE
Transit: Take TransLink Bus 250 (Horseshoe Bay) to Marine Drive at Beacon Lane. Walk down Beacon Lane to enter the park.
Vehicle: Follow Marine Drive west through West Vancouver to Beacon Lane, which is 350 m beyond a firehall; turn left at the Lighthouse Park sign. Park at the road's end. Alternatively, from Highway 1/99 (Upper Levels Highway), take Exit 4 (Caulfeild Road–Woodgreen Drive) and go left. Turn left onto Headland Drive, make a quick right–left jog at Meadfeild Road, meet Keith Road and turn left onto The Dale, which leads to the firehall at Marine Drive.

CYPRESS FALLS PARK

Distance: 3.4 km (1.9 mi)
Time: 1.5 hours
Surface: trail, road
Elevation gain: 152 m (500 ft)
Quality: ★★★★
Difficulty: ■

Season: all year
Car GPS entry: Woodgreen Pl &
Woodgreen Dr West Vancouver, BC
Trailhead: 49°21'07" N 123°14'28" W

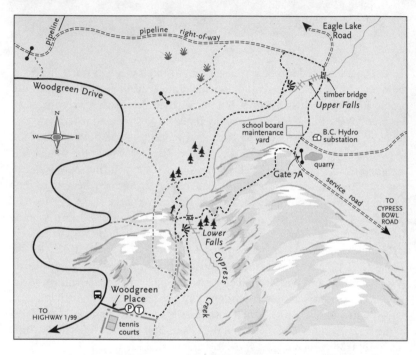

HARBOURING GROVES of fine old-growth Douglas-fir and two sets of water-falls, this low-elevation forest park makes a good destination at any time of year. It is popular with dog walkers.

The trail begins across a grassy area at the east end of the parking lot. Go left on the main trail after entering the trees. After a short distance, drop right to a path paralleling the main trail and note the bits of wood and wire poking through the surface, remains of a wood-stave water pipeline installed in the 1910s.

In about 10 to 15 minutes, you arrive first at a fenced view of the lower falls tumbling through a little canyon and then, a little higher, at another

The upper falls on Cypress Creek.

fenced view at the top of the falls. Years ago, someone cut steps into the rounded rock and fashioned a bench from a large log, now tired and mossy. A footbridge crosses to the east side of the creek and a trail that you may choose to descend on your return.

Staying on the west side of the bridge for now, head uphill on a rooty trail beside a once-functional set of stairs and watch for the impressive grove of towering Douglas-fir, some approaching 2 m (6 ft) in diameter and perhaps 400 years in age, that escaped both fire and logging. The trail continues and, in the wet season, crosses small watercourses that nourish Western red cedars. There are a couple of short side trails where you can access the creek. Within 30 minutes, your ears alert you to the nearness of the upper falls, which freefall about 10 m into a small pool. The edge of the viewpoint is unfenced and precipitous.

Now, you may return by either the same route or the aforementioned alternative. If you choose the latter, ascend until you exit onto a wide clearing with a power line. This is the pipeline route that carries water from Dick (Eagle) Lake to West Vancouver. (This junction also overlaps with Walk 10.) Turn right, then right again at the road, cross the vehicle bridge over Cypress Creek and proceed past the school board maintenance yard on the right and a B.C. Hydro substation on the left. Immediately thereafter, opposite Gate 7A at a quarry site, find a signposted trail heading into the bush on your right. This leads to the footbridge at the lower falls and your return route.

There are other trails in the park that you may wish to explore if you just want a longer wander; some lead to the residential area on Woodgreen Drive, but none anywhere in the park is marked.

GETTING THERE

Transit: Take TransLink Bus 253 (Caulfield/Vancouver/Park Royal) to the flag stop on Woodgreen Drive at Woodgreen Place, then as below.
Vehicle: From Highway 1/99 (Upper Levels Highway), take Exit 4 (Caulfeild Road–Woodgreen Drive). Turn right, then north onto Woodgreen Drive and then right onto Woodgreen Place; a gravel road at its end angles to the left for parking.

HOLLYBURN HERITAGE TRAILS

Distance: 6.7 km (4.2 mi)
Time: 3.5 hours
Surface: trail
Elevation gain: 315 m (1033 ft)
High point: 665 m (2182 ft)

Quality: ★★★★
Difficulty: ♦
Season: May to November
Car GPS entry: Chartwell Dr & Pinecrest Dr West Vancouver, BC
Trailhead: 49°21'10" N 123°09'38" W

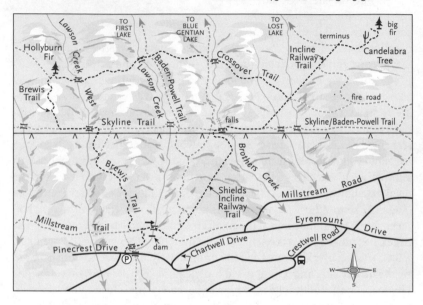

THIS FASCINATING walk, a combination of two heritage circuits, winds through regenerated forest that was logged for local use and export during Vancouver's early years. Your route passes visible remnants of logging road-work and other landscape modifications that are described in the informative Lawson Creek and Brothers Creek Forest Heritage Walk brochures (www .westvancouver.ca). A granite cairn and a signpost for Lepp Trail on the west end of the bridge spanning Lawson Creek on Pinecrest Drive mark your start-ing point.

On the Lawson Creek Trail, the first stop of historical interest is Shields log dam and flume pond, with a block of red cedar (shinglebolt) on the ground nearby. The pond was built in 1917 to store shinglebolts before flushing them down a flume (wooden channel) to a shingle mill 2 km (1.2 mi) below. Con-tinuing uphill, turn right at a fence onto Millstream Trail, cross Lawson Creek, then turn uphill on a gravel road at a junction 5 minutes beyond. After another

Lawson Creek below Shields log dam.

5 minutes, you have a choice: stay on the gravel road until you go right at the Skyline Trail or bear right onto a narrower, overgrown path, the Shields Incline Railway Trail. This leads to an overlook of Brothers Creek and overlaps Walk 15, which explores the Brothers Creek area. Fifty metres farther uphill, look for an unnatural trench in the ground, dug by loggers to skid logs down the mountain using steam-powered cable systems. After crossing the road at the power lines, turn right at the Skyline Trail and drop steeply to cross Brothers Creek. There is a lovely waterfall here, worth a photo.

Continue to a fork where you rejoin the Incline Trail. Pass the Crossover Trail and continue uphill to where the road turns sharply left. Pause here. To see the Candelabra, a large Douglas-fir snag with a distinctive pitchfork-like shape, go straight ahead a few paces and then right to descend for 5 minutes to its base. Now continue downhill through a graveyard of large snags to meet a Douglas-fir that is 43 m (140 ft) tall with a diameter of 2.7 m (8.8 ft), a living giant amongst the dead.

Next, retrace your steps to the Crossover Trail, where you turn right, ascending gradually towards a crossing of Brothers Creek. At the Baden-Powell Trail junction, you may turn downhill to return to your start or continue onward, across Lawson Creek, to experience the Hollyburn Fir. This giant is nearly 1,100 years old, 3 m in diameter and 44 m to its broken top. Now you head downhill on the Brewis Trail, sometimes a bit vague in the open understory, to the power line and Skyline Trail, where you turn left. A few hundred metres later, turn right to rejoin the Brewis Trail. After about 1 km (0.6 mi), at the Millstream Trail junction, go left, through the fence you passed earlier, downhill on the Shields Dam Trail and back to your vehicle.

GETTING THERE

Transit: Take TransLink Bus 254 (British Properties/Park Royal/Vancouver) to Chartwell Drive and Crestwell Road; walk west on Chartwell to Pinecrest Drive, then along Pinecrest to the trailhead.

Vehicle: From Highway 1/99 (Upper Levels Highway), take Exit 11 (15th Street) and go north on 15th Street and then up Cross Creek Road to Chartwell Drive, which climbs steeply to Pinecrest Drive. Turn left and park near the bridge.

BROTHERS CREEK TRAILS

Distance: 11 km (6.8 mi)
Time: 4.5 hours
Surface: unpaved roads, trails
Elevation gain: 450 m (1475 ft)
High point: 830 m (2725 ft)

Quality: ★★★★
Difficulty: ◆
Season: May to November
Car GPS entry: Chartwell Dr & Millstream
Rd West Vancouver, BC
Trailhead: 49°21'17" N 123°9'11" W

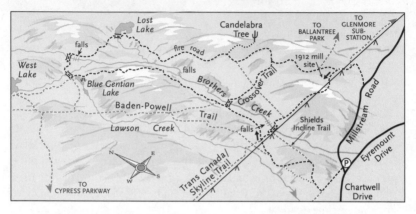

BLUE GENTIAN Lake, with its boardwalks, water lilies and picnic table, provides a fine reward at your turnaround point after a variety of sights, including falls and canyons, enormous snags and logging artifacts.

Begin your outing by walking along the road-width Millstream Trail. Within 5 minutes, turn right on a fire access road towards the Baden-Powell/ Skyline Trails, your path now a steady uphill. Continue past the ancient truck remains, then watch for a trail heading off to the right. A wooden sign for Brothers Creek/Lost Lake is visible high up in the trees as soon as you turn right off the road. If you get to the power lines, you've gone too far; go back down the hill to the turnoff. Within a few minutes, cross the power line right-of-way and continue straight ahead, the creek well below on your right. A footbridge over Brothers Creek on the Crossover Trail leads to a shorter return route, for a round trip of 6 km (3.7 mi).

Staying left and continuing up the main trail, you enjoy a level stretch where the creek is a pleasant stream before you rise again to view a set of falls. The trail stays away from the bank, but you will see where it led to another bridge, which at time of writing is washed out. There is no way to cross the creek here, so continue on the trail west of the creek for about 20 minutes to reach picturesque Blue Gentian Lake.

From the lake, stay right to go to Lost Lake, stepping across two creeks, just beyond which are views into the gorge of the upper falls. The track here is rough and eroded; fallen trees obscure the path in a few spots. From Lost Lake, use the trail down the east side of Brothers Creek to join and descend the fire road. Some portions of the route coincide with Hollyburn Heritage Trails (Walk 14). Stay on the fire road. Lower still, the Crossover Trail enters from the right and departs later for Ballantree by the site of a 1912 sawmill. Keep right, continue down and just before the power line, turn right on Skyline Trail. You rise some 100 m, then drop sharply to Brothers Creek's lower falls. Cross the creek, rise equally fast out of its ravine, then

A sign high in the trees marks the trail to Brothers Creek. *Photo: Amanda Halliday*

continue to the intersection of the Brothers Creek/Lost Lake trail. Turn left, cross the power lines, continue downhill and so back to your transportation.

GETTING THERE
Transit: Take TransLink Bus 254 (British Properties/Park Royal/Vancouver) to Eyremount Drive and Crestwell Road; walk two blocks west to Millstream Road and then up to the gate.
Vehicle: From Highway 1/99 (Upper Levels Highway), take Exit 11 (15th Street) and turn north at 15th Street onto Crosscreek Road, turn left onto Chartwell Drive, then left on Millstream Road. Park here near a gated forest road reached immediately after turning.

AMBLESIDE TO DUNDARAVE SEAWALK

Distance: 8.5 km (5.3 mi)
Time: 2.5 hours
Surface: gravel, paved
Quality: ★★★
Difficulty: ●

Season: all year
Car GPS entry: Taylor Way & Marine Dr
West Vancouver, BC
Trailhead: 49°19'28" N 123°08'05" W

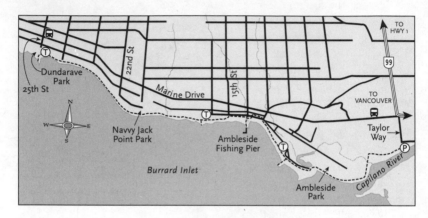

PANORAMIC VIEWS of the West Vancouver shoreline, Lions Gate Bridge, Stanley Park and Burrard Inlet with its variety of marine activity are your reward on every step of this popular waterfront walk. Information panels about the local history and people-watching add to the interest on this route.

Begin your walk at the end of Taylor Way, where the Capilano Pacific Trail (Walk 17) ends. Follow the path west to Ambleside Park as it passes under the railway and emerges at the mouth of the Capilano River. To your left is the Lions Gate Bridge, completed in 1938, and ahead across Burrard Inlet are Stanley Park and Siwash Rock (or Standing Man, to the Squamish). As the trail curves to the west, you pass through a gate and enter what is for the rest of the walk a bicycle-free zone. Dogs are permitted until you reach Ambleside Park and exit the off-leash dog zone.

As you approach the Hollyburn Sailing Club, jog right onto a short section of the Spirit Trail with the option of visiting the beach at the Ambleside Fishing Pier. Continue on Argyle Street to Painters' Landing, where you rejoin the oceanfront path and continue through John Lawson Park, cross Lawson Creek (which you explore at a higher elevation in Walk 14) and pass the *Big Chairs* sculpture by Bill Pechet at 18th Street, where you transition to West Vancouver's Centennial Seawalk. Follow the Seawalk to Dundarave Park.

The Centennial Seawalk near John Lawson Park on a dismal day.

Consider a rewarding break at one of Dundarave Village's many foodie shops and cafés before retracing your steps to your starting point.

GETTING THERE

Transit: Take TransLink Bus 239 or 250–258 to Park Royal South Mall. Walk to the south end of Taylor Way.

Vehicle: From Highway 1/99 (Upper Levels Highway), take Exit 13 (Taylor Way) and drive south on Taylor Way, crossing Marine Drive, to Park Royal South Mall in West Vancouver. Or drive north over the Lions Gate Bridge, take the exit for West Vancouver and find yourself heading west on Marine Drive. Turn left onto Taylor Way. Drive to the end of Taylor Way and park in the southeast corner. You may also find curbside parking nearby.

BOWSER TRAIL PLUS

Distance: 7.9 km (4.9 mi)

Time: 3 hours

Surface: paved, trail, stairs

Quality: ★★

Difficulty: ●

Season: all year

Car GPS entry: Marine Dr & Taylor Way
West Vancouver, BC

Trailhead: 49°19'28" N 123°08'05" W

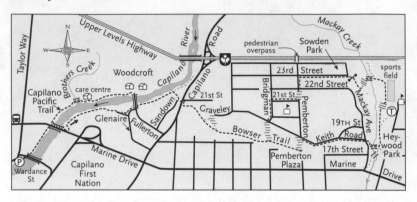

BOWSER TRAIL itself, the namesake of this walk, is only a 15-minute stretch; however, tagging on a stroll along the Capilano River to the west and a vigorous walk through Mackay Creek Park to the east makes for a very worthwhile outing.

Begin your walk at the end of Taylor Way on the Capilano Pacific Trail. Across the river is X̱wemelch'stn village, one of the oldest and major villages of the Squamish First Nation. Heading upstream, pass under two roads, the second of which is Marine Drive. Here, you go left and up onto the sidewalk, cross the bridge and follow the first paved path left and down to a wider paved path. Without turning left or right, continue across the lawn to find a trail into the woods on the riverbank. About 5 minutes later, head along the side of playing fields, cross a parking lot, step between the barrier at Glenaire Drive, then go left at Fullerton Avenue to Woodcroft Bridge. Without crossing the bridge, find the track at its southeast corner that drops to the riverbank behind shrubbery. Just beyond the last house on this beautified path, a track leads right amongst young conifers to Capilano Road and a pedestrian crossing at West 21st Street. A few paces south lies Bowser Trail, a pleasant surprise close to Marine Drive. The official trail ends behind a shopping centre at Pemberton Avenue, but you may continue by ascending the many flights of wooden steps to tiny Ashdown Park, with its peek-a-boo view of Vancouver. Now go

A lovely wooded section of Capilano Pacific Trail.

right on Keith Road, past West 19th Street, to reach Mackay Avenue and a track into Heywood Park across the road. Once in the park, descend to cross Mackay Creek, then turn immediately upstream on a rough track along the ravine. Keep to the left and creekside at a fork, continue over a rather long boardwalk and ascend steps that lead to sports fields.

At the north end of the fields, descend to a bridge over Mackay Creek, cross it, then climb out of the ravine; turn right onto a path at the edge of the trees and follow this to its end, emerging at the playing field of Sowden Park. Now on quiet residential streets, work your way west on West 23rd Street, south on Pemberton Avenue and up a few steps, west on West 21st Street, then south on Bridgman Avenue to cross Keith Road. Now you return to Bowser Trail by descending more than 200 steps.

Retrace your route as far as Fullerton Avenue, but this time cross the bridge, turn downstream on the Woodcroft side and follow the west bank on the Capilano Pacific Trail over Brothers Creek and under Marine Drive, to arrive back at your starting point.

GETTING THERE
Transit: Take TransLink Bus 239 or 250–258 to Park Royal South Mall. Walk to the south end of Taylor Way.
Vehicle: From Highway 1/99 (Upper Levels Highway), take Exit 13 (Taylor Way) and drive south on Taylor Way, crossing Marine Drive, to Park Royal South Mall in West Vancouver. Or drive north over the Lions Gate Bridge, take the exit for West Vancouver and find yourself heading west on Marine Drive. Turn left onto Taylor Way. Drive to the end of Taylor Way and park in the southeast corner. You may also find curbside parking nearby.

MOSQUITO CREEK

Distance: 8 km (5 mi)
Time: 2.5 hours
Surface: trail, paved
Elevation gain: 210 m (689 ft)
High point: 240 m (787 ft)

Quality: ★★★
Difficulty: ■
Season: all year
Car GPS entry: Marine Dr & Fell Ave
North Vancouver, BC
Trailhead: 49°19'28" N 123°05'38" W

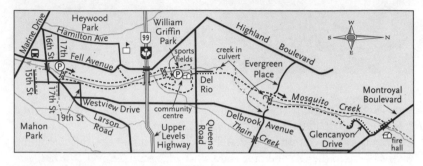

NUMEROUS CREEKS run down the slopes of the North Shore mountains, and their ravines provide pleasant outings in a modified natural setting. Mosquito Creek has been altered to protect properties from flood damage, and now the wide, hard-surfaced path beside the rushing waters is an inviting place to walk.

From the trailhead on 17th Street, stay on the west side of Mosquito Creek to head upstream. Within a minute or two, you'll notice a side trail passing through a fence and across a small watercourse on your left. You may follow this diversion over boardwalks and on a narrow footpath that wanders through a small eco-sensitive wetland. Since the mid-1990s, this area has been improved to restore habitat for spawning salmon and other wetland flora and fauna. (Please remember that lively dogs can do damage that we may not readily observe.) Back on the multi-purpose path, you continue to ascend gently, then pass under the Upper Levels Highway, where you begin rising to William Griffin Park and Community Recreation Centre (and alternate parking) on Queens Road. Look for the row of cut stones cleaved by growing trees, a dynamic art sculpture that changes slowly over time through natural forces. For a short outing, this is a convenient place to turn back.

Before continuing upstream, note, during high water, the creek falling over a short drop behind an enclosed area. This is where the water exits from its journey through a pipeline, begun approximately 1 km (0.6 mi) above. Now,

The path passes through restored wetland that is an important fish habitat.

cross Queens Road to Del Rio Drive, opposite the William Griffin Park sign, and proceed to its end, where the trail resumes. Initially, you travel through a thinly treed area, overgrown with ivy, to a paved cross path and a bridge on your right at Evergreen Place. Below the bridge is the pipeline intake that carries the creek to where you saw it emerge earlier. Without crossing the bridge, you continue through a surprisingly wide valley that gradually narrows and steepens while the forest envelopes you with wonderful second-growth cedar, hemlock and Douglas-fir. Too soon, you reach the substructure of the bridge on Montroyal Boulevard. This is your turnaround point, as the deteriorating trail continuing upstream has sloughed and is now closed.

To vary your downstream return with a "woodsy" experience, climb the steps to Montroyal Boulevard, cross to the east side, then go right on Glencanyon Drive to its end. Enter the woods on the right-hand trail to descend on a rough track, popular with dog walkers, until you arrive at the path from Evergreen Place, where you cross the footbridge to join your outward route.

GETTING THERE
Transit: Take TransLink Bus 239, 240, 241 or 255 along Marine Drive to Fell Avenue. Walk 350 m north on Fell Avenue to 17th Street and turn right.
Vehicle: From Marine Drive in North Vancouver, turn north onto Fell Avenue and park near 17th Street.

MAHON PARK

Distance: 5 km (3.1 mi)
Time: 1.5 hours
Surface: trail, stairs
Quality: ★★★★
Difficulty: ●

Season: all year
Car GPS entry: Jones Ave & 18th St W
North Vancouver, BC
Trailhead: 49°19'32" N 123°04'54" W

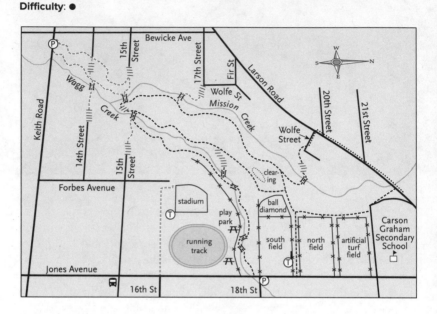

KNOWN AS the "jewel of the city," this little park, named for Edward Mahon (pronounced Mann), a pioneering visionary of conservation, offers a breath of nature and an ideal location for shinrin-yoku. Large trees and two pretty streams in adjacent ravines mute the surrounding city noise. Numerous bridges sport fragments of running verse, such as "step into a forest" and "a creek flows at your feet."

On foot, cross Jones Avenue to the trailhead opposite the parking lot, then pause at the information kiosk to learn about the cultural and natural history of the area. As you enter the forest, descending a well-made trail against a steep slope, you might consider the contrast of this natural environment with the playing fields above. As you cross the bridges back and forth over Wagg Creek, avoid the one leading west (right) up a long flight of stairs; instead, continue downstream on the creek's left bank and, at a T-junction, cross the bridge and climb a short set of stairs. Going left over another bridge leads you quickly to the Keith Road exit, but your route turns hard right onto a

Wagg Creek ravine is a natural oasis.

trail that climbs gently out of the ravine to the crest of the ridge between Wagg and Mission Creeks. Watch the left-side slope for the cedar tree with a rock amongst its roots. Do you think of a mother bird hugging its egg? Pass a descending set of stairs—the flight mentioned earlier—and you soon arrive at a flat clearing. Playing fields are a short distance beyond. Keeping the ball diamond on your right, walk between the south and north fields and exit onto Jones Avenue, not far from your vehicle.

It's hard to do two loops on three trails without repeating one of the legs, so this might be a good time to rest by the sports track. If you choose to explore the Mission Creek ravine, retrace either your descending or ascending track to arrive back at the trail junction below West 15th Street. Now, with Mission Creek at your left and ignoring a bridge, follow the ravine trail uphill to a fork: right leads to the familiar fields and back to your starting point, left to Wolfe Street via a stairway beside an enormous stump. Choosing the latter path up to Wolfe Street, go left to Larson Road, turn right, walk 250 m to a substantial path leading to Carson Graham School, follow the service/bike road to a gate, then turn right onto a narrow path west of the playing field. This goes between the north and south fields and so back to your starting point.

GETTING THERE
Transit: Take TransLink Bus 240 (15th Street/Vancouver) or 255 (Dundarave/ Capilano University) to Jones Avenue and 15th Street. Walk north on Jones Avenue to the trailhead at 18th Street.
Vehicle: From Highway 1/99 (Upper Levels Highway), take Exit 17 (West-view Drive) and go south. Turn left on 23rd Street and right on Jones Avenue to West 18th Street. Park in the lot on the northeast corner. Street parking is also available.

20 NORTH VANCOUVER

SPIRIT TRAIL

Distance: 8 km (5 mi)
Time: 3 hours
Surface: paved
Quality: ★★★
Difficulty: ●

Season: all year
Car GPS entry: Gladstone Ave & 4th St E
North Vancouver, BC
Trailhead: 49°18'34" N 123°02'38" W

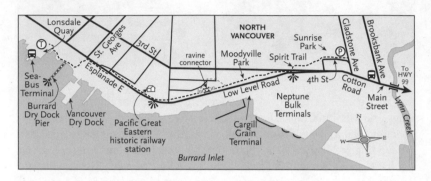

THE NORTH Shore Spirit Trail is a collaboration amongst three municipalities, the Squamish and Tsleil-Waututh First Nations and the provincial and federal governments to create a continuous greenway across the entire North Shore from Deep Cove to Horseshoe Bay. This North Vancouver portion of the Spirit Trail, completed in 2017 and open to walkers, cyclists and rollerbladers, is a real treat for those who enjoy expansive views of Burrard Inlet and its industrial activities. Note that you could start this walk at Lonsdale Quay after crossing the inlet by SeaBus.

Your walk begins where the Spirit Trail's swirly logo, Shewalh Stelmexw (pronounced Sha-woth Stol-molth), or People's Path in the Squamish language, is emblazoned on the sidewalk. Head west past the soccer pitch and uphill to cross Heywood Street and then to cross the pedestrian bridge to a viewpoint over Neptune Coal port. Veer right on the upper path, where the view expands to include the Neptune terminal's mammoth robin's-egg-blue coal-handling machinery, Burrard Inlet and Vancouver's New Brighton and Hastings Parks (Walk 41). After entering a forested section through historic Moodyville Park—the site of a thriving sawmill town in the late 1800s—a Y-junction presents the choice of remaining on the paved trail or taking the ravine connection with its stairs and suspension bridge through Moodyville Ravine. The routes converge on the other side of the ravine, where views expand to encompass the Vancouver skyline across the water. Stanley Park

The Spirit Trail offers many views across Burrard Inlet to the Vancouver skyline.

comes into view as you approach the B.C. Ferries drydock. On your right, look for the temporary location of the Pacific Great Eastern Historic Railway Station, an artifact of the "Prince George Eventually" railroad.

Follow the well-marked trail along Esplanade Avenue past the pole art to cross at St. Andrews Avenue. Continue on the south side of Esplanade to St. Georges and go left towards the waterfront where what was once a ship-building area is now high-rise residences. A short diversion to the Burrard Dry Dock Pier rewards you with unobstructed views of the container port, downtown Vancouver and Stanley Park, while in the foreground are anchored freighters and the busy SeaBus crossing between downtown Vancouver and Lonsdale Quay.

Finally, after passing the new Polygon Gallery, you reach Lonsdale Quay, your turnaround destination. Relax and reward your efforts with a treat from one of the many specialty shops before retracing your steps and taking in the excellent views again en route to your starting point.

GETTING THERE

Transit: Take TransLink Bus 239 to Cotton Road and Brooksbank Avenue. Walk west past the Park & Tilford mall, turn right onto Gladstone Avenue and walk north to the soccer pitch on 4th Street.

Vehicle: From Highway 1, take Exit 23A (Main Street) to Main Street and travel west to Gladstone Avenue. Turn right and park beside the soccer pitch on 4th Street.

LYNN HEADWATERS LOOP

Distance Lynn Loop: 5.2 km (3.2 mi)
Time: 1.5 hours
Distance Debris Chute: 9 km (5.6 mi)
Time: 3 hours
Surface: road, trail
Elevation gain: 200 m (656 ft)
High point: 380 m (1245 ft)

Quality: ★★★★
Difficulty: ● to ■
Season: most of the year
Car GPS entry: Lynn Valley Rd &
Dempsey Rd North Vancouver, BC
Trailhead: 49°21'35" N 123°01'41" W

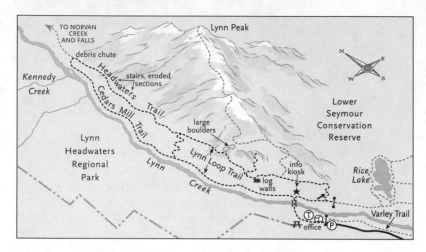

YOU MAY customize your own outing here at Lynn Headwaters Regional Park: an easy return stroll along Lynn Creek on the Loop and Cedars Mill Trails to a wide clearing opposite Kennedy Creek Valley; a moderate workout on a rough forest trail with noticeable elevation changes to the same clearing; or a shorter loop combining the two. Note that this is a popular destination and, on a busy day, you may have to park up to 1 km (0.6 mi) from the trailhead.

From the picnic area, cross Lynn Creek Bridge to an information kiosk where the easy upstream walk begins to the left. To follow the more demanding route, go right for some 5 minutes to the signed Lynn Loop trailhead heading left into the trees. Along the way are moss-covered trees and tangles of blowdowns, trees toppled in strong windstorms. Within 15 minutes, you pass the trailhead to Lynn Peak on your right and then, a little later, a possible (signed) side trip up a short, steep track that rises 70 m (230 ft) to a rocky outcrop with a broken view across Burrard Inlet. Still later, another side path to the right takes you to a pair of huge boulders, or erratics, deposited well over 10,000 years ago by a retreating glacier. Next comes a point of

Lynn Creek's cool waters and natural pools are a draw for salmon—and walkers.

decision: you may complete Lynn Loop by dropping steeply—note the pair of enormous cedar stumps flanking a staircase—to the Lynn Creek Trail, where you turn left downstream, or you may continue north another 2 km (1.2 mi).

If you continue, now on the Headwaters Trail, you gradually start descending, occasionally on a staircase. The trail crosses small watercourses and one or two debris torrents, potentially dangerous during high runoff. A largish creek, which you cross on stepping stones, marks your return junction where you go left. (Headwaters Trail continues a farther 2.3 km/1.4 mi north to Norvan Falls.) Descend to a large clearing with a superb view to the wild country north of Grouse Mountain; access to Lynn Creek, where you might want to dawdle; and the head of the riverside Cedars Mill Trail, your return route.

Travelling downstream, you pass the long-vanished Cedars Mill (where only a few pieces of rusted machinery remain), the T-junction with the Lynn Loop connector, and wire coils, remnants of wood-stave pipes that once carried water to North Vancouver. And so back to your starting point.

LONGER OPTION
Reluctant to leave? You could add the Rice Lake loop (Walk 22), which begins 1.5 km (0.9 mi) along the road from the Lynn Creek Bridge.

GETTING THERE
Transit: Take TransLink Bus 228 (Lynn Valley/Lonsdale Quay) to Lynn Valley Road at Dempsey Road. From there, walk north on Lynn Valley Road or, after 100 m on Lynn Valley Road, take Rice Lake Road to your right and continue on Marion Road to reach the Varley Trail, which connects with the trailhead. Either option adds a 3 km (1.9 mi) return to your walk.
Vehicle: From Highway 1 eastbound (Upper Levels Highway) take Exit 19 (Lynn Valley Road) and travel north. If westbound, take Exit 21 (Mountain Highway) and travel north to Lynn Valley Road. Continue on Lynn Valley to a park gate (note the hours). Follow the narrow road to the last parking lot.

RICE LAKE

Distance: 6 km (3.7 mi)
Time: 2 hours
Surface: trail
Quality: ★★★★
Difficulty: ●
Season: all year
Car GPS entry (LSCR): Lillooet Rd &
Monashee Dr North Vancouver, BC

Trailhead (LSCR): 49°21'01" N
123°00'53" W
Car GPS entry (Varley): Lynn Valley Rd &
Dempsey Rd North Vancouver, BC
Trailhead (Varley): 49°21'35"
N 123°01'41" W

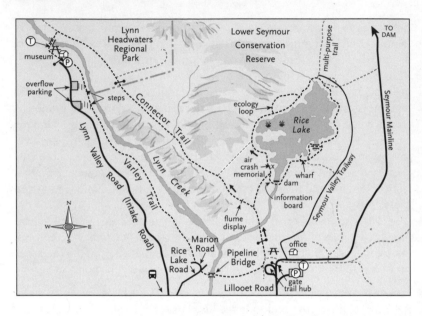

RICE LAKE is a "well-groomed" destination, with wide paths and stops of interest: a flume and shinglebolt display, a plane-crash memorial and a large, wide fishing wharf. This description begins from the Lower Seymour Conservation Reserve (LSCR) with the walk around Rice Lake, then describes an optional stroll to nearby Lynn Creek.

Your trail begins at the 0 km signpost, northwest from the parking lot, past the Rice Lake gatehouse and north from the information kiosks. From the signpost, bear left on a wide gravel path that soon branches right to Rice Lake. Immediately on your left is a display about local logging activities more than a century ago and about the lake's more recent role as a reservoir. Next, the memorial to a 1947 plane crash will catch your attention before you come

Rice Lake invites reflection.

to the unannounced, short Forest Ecology Loop Trail. Continue around the lake, ignoring a broad multi-purpose trail leading to the north, until you arrive at the Douglas Mowat Memorial Special Fisheries Wharf. Rice Lake is stocked regularly with rainbow trout for local fisherfolk (licence required).

Back on the main trail, turn left to return to your starting point or right to continue an additional 1.5 km (0.9 mi) to the bridge over Lynn Creek and the decrepit water intake dam at Lynn Headwaters Regional Park (see also Walk 21). To complete the circuit, proceed to the southeast end of the upper parking lot to read about Frederick Varley, the Group of Seven artist who lived and painted in the area, then join the trail named for him. Note that staircases along the route lead to parking lots above. Twenty minutes later, you emerge onto Marion Road and immediately meet Pipeline Bridge over Lynn Creek, the upper reaches of Lynn Canyon. Five minutes more, up the road with the unusual street lamps, and you're back at your vehicle.

GETTING THERE
Transit: To begin at the LSCR and Lynn Valley, take TransLink Bus 228 (Lynn Valley/Lonsdale Quay) to Lynn Valley Road at Dempsey Road. Walk north 100 m on Lynn Valley Road, turn right on Rice Lake Road and follow to a bridge, cross this and walk to the Lower Seymour Conservation Reserve (LSCR) parking lot, about 800 m. To begin at the Varley Trail, continue straight along the gravel road to Marion Road and the trailhead.
Vehicle: To begin at the LSCR, from Highway 1 northbound take Exit 22A (Capilano College/Lillooet Road)—or, if southbound, take Exit 22—and drive 5 km (3.1 mi) north on Lillooet Road to park. To begin in Lynn Valley, from Highway 1/99 (Upper Levels Highway), take Exit 19 (Lynn Valley Road) and travel north to a park gate (note the hours). All lots link to the Varley Trail.

FISHERMAN'S TRAIL

Distance: 13.6 km (8.5 mi)

Time: 4 hours

Elevation gain: 140 m (460 ft)

Surface: trail, paved road

Quality: ★★★★

Difficulty: ■

Season: most of the year

Car GPS entry: Lillooet Rd & Monashee Dr North Vancouver, BC

Trailhead: 49°21'01" N 123°00'53" W

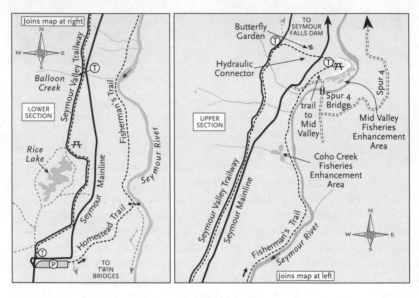

THIS TRAIL, one of many in the Lower Seymour Conservation Reserve (LSCR), provides a pleasant walk through forest and along the riverbank, with views of Mount Seymour and its neighbours from an unusual perspective.

Area information is available at a kiosk at the parking lot and at the gatehouse just beyond. Your trail begins at the northeast corner of the lot, between works-yard fences. Initially, you follow a narrow passage beside a high fence to a service road, which you cross to enter open forest on the wide Twin Bridges Trail. A moment later, go left on the Homestead Trail, where you enter the forest and descend about 100 m to meet the Fisherman's Trail, where you turn upriver at a wooden gate. The well-made path rolls along through maturing second-growth conifers hiding large moss-covered stumps; from time to time it wanders beside the riverbank. After the trail widens into a rough service road, bridges facilitate crossing the several streams, some of which become quite swollen during heavy rains, even

Watch for black-tailed deer feeding on trailside clover.

causing small mudslides from the slopes above. One such unmarked stream drains the hidden Coho Creek Fisheries Enhancement Area, one of several in the LSCR. Views of treed mountain slopes emerge to your right. After about 90 minutes, you arrive at a junction with the service road. Cross this to begin a steady ascent to the mid-valley destinations. Within 10 minutes, and after rounding a bend, a picnic and viewing area greets you—a good spot to study both mountain and valley.

To return, you may retrace your steps along the tranquil Fisherman's Trail (recommended) or complete your loop as you hoof it on the Seymour Valley Trailway, a paved multi-use recreational road that is popular with cyclists and rollerbladers. To reach the trailway, take the Hydraulic Connector Trail from the northeast corner of the picnic area. A short diversion to the Butterfly Garden, a one-time RCMP bomb disposal site, is worth a look in season.

Along the 5.7 km (3.4 mi) of the trailway that make up your return journey are picnic tables, toilets and signed stops of interest, one of which was the site of an experimental balloon-logging operation in 1967. Another signed stop, near a side trail leading to Rice Lake (Walk 22), provides information about homesteading in the area. Finally, you arrive at the 0 km signpost and the gatehouse. The parking lot, and the end of your journey, is just a few paces beyond.

GETTING THERE

Transit: Take TransLink Bus 228 (Lynn Valley/Lonsdale Quay) to Lynn Valley Road and Dempsey Road. Walk north to follow gravelled Rice Lake Road to a bridge, cross this and walk to the Lower Seymour Conservation Reserve (LSCR) parking lot, about 800 m.

Vehicle: From Highway 1 northbound, take Exit 22A (Capilano College/Lillooet Road)—or, if southbound, take Exit 22—and drive 5 km (3.1 mi) north on Lillooet Road to park.

MAPLEWOOD FLATS

Distance: 3.3 km (2 mi)
Time: 1 hour
Surface: trail
Quality: ★★★
Difficulty: ●

Season: all year
Car GPS entry: 2645 Dollarton Hwy
North Vancouver, BC
Trailhead: 49°18'23" N 123°00'07" W

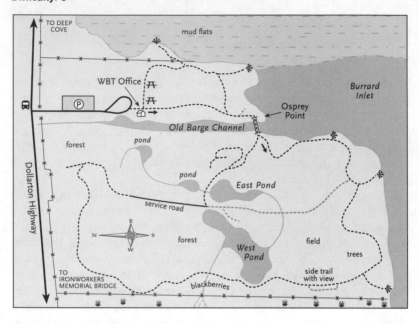

THIS LITTLE wilderness retreat on Tsleil-Waututh Nation territory is hidden amongst industrial and urban activities on North Vancouver's bustling waterfront. It provides an easily accessible opportunity to enjoy birdsong and wildlife viewing throughout the year. Well over 200 bird species have been sighted, as well as mammals small and large. Sightings are noted on a board outside the Wild Bird Trust of British Columbia (WBT) office. The conservation area is operated by the WBT on what was once an industrial site until public interest groups initiated actions to restore the degraded land to a natural state. The land, which includes a meadow, ponds, woods and shoreline and preserves a remnant of the once-common waterfront wetland ecosystem on the north shore of Burrard Inlet, is now leased to Environment Canada, whose Pacific Environmental Science Centre occupies an area at the sanctuary's entrance.

Start your walk at the WBT office, then head south towards Burrard Inlet and Osprey Point. You may be lucky enough to spot an osprey, whose population has been slowly growing since the conservation area was established. Note the breeding boxes for purple martins on the old pilings, once used for mooring. Proceed to the bridge over the Old Barge Channel,

Old Barge Channel protects birds and this replica by Vancouver artist Ken Lum of the squatters' shacks that existed here in the late 1800s to the 1950s.

pause to watch the activities below, then at the fork continue left, the more interesting direction. The trail meanders through woods, approaches the shoreline, where occasional benches are placed at viewpoints, pauses at a salt marsh backdropped by industrial activity, then reaches a pond fringed with water-loving plants where several waterfowl are in residence.

Beyond the pond, you enter an area of forest where the ubiquitous wild blackberry is overrunning flowering shrubs and ferns. (The berries are delicious in season, if you can pluck them from amongst the thorns.) After a small piece of paved service road, you swing to the left on a trail passing between two ponds and continuing to yet another left fork. This leads to a miniature summit, where once-fine views are now obstructed by towering cottonwood trees. Descend and walk left to recross the bridge over the Old Barge Channel. The eastern part of the conservation area is quite small, with paths leading to viewpoints, where you may observe the intertidal marshes and the vast mud flats that stretch out across the bay at low tide. Finally, the path returns you to the WBT office, where there are a few picnic tables.

The WBT sponsors free guided walks and other activities. For more information, call 604-929-2379 (limited hours) or visit the website: www .wildbirdtrust.org.

GETTING THERE

Transit: Take TransLink Bus 212 (Deep Cove/Phibbs Exchange) or 215 (Indian River/Phibbs Exchange) to the 2500 block of Dollarton Highway.
Vehicle: From Highway 1 northbound, take Exit 23B (Main Street/Dollarton Highway)—or, if southbound, take Exit 23A (Main Street)—and drive east along the Dollarton Highway. Park either within the gates (note the hours) or on the street outside.

HISTORIC MUSHROOM LOOP

Distance: 6.4 km (4 mi)
Time: 2.5 hours
Surface: trail, paved road
Elevation gain: 275 m (902 ft)
High point: 570 m (1870 ft)

Quality: ★★★
Difficulty: ■
Season: May to early November
Car GPS entry: Mt Seymour Rd & Mt Seymour Pkwy North Vancouver, BC
Trailhead: 49°20'18" N 122°57'25" W

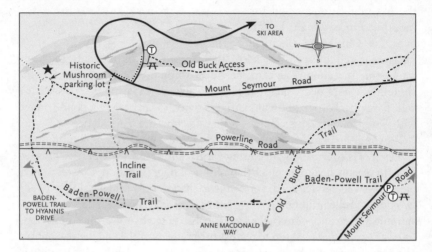

DURING THE 1930s and 1940s, the "mushroom," a large roofed-over stump at the end of a drivable road with a parking area, served as a rendezvous point, message board and trailhead for mountain enthusiasts. Today, an information board with historic photos helps you imagine those days. Of further interest is the history of the Baden-Powell Trail, which stretches 48 km (30 mi) across the North Shore mountains, from Horseshoe Bay to Deep Cove. The Boy Scouts and Girl Guides of B.C. built it in 1971 to celebrate British Columbia's centenary.

From the parking lot, cross the Mt. Seymour Road and enter the forest westbound. The trail rises gently to reach an intersection with the Old Buck Trail. Here, drop left a few paces to regain the Baden-Powell Trail by going right, over a bridge. Carry on for 20 to 30 minutes, ignoring any side branches that are used by mountain bikers, until the Baden-Powell Trail veers sharp left, but your route continues straight ahead. Shortly thereafter, cross the power line cut, continue climbing and before long you reach a confusing conjunction of trails. This is the historic mushroom site. Today, only remnants

Second-growth forest along Old Buck Access trail.

of the "mushroom stump" remain and nothing of the former parking lot. Go right to where the information board is located; if you pass the signpost for Ned's Atomic Dustbin trail, retrace your steps and now go left.

Continue onward until you reach another junction, where you turn left to ascend a steepish slope over a number of horizontal logs, well sculpted by water and use, set into the trail. In a few minutes, you reach the road, cross it and head downhill a few paces to the entrance to the Vancouver Picnic Area. Once part of the original road up Mount Seymour, this is a comfortable place to relax and enjoy the amenities before continuing.

The next part of your route is the most pleasant (no pedal-pushers permitted), as it descends gently to the junction with Old Buck Trail. Turn right onto this former logging road, which leads to the highway; cross and head uphill to regain the trail. Soon thereafter, as you cross the power line, you may glimpse the tops of Buntzen and Eagle Ridges, the only view available on this walk. Re-entering the forest, you continue to descend. Watch for the sharp turn left onto your original trail, which will take you back to your starting point. (All junctions are well signed.)

LONGER OPTION

For a walk taking another hour or so, you may start lower on the mountain, going left off Mt. Seymour Road onto Anne Macdonald Way and then immediately right into a parking lot at the Old Buck trailhead. From here, the Old Buck Trail rises 215 m in 2.3 km (1.4 mi) to meet the Baden-Powell Trail.

GETTING THERE

Transit: Take TransLink Bus 215 (Indian River/Phibbs Exchange) to Indian River Drive at Mt. Seymour Parkway. Walk north on Mt. Seymour Parkway for 200 m, turn left at Anne Macdonald Way and reach the Old Buck trailhead, to begin the longer option.

Vehicle: From Highway 1 northbound, take Exit 22B (Mount Seymour Parkway)—or, if southbound, take Exit 22—and travel east to Mt. Seymour Road and go left (north). About 2.5 km (1.6 mi) from the entrance to Mt. Seymour Park, park at a small lot opposite the Baden-Powell trailhead.

THREE CHOP/OLD BUCK LOOP

Distance: 7.7 km (4.8 mi)
Time: 3 hours
Surface: rough, eroded, unmaintained trail
Elevation gain: 545 m (1788 ft)
High point: 764 m (2507 ft)

Quality: ★★★★
Difficulty: ◆
Season: June to November
Car GPS entry: Mt Seymour Rd & Mt Seymour Pkwy North Vancouver, BC
Trailhead: 49°20'18" N 122°57'25" W

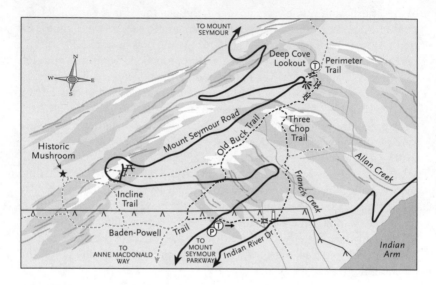

LOCATED ON the lower slopes of Mount Seymour, this walk in the woods avoids the high-use areas of the provincial park and can be enjoyed while higher trails (Walks 27, 28 and 29) are snowbound. The highlights are the challenge of a steady ascent on a rough wilderness trail and an optional expansive view from Deep Cove Lookout on Mt. Seymour Road.

Begin your walk from the parking lot on the Baden-Powell Trail as it descends an easy grade through attractive forest to Indian River Road. Here you join Three Chop Trail to the right of the gate on the service road, climbing to arrive in short order at the power line right-of-way, where the trail lies directly in front of you in the forested slope ahead as you pass underneath the wires. Keep left at a fork on a rough path and ascend steadily on an eroded trail in fairly old second-growth trees, until you come to Francis Creek; this is easy to cross, with care, most of the year. Look for orange markers on trees to stay on route. After the creek crossing, the grade steepens and the trail is even

The Francis Creek crossing in summer.

more eroded, but eventually relief comes just as the forest cover becomes deciduous, with berry bushes and ferns crowding in on the trail. Then you work left to join Old Buck Trail, some 2 km (1.2 mi) from the start.

Now turn right on Old Buck Trail, a rehabilitated logging road, continuing on its gentler grade, with bridges and fine views of many little waterfalls along the way. The appearance of a large rockslide on your left signals the Mt. Seymour Road immediately above. At a junction, you turn left over a final bridge with a view both up- and downstream of the falling waters of Allan Creek. Soon you arrive at Deep Cove Lookout on the Mt. Seymour Road— at first a seemingly anticlimactic destination. Walk around the perimeter, however, and there before you lies the wide sweep of the Fraser Valley and its delta, from Mount Baker to the southern Gulf Islands across the Strait of Georgia. Unfortunately, trees now obstruct the view of Deep Cove itself.

Returning from the lookout, take Old Buck Trail, staying with it as it swings gradually west across the face of the mountain, bridging numerous streams. Ignoring all forks, continue directly down to the Mt. Seymour Road, cross it, walk 50 m uphill to pick up the route again, keep going to the power line and cross that as well. Then continue down, watching for the sharp turn left onto Baden-Powell Trail (right connects with Walk 25). Within 10 minutes, you'll meet Mt. Seymour Road again and be back at your starting point.

GETTING THERE

Vehicle: From Highway 1 northbound, take Exit 22B (Mount Seymour Parkway)—or, if southbound, take Exit 22—and travel east to Mt. Seymour Road and go left (north). About 2.5 km (1.6 mi) from the entrance to Mt. Seymour Park, park at a small lot opposite the Baden-Powell trailhead.

GOLDIE AND FLOWER LAKES

Distance: 4 km (2.5 mi)
Time: 1.5 hours
Surface: trail
Elevation gain: minimal
High point: 1020 m (3345 ft)

Quality: ★★★★
Difficulty: ■
Season: June to October
Car GPS entry: Mt Seymour Rd & Mt Seymour Pkwy North Vancouver, BC
Trailhead: 49°21'59" N 122°56'54" W

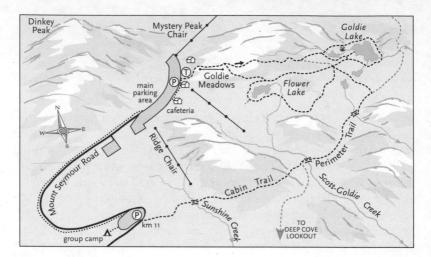

WOULD YOU like to take a cool walk in the forest on a hot day with the promise of wild blueberries in season? Goldie Lake makes an attractive destination, and you could include Flower Lake as well to extend your outing. Both Goldie and Flower are subalpine lakes with marshy shores that are slowly being invaded by surrounding plant life. They are situated near the ski runs in the popular Mt. Seymour Provincial Park. Note that dogs must be leashed in the park.

The trail begins at a large signpost located behind the first-aid building, near the Magic Carpet tow in the Goldie Meadows beginners' ski area. Descend beside the covered ski lift and follow the signed trail as it winds through forest for 560 m to a junction, the right arm of which leads to Flower Lake (320 m), which you can save for later. Continue on the main path about 200 m farther to another junction. Watch the signs carefully, because in this area there is a confusion of junctions and trails amongst the marshes and ponds that form the western side of Goldie Lake. Goldie Lake lies to your left, nestled in a shallow basin; you may make the 1 km (0.6 mi) loop of the lake

Goldie Lake on an overcast day.

in either direction. Note the variety of flowery plants and sedges that thrive in the marshes, beyond which the sometimes-muddy trail lies close to the lake's edge. Note that trees and shrubs are smaller here than lower on the mountain because of the harsher growing conditions (with the exception of towering yellow cedars).

At one of the trail crossings west of Goldie Lake, a signpost indicates the Perimeter/Flower Lake junction. The route to Flower Lake includes a stepping-stone creek crossing when water levels are high. Alternatively, there is a bridge just downstream. The trail wanders through forest and eventually meets, at a signed junction, an optional return to the parking lot. However, you continue past the end of Flower Lake and back to the first Goldie/Flower junction, the one you noted early in your outing. From here, turn left and ascend the gently sloping path back to your vehicle.

LONGER OPTION

The Cabin/Perimeter Trail provides a somewhat strenuous challenge (and additional time), best approached from Mt. Seymour Road. Watch for a large parking lot on a hairpin turn at km 11; the route begins at the Old Cabin Trail across the road. Be aware that this 1.6 km (1 mi) sinuous trail requires careful attention to footing and occasional use of hands, especially in wet weather. It takes you to the Goldie Lake junction and the lake circuits. To return, either retrace your route or continue to the upper parking lot and then walk beside Mt. Seymour Road for 1.5 km (0.9 mi) to your vehicle.

GETTING THERE

Vehicle: From Highway 1 northbound, take Exit 22B (Mount Seymour Parkway)—or, if southbound, take Exit 22—and travel east to Mt. Seymour Road and go left (north). Drive to the top parking lot.

DOG MOUNTAIN AND DINKEY PEAK

Distance to Dog Mountain: 5 km (3.1 mi)
Time: 2.5 hours
Distance to return via Dinkey Peak: 6 km (3.7 mi)
Time: 3 hours

Quality: ★★★
Difficulty: ■
Season: June to October
Car GPS entry: Mt Seymour Rd & Mt Seymour Pkwy North Vancouver, BC
Trailhead: 49°22'03" N 122°56'57" W

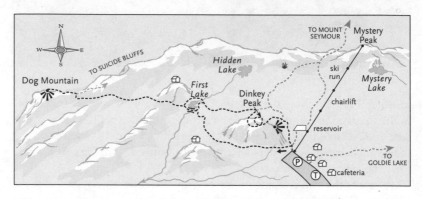

PANORAMIC VIEWS of city, mountains and ocean are your reward at the end of this trail. Despite its name, Dog Mountain is a family-friendly rocky bluff on the shoulder of Mount Seymour, reached with little elevation gain. Ease of access makes this a very popular outing, which, unfortunately, has resulted in deterioration of the trail bed. Take care as you pick your way over deeply exposed roots and loose rocks and through ever-widening muddy patches. While Dog Mountain is accessed from Mount Seymour Provincial Park, it lies in the Lower Seymour Conservation Reserve.

Start your walk at the far end of the parking lot by the information kiosk and enter the forest at the first opening on the left, where a trail map depicts your route. Due to work on improvements to the trail, there is no signpost. After some 20 minutes, you arrive at pond-size First Lake, set in a picturesque wooded basin overlooked by a search and rescue cabin perched on a bluff above. Before crossing the bridge at the lake's outlet, note the trail that joins from the right; it can provide a variation of your return route. Again, you travel up and down through forest over a tangled and rocky trail for 1.5 km (0.9 mi) until you arrive at the outcrops and bluffs of Dog Mountain. Here, you can see Mount Baker watching over the Fraser Valley, the neighbouring North Shore mountains, the Salish Sea and the mountains of Vancouver

View from Dog Mountain over Burrard Inlet towards Vancouver and Point Grey.

Island to the west, the sprawl of Metro Vancouver below and the Seymour River Valley at your feet.

To return via Dinkey Peak, a bluff that overlooks the parking lot below and Mount Baker in the distance, watch for the signed fork to Dinkey Peak at First Lake. Follow the gently rising trail to the next junction, this one providing the option of a short walk, left, to join the Mount Seymour Main Trail (see Walk 29) or a longer detour, right, over Dinkey Peak. For the latter, continue over the first rocky knobs, which form the actual "peak," then descend on a trail until you are surprised by a sturdy staircase on your right leading onto a bluff and your viewpoint. When you are ready to move on, return to the trail below the staircase and continue downhill a short distance to the main trail, where you turn right and descend to your vehicle.

SHORTER OPTION

Should you wish to avoid Dog Mountain and reach only the Dinkey Peak viewpoint, a walk of about 40 minutes one way, proceed up the Mount Seymour Main Trail from the parking lot for just over 500 m to a signpost pointing the way. Follow to the staircase leading to Dinkey Peak.

GETTING THERE

Vehicle: From Highway 1 northbound, take Exit 22B (Mount Seymour Parkway)—or, if southbound, take Exit 22—and travel east to Mt. Seymour Road and go left (north). Drive to the top parking lot.

MYSTERY LAKE AND PEAK

Distance: 4.2 km (2.6 mi)
Time: 2 hours
Surface: trail
Elevation gain: 200 m (656 ft)
Quality: ★★★
Difficulty: ■

Season: July to October
Car GPS entry: Mt Seymour Rd & Mt Seymour Pkwy North Vancouver, BC
Trailhead: 49°22'03" N 122°56'57" W

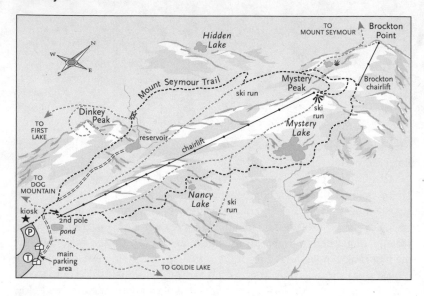

MYSTERY LAKE, though close to the Mount Seymour ski slopes, rests in an appealing setting, with rocky places to sit and enjoy the peace of nature. Please keep dogs on leash and leave drones at home.

From the kiosk at the far end of the parking lot, head briefly up the main trail. Then, at a signed junction just past the Mystery Peak chairlift terminal, make your way towards the second chairlift pole, which stands just beyond a pond. Near this pole, a narrow trail goes into the trees and immediately starts rising. Your climb continues over rough ground and through the coniferous forest for about 15 minutes until you reach Nancy Lake, an attractive little body of water best viewed from the boardwalk on its uphill side.

A few minutes later, the trail crosses a wide ski run and then re-enters the trees, where orange markers indicate the route. The trail, which also serves as a rather eroded creek bed during heavy rains and melting snow runoff, becomes stonier as it continues to rise for another 10 minutes or so. That's

The memorial to Tim Jones.

when you may hear the sound of Mystery Creek, signalling that the lake is not far. The trees gradually thin, and your surroundings become more subalpine as you near your objective in its rocky basin.

After a break at the lake you could retrace your steps, but the more pleasant way is to continue forward. Go counter-clockwise and follow the track north on the lake's east side, rising slightly, dropping, then rising again to the foot of the Brockton Point chairlift and a signposted junction. From here, you can continue around to a descending ski run. If, however, you want to enjoy the expansive views from Mystery Peak, you walk about 100 m west, then go left to climb and circle around to the summit and the upper terminus of the Mystery Peak chairlift. When ready to descend, leave the summit by taking the Manning ski run (signed), which swings around the summit and descends towards the parking lot.

On your way down the ski run, look for a signpost indicating the parking lot via Mount Seymour Main Trail. This original, well-used trail provides a "woodsier" alternative to the wide ski-run swath for the remaining 1.2 km (0.7 mi) to the parking lot. En route, and not far from the parking lot, you pass a memorial to Tim Jones, an advocate and team leader for North Shore Rescue who died in 2014, and the two ends of the Dinkey Peak Loop Trail (Walk 28), which may entice you to a final view before arriving back at your vehicle.

GETTING THERE
Vehicle: From Highway 1 northbound, take Exit 22B (Mount Seymour Parkway)—or, if southbound, take Exit 22—and travel east to Mt. Seymour Road and go left (north). Drive to the top parking lot.

INDIAN ARM PARKS

Distance: 10.5 km (6.5 mi)
Time: 3 hours
Surface: trail, paved
Quality: ★★
Difficulty: ■

Season: all year
Car GPS entry: Cates Park North Vancouver, BC
Trailhead: 49°18'12" N 122°57'18" W

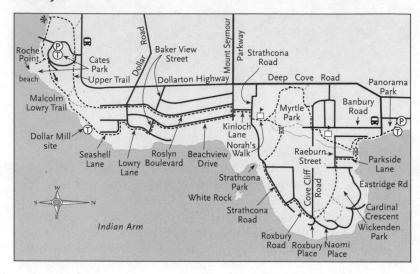

THIS WALK on Tsleil-Waututh First Nation territory begins in the family-oriented Cates Park at the mouth of Indian Arm, strolls along residential streets with harbour views, winds through a cluster of little parks near Deep Cove and finishes in the village where you can explore, rest and watch the various water-based activities. Your return route is more direct, or you can ride the bus back to Cates Park.

The walk begins in what was a food-gathering place for the Tsleil-Waututh, who call it Whey-Ah-Wichen, or "facing the wind." In the 1950s, the area was dedicated to the memory of Charles H. Cates, founder of the Cates Towing Company, and the park developed. Follow the shoreline in the park or walk on the beach around Roche Point, past a swimming beach and totem pole to the Malcolm Lowry Trail, which is named for the writer who lived in a shack along the shoreline here in the 1940s and '50s. This trail traverses the shoreline to the park's boundary, a historical information plaque and the concrete foundation of a beehive sawdust burner from the (Robert) Dollar lumber mill established in 1916.

Looking southeast from Roche Point towards Port Moody.

Continue along Sea Shell Lane, go left briefly to Beachview Drive, right onto Lowry Lane with its pocket park where kayakers launch their craft, left on Baker View Street and back to Beachview Street with its grand houses and expansive views. At Mount Seymour Parkway, jog left then right onto Kinloch Lane, then right again onto Norah's Walk. Go straight across the Seycove Secondary School parking lot, circle behind the school, find a trail between two portable buildings and follow this through the open woods of Myrtle Park, watching for nurse stumps en route. As you reach a dog park, go right over a bridge and soon exit at a small picnic and play area at Strathcona Road. Go left, pass the attractive Strathcona Park with its little bay, ascend to Roxbury Road and then, just at Cove Cliff Road, enter Wickenden Park. Descend some stairs and go left where the boardwalk forks. Exit at leafy Raeburn Street and follow this to a trail gate on the right, opposite the entrance to Cove Cliff Elementary School. This final path leads to Deep Cove, Panorama Park and a well-earned rest.

To return, retrace your steps to Raeburn Street, cross it and find a path that hugs the fence around the elementary school yard. Emerge onto Banbury Road, where you go left to cross Cove Cliff Road and arrive once again at the Myrtle Park dog area. This time, you may take the lower trail until you reach an obvious path leading to the secondary school. Staying right leads to the sports fields. Continue to Kinloch Lane, jog right, then head left along Roslyn Boulevard, which leads back to Cates Park. Trail maps may invite you to further explore this park.

SHORTER OPTION
For a walk of 4.5 km (2.8 mi), take the #212 bus back to Cates Park.

GETTING THERE
Transit: Take TransLink Bus 212 (Deep Cove/Phibbs Exchange) to both Cates Park and Deep Cove. For Cates Park, get off at the 4000 block of Dollarton Highway and walk 350 m east to the entrance. For Deep Cove, get off at the last stop, Banbury Road at Deep Cove Road.
Vehicle: From Highway 1 northbound, take Exit 23B (Main Street/Dollarton Highway)—or, if southbound, take Exit 23A (Main Street)—and drive east along Dollarton Highway to Cates Park and park in the upper lot. Lower lots have a 3-hour limit, as does Deep Cove from May to Labour Day, when finding parking may be difficult.

POINT GREY/WRECK BEACH

Distance: 10 km (6.2 mi)
Time: 3.5 hours
Surface: trail, sand, pebble beach
Quality: ★★★
Difficulty: ■

Season: all year; some sections unpass-
able at high tide
Car GPS entry: SW Marine Dr & W 16th
Ave University Endowment Lands, BC
Trailhead: 49°15'09" N 123°15'02" W

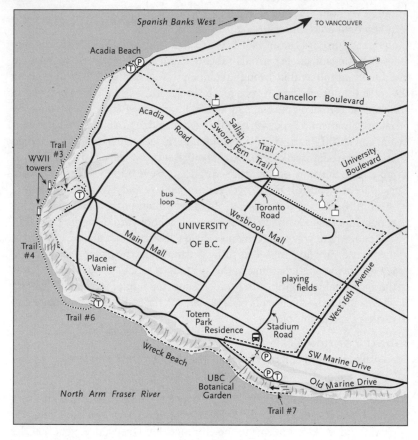

GEOGRAPHIC AND cultural characteristics combine to make this walk
unique. Part of the Pacific Spirit Regional Park, Wreck Beach is where river
meets ocean, and travel is determined by the height of the tide (check www
.tide-forecast.com for Point Grey). As well, Wreck Beach is a popular summer
destination for nude sunbathing. Several stairways connect the beach to the
road, allowing you the option of shortening your walk.

Cobblestones near Acadia Beach.

Your outing begins with a descent on stairs beside a creek to a rough track. Turn right and, after a short beach section, follow a trail in the woods to avoid the river's marshy edge. You also pass many pockets of sandy beach tucked in amongst logs—an area particularly popular with nude sunbathers in season—as you continue to the "heart" of Wreck Beach at Trail 6.

Here, the long North Arm Breakwater marks the mouth of the Fraser River and your route begins to curve northward. (Trail 6 offers a shortcut back to your transportation. From the top, go right along SW Marine Drive.) Continuing around the bend, you pass spectacular actively eroding cliffs that are fully exposed to fierce storms. Although protective berms have been built and cobblestones dumped on the beaches, wind and waves continue to scour away below while unseen internal forces loosen the cliffs from above. (Trail 4 offers a shortcut on this stretch, leading up to the Museum of Anthropology [MOA] and NW Marine Drive. Go right along NW Marine Drive.)

Ahead stands the first of two searchlight towers that were part of the Canadian military's defence system during World War II. (Trail 3, at the second tower, climbs to Marine Drive, where you turn left to reach Acadia Beach on an easy path.) Finally, after about 20 minutes of rocky terrain, which may be slippery, you reach the Acadia Beach parking lot.

Several options exist for your return. To remain on trails, cross NW Marine Drive to Admiralty Trail then onto Salish Trail, which leads to Chancellor Boulevard. Cross here, continue on Salish Trail for a short distance, then turn right onto Sword Fern Trail. At University Boulevard, cross to Toronto Road, then go left along Acadia Road and, just past Norma Rose Point School, regain Sword Fern Trail. At 16th Avenue, turn right and, at SW Marine Drive, go right to Old Marine Drive to reach your vehicle. To find a bus or to explore the UBC campus, walk up NW Marine Drive for 15 minutes to Chancellor Boulevard, where you can catch a #68 bus back to your starting point or wander back at will through campus, taking in parts of Walk 33 along the way.

GETTING THERE

Transit: From the UBC Exchange, take TransLink Bus 68 (UBC Exchange/Lower Mall) to West Mall and Stadium Road. Walk west on Stadium to SW Marine Drive, go right to Old Marine Drive, then follow to Trail 7.

Vehicle: Park near the Trail 7 sign on Old Marine Drive, which forks off SW Marine Drive halfway between West 16th Avenue and Wesbrook Mall.

CHANCELLOR WOODS

Distance: 6 km (3.7 mi)

Time 2 hours

Surface: trail, gravel

Quality: ★★★

Difficulty: ●

Season: all year

Car GPS entry: Blanca St & W 4th Ave
Vancouver, BC

Trailhead: 49°16'15" N 123°13'46" W

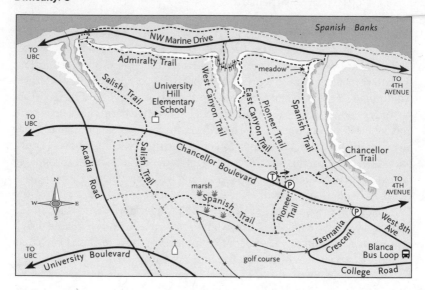

THE NORTHERN segment of Pacific Spirit Regional Park, extending from Chancellor Boulevard to Spanish Banks, contains a number of trails, mostly in forest. The area features a considerable variety of trees, some quite deep ravines and, optionally, the beach. The trail system lends itself to circular walks; two that start from the same point are described here.

From the information kiosk at the trailhead, head east into the forest along Chancellor Trail, a connector to Spanish Trail, which then leads north amongst tall second-growth Douglas-fir, cedar and hemlock growing on the flats above Spanish Bank Creek. After some 20 minutes of gentle descent, you meet a junction with a stile; the track behind the stile leads to Pioneer Trail and the site of a pioneer homestead of which only a small "meadow" remains. From here, an unmarked trail connects to the Admiralty Trail below.

From the junction at the stile, continue downhill to another stile, at which the Admiralty Trail goes left. (From here, you can also drop down to Marine Drive and the beach.) Admiralty Trail follows the edge of the bluffs until you

Stairs along the East Canyon Trail, descending into the ravine.

meet the junction with East Canyon Trail, which leads back to the trailhead to complete the shorter outing. This route follows the ravine's edge fairly closely, though it is sometimes forced away from the main canyon by washouts.

The longer loop continues on Admiralty Trail from the East Canyon Trail junction and winds down to the depths of the ravine, where another option presents itself. The more challenging route climbs back up over what may seem like endless stairs, but these eventually land you on a continuation of the easy Admiralty Trail along the bluffs—which afford winter views of Burrard Inlet and beyond—until it meets the Salish Trail.

The second option from the ravine's floor is to cross NW Marine Drive, walk left along the beach, ascend to the Acadia Beach parking lot (see Walk 31) and, a few paces beyond, recross the road and pick up the Salish Trail. This broad packed-gravel path ascends gently to University Hill Elementary School and Chancellor Boulevard. Use the pedestrian crossing and stay with Salish Trail south to its intersection with Spanish Trail, where you go left. This track goes through deciduous scrub and crosses a marsh before entering pleasant, open forest. Finally, going left on Pioneer Trail takes you back to Chancellor Boulevard and your transportation.

SHORTER OPTION
For an hour-long walk covering 3.9 km (2.4 mi), at the junction of Admiralty Trail with East Canyon Trail, follow East Canyon back to your starting point.

GETTING THERE
Transit: Take TransLink Bus 4 (Powell/Downtown/UBC) or 14 (Hastings/UBC) to Blanca Loop. Walk north on Blanca Street to 8th Avenue, walk 700 m west to Tasmania Crescent, then, 100 m farther, go north to join the route at Spanish Trail.
Vehicle: On West 4th Avenue, head west past Blanca Street near the University of British Columbia and continue 800 m west of Drummond Drive to an obvious roadside parking area. Note the 2-hour time limit.

UBC GARDENS TOUR

Distance: 5 km (3.1 mi)
Time: 2 hours
Surface: paved; trail
Quality: ★★
Difficulty: ●

Season: all year
Car GPS entry (Rose Garden parkade):
6278 NW Marine Dr Vancouver, BC
Trailhead (outside parkade): 49°16'11" N
123°15'23" W

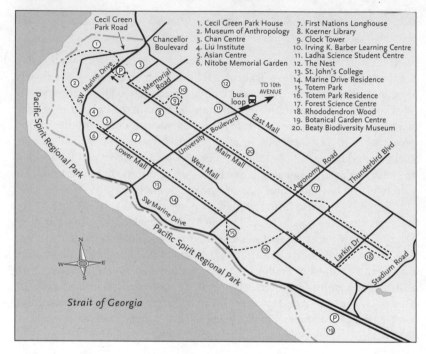

1. Cecil Green Park House
2. Museum of Anthropology
3. Chan Centre
4. Liu Institute
5. Asian Centre
6. Nitobe Memorial Garden
7. First Nations Longhouse
8. Koerner Library
9. Clock Tower
10. Irving K. Barber Learning Centre
11. Ladha Science Student Centre
12. The Nest
13. St. John's College
14. Marine Drive Residence
15. Totem Park
16. Totem Park Residence
17. Forest Science Centre
18. Rhododendron Wood
19. Botanical Garden Centre
20. Beaty Biodiversity Museum

GARDENS AND attractive treed avenues have fortunately been left intact as the large campus—in reality, a city within a city—undergoes continual change and growth. This walk links some natural highlights; you could, in fact, begin anywhere along the circuit and adapt it to your own inclinations. (To assist your route-finding, see www.maps.ubc.ca and parking.ubc.ca.) This walk also links nicely with Walk 31.

From the parkade, cross NW Marine Drive, go right a few paces, then cut left beside a parking lot and between buildings to reach Cecil Green Park Road. Cross this and find your way behind some buildings to Cecil Green Park, with its attractive grounds and fine view. Next, go west and south along the clifftop opposite the Museum of Anthropology, continue past Haida

The garden at the Asian Centre is known for its second-growth forest, Asian wild plants and shrine. *Photo: Ellen Halliday*

House with its totems and follow a wooded path to exit on NW Marine Drive opposite the Liu Institute. The path continues a few paces to the right across the road to Lower Mall, and almost immediately, you arrive at the Nitobe Memorial Garden. Behind the walls (entrance fee) lies a miniature Japanese landscape. Opposite this garden sits the Asian Centre with its commemorative Pacific Bell in a pagoda; take a diversion on Memorial Road to visit it. Your next stop is the First Nations Longhouse, built amongst trees that were once part of a larger arboretum.

Continuing south along Lower Mall, you cross University Boulevard, pass St. John's College and the Marine Drive Residences, then cross the northern jog of Agronomy Road. Now cross diagonally through Totem Park, an open woodland of red cedar and Douglas-fir, then wend your way east (left) through the residence grounds to West Mall. Here, you go right to reach Larkin Drive, on which you soon go right into Rhododendron Wood, which, despite its name, is another woodland of cedar and fir. Stroll along the path to its end, then jog left to the broad pedestrian Main Mall Greenway, where you turn left again and begin your return journey.

The first stop of interest here is a community garden followed by a carved wooden arch, Hungarian style, at the Forestry complex. Note the adjacent pole, carved from an 800-year-old Western red cedar that was blown down in Stanley Park during a major storm in 2006. Thereafter, continue along Main Mall past the Beaty Biodiversity Museum—with its Blue Whale skeleton suspended in a glass atrium—until you reach the clock tower in the grounds of the Irving K. Barber Learning Centre, which hugs the original library building built of stone.

From here, continue north for another minute or two to the lovely rose garden, with its balcony views of the garden itself, the entrance to Howe Sound and the mountains beyond. Now you need only descend some steps to arrive at the parkade entrance, thus completing your loop.

GETTING THERE

Transit: TransLink Buses 1 to 14 service UBC. From the UBC Exchange bus loop, walk west along Student Union Boulevard, cross East Mall and join the walk at the clock tower.

Vehicle: Make your way to NW Marine Drive at UBC and the Rose Garden Parkade near the Chan Centre.

MUSQUEAM/FRASER RIVER

Distance: 8 km (5 mi)
Time: 2.5 hours
Surface: road, trail, bridle trail
Quality: ★★★
Difficulty: ●

Season: all year
Car GPS entry: SW Marine Dr & Crown St
Vancouver, BC
Trailhead: 49°14'00" N 123°11'38" W

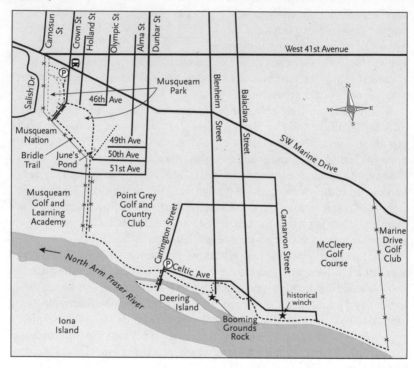

OVER THE centuries, this former wetland has supported wildlife, First Nations, immigrant farmers, a cannery, shipbuilding, forestry activities and now golf courses and residences. This walk on Musqueam Nation territory provides a taste of each.

From your vehicle, head south until, at the foot of Crown Street, you enter the Musqueam Reserve (private land). Cross two closely situated bridges, and at the second, turn left onto a bridle trail that runs behind houses and briefly beside a stream. (Bridle trails can be very muddy.) Continue across a large covered water main, keeping right, and cross 51st Avenue, still on the bridle path, which now runs between the Musqueam Golf and Learning Academy

Looking out over the Fraser River from Deering Island Park.

on your right and the Point Grey Golf and Country Club on the left. How many golf balls can you spot in the deep drainage ditch? Then comes the river, with views up, down and across to Iona Island; log booms lining the shore; and planes using the airport just beyond. Before long, you arrive at Carrington Street (where there is parking) and the bridge to Deering Island, the west end of which is a park where there are benches, a great place to watch river traffic. To think that this island sold for four dollars in 1900!

Back on the mainland, continue eastwards past luxury homes with stables to your left and a slough to your right, on which are moored pleasure craft below the island houses. At the next street end (Blenheim) you encounter the Booming Grounds Rock, a large boulder inscribed with memories of the life of a boy growing up on the booms. Then, from Celtic Avenue, you follow a bridle trail through forest to Balaclava Street, where you follow a public path between a works yard on your right and new housing on your left, built on land previously occupied by different owners who built boats and ships until 1994. Still heading upstream, and stopping at the info-boards, you come to a stretch with views over the pleasant, public McCleery Golf Course and then an End of Trail sign at the Marine Drive Golf Club grounds.

Retrace your steps until, having turned north at the Musqueam Golf Academy, you go half right on the water-main path just beyond June's Pond where a plaque commemorates her work to protect the Musqueam Park wetlands. Proceed across a wide grassy field to its northern edge to cross to 46th Avenue. When 46th ends at Holland Street, go straight ahead on the little lane to Crown and back to your starting point via road or wooded trail.

GETTING THERE
Transit: Take TransLink Bus 41 (Joyce Station/Crown/UBC) or 49 (Metrotown Station/Dunbar Loop/UBC) to SW Marine Drive and Crown Street.
Vehicle: Drive to Crown Street south of SW Marine Drive. A few parking slots jut into Musqueam Park.

ARBUTUS GREENWAY

Distance: 12 km (7.5 mi)
Time: 3.5 hours
Quality: ★
Difficulty: ●

Season: all year
Car GPS entry: W King Edward Ave &
Arbutus St Vancouver, BC
Trailhead: 49°15'05" N 123°09'10" W

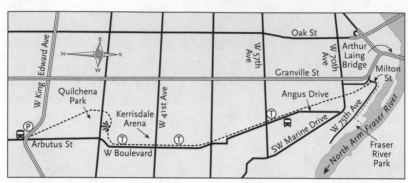

THE ARBUTUS Greenway is a 9 km (5.4 mi) traffic-free pathway for people to walk, bike or roll through Vancouver neighbourhoods. In 2016, the City of Vancouver purchased the Arbutus Corridor from Canadian Pacific Railway (CPR), immediately removed the railway tracks, built a temporary paved path and renamed it as a greenway for everyone to enjoy. A public consultation process, which will result in a master plan by 2022, is underway. This walk takes you through Arbutus Ridge and Kerrisdale Village and ends in Marpole. The proximity to transit routes allows you to shorten your walk almost anywhere and return to your starting point by bus.

From the southwest corner of Arbutus Street and King Edward Avenue, head south, keeping to the left side of the path designated for walkers. On most days, swarms of cyclists buzz by in both directions on the opposite side of the path. On your right, Quilchena Park, which means "flat place near the water" in the Salish language, is worth a visit to experience its green space and mountain views. Now the path climbs gradually to Arbutus Ridge. As you rise above the rooftops, a panorama of English Bay and the North Shore mountains is revealed.

Next up is Kerrisdale Village with its many shops and the venerable Kerrisdale Arena, which was built in 1949 and was the site of the city's first-ever rock concert, by Bill Haley and His Comets on June 27, 1956. After the path crosses 49th Avenue, vegetable and flower gardens appear alongside and quirky scarecrow figures—Bart, Pot Head and Charley—calmly observe the passing parade.

Approaching the southern end of the Arbutus Greenway.

A slow descent into Marpole brings you to a crossing at SW Marine Drive and the end of the greenway at Milton Street. A visit to Colbourne House in William Mackie Park, the home of the Marpole Museum & Historical Society, may persuade you to linger before your return.

To take transit as part of your return, board the #16 bus at 64th Avenue or later along West Boulevard.

LONGER OPTION
From the end of Milton Street, head west for 750 m on 75th Avenue to enter Fraser River Park, which has boardwalks that cross restored tidal marshes and great views of the Fraser River and Sea Island.

GETTING THERE
Transit: Take TransLink Bus 16 (29th Avenue/Arbutus) or 25 (Brentwood Station/UBC) to Arbutus Street and King Edward Avenue.
Vehicle: From Granville Street (Highway 99), go west on King Edward Avenue (25th Avenue) to Arbutus Street. Park on a neighbourhood side street.

HASTINGS MILL TO SPANISH BANKS

Distance: 6 km (3.7 mi)
Time: 2 hours
Surface: paved
Quality: ★★
Difficulty: ●

Season: all year
Car GPS entry: Alma St & W 4th Ave
Vancouver, BC
Trailhead: 49°16'21" N 123°11'09" W

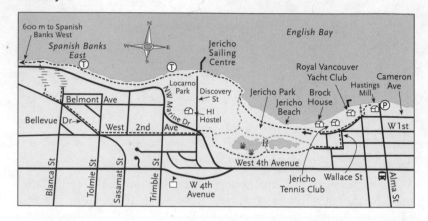

BRING ALONG your swimming kit (in season!) on this walk, which features a touch of history, sandy beaches, well-groomed paths, lawns and copses of trees. Once home to a Musqueam First Nation village (Ee'yullmough), then a logging camp known as Jerry's Cove—hence Jericho—and then a base for the Department of National Defence (now only the building used by the Jericho Sailing Centre remains), water and beach make this a popular destination nowadays.

On foot, go to the north end of Alma Street to see the Hastings Mill Store Museum (limited hours). This 1865 structure was built in Gastown and served as the first post office and community centre on Burrard Inlet. A lucky survivor of the 1886 Gastown fire that nearly levelled that settlement, it was barged to its present location in 1930.

Starting at the museum, cross the park to Point Grey Road and head west past the Royal Vancouver Yacht Club, the Jericho Tennis Club and the Brock House Senior Centre (once the Brock family home), before angling towards the beach and a small Parks Board pavilion. From now on, you see the North Shore mountains across the inlet on your right and Bowen Island more or less ahead. Continuing past the Jericho Sailing Centre and half left towards a grove of trees, you reach the pavilion at Locarno Beach. A farther 600 m

English Bay and Crown Mountain seen from Jericho Beach.

on, travelling amongst dog walkers, cyclists and beach-goers, you reach the Spanish Banks East pavilion. Should you wish to continue yet another 600 m to the pavilion at Spanish Banks West, you will meet the boundary of Pacific Spirit Regional Park at Spanish Bank Creek and the beginning of that park's web of trails (see Walk 32).

To add an interesting variation to your return route, cross NW Marine Drive immediately behind the Spanish Banks East pavilion to a set of stairs. This ascends the steep, 30 m bank to the foot of Blanca Street and a short walk uphill leads to a five-way intersection. Alternatively, another set of stairs, steeper and longer (45 m), climbs the hill from a point farther west, about halfway along the parking lot. You must keep a sharp eye to spot either set. The second set emerges on Belmont Avenue. Turning left along this street of majestic homes takes you to the aforementioned five-way intersection. Go half right onto Bellevue Drive and along West 2nd Avenue, passing the Aberthau Community Centre, a former family residence. Cross NW Marine Drive to Jericho Park, then make your way back to Hastings Mill Pioneer Park and your starting point.

GETTING THERE

Transit: Take TransLink Bus 44 (UBC/Downtown) or 84 (UBC/VCC-Clark Station) to West 4th Avenue at Alma Street. Walk 400 m north on Alma Street to Point Grey Road.

Vehicle: From West 4th Avenue, drive north on Alma Street to Point Grey Road, turn west and park in a strip-lot beside Hastings Mill Pioneer Park.

KITSILANO/FALSE CREEK

Distance: 7 km (4.3 mi)

Time: 2 hours

Surface: paved

Quality: ★★

Difficulty: ●

Season: all year

Car GPS entry: Arbutus St & Cornwall Ave
Vancouver, BC

Trailhead (parking lot): 49°16'36" N
123°09'07" W

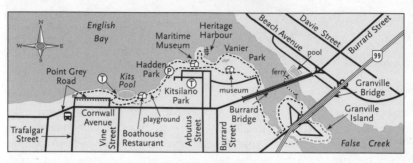

ARE YOU looking for a walk with the option of other sideline activities? You could happily spend several hours at this popular destination that offers a lovely walk with great views as well as swimming, history and culture. You can determine your own walking distance, as this part of the path is but a small section of the 30 km (18 mi) Seaside Greenway biking and walking route that stretches between Stanley Park and Spanish Banks (Walk 36).

From the beach at the parking lot described, walk east around the point to arrive at Hadden Park. Here you can explore Kits Point, the Heritage Harbour and the Maritime Museum, which houses the RCMP schooner *St. Roch*. This vessel, built in 1928, was the first to navigate the Northwest Passage in both directions and the first ship to circumnavigate North America. Outside the museum sits the *Ben Franklin*, a historic submarine. Continuing on takes you around Vanier Park on a bulge of land that marks the entrance to False Creek on its southern side. Have a kite? This is a good place to fly it. Like Shakespeare? This is the home of the popular Bard on the Beach theatre during the summer. Next, you pass under the 1932 Art Deco–style Burrard Bridge, and shortly thereafter, you arrive under the Granville Street Bridge. From here you may retrace your steps or, with more time, extend your walk by continuing left under the bridge to Granville Island, where there is a wonderful market and a host of shops to explore.

If you still want to continue along the Seaside Greenway, hop aboard a ferry (fare required) at Granville Island to cross False Creek and join the path

View across the entrance of Heritage Harbour to Vanier Park.

that parallels Beach Avenue to Stanley Park. This will double your distance, but turnabout is always an option, as is a return by bus. (This walk links to Walk 38 at Granville Island.) Eventually, back at your starting point, you may continue your walk by heading west past the heated saltwater Kits Pool to find a narrow path that runs unobtrusively below houses and above the beach. At its end, a flight of stairs rises to Point Grey Road, here a quiet residential street below whose houses you have just travelled. A return by the path or a stroll along Point Grey Road to rejoin the Seaside Greenway takes you back to the park and your transportation.

GETTING THERE

Transit: Take TransLink Bus 2 (Macdonald/Downtown) to Cornwall Avenue and Trafalgar Street or Bus 4 (Powell/Downtown/UBC) or 7 (Nanaimo Station/Dunbar) to West 4th and Trafalgar and walk 550 m north on Trafalgar. Begin at the west end of the walk.

Vehicle: At the north end of Arbutus Street in Kitsilano, park in the pay lot near the playground. If full, there are other lots to the east.

FALSE CREEK

Distance: 8 km (5 mi)
Time: 2.5 hours
Surface: paved
Quality: ★★
Difficulty: ●

Season: all year
Car GPS entry: Terminal Ave & Quebec St
Vancouver, BC
Trailhead: 49°16'23" N 123°06'08" W

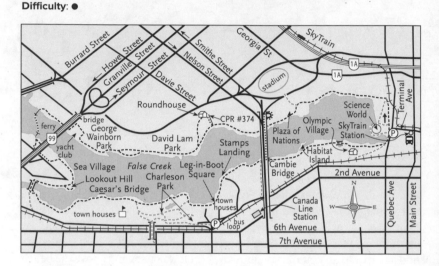

THE TERM "urban wonderland" aptly describes this walk around False Creek, which encircles what was once Vancouver's clanging industrial core. Strolling the seawall provides stunning views, green spaces, artistic décor, glimpses into history, a mini-ferry ride and the eclectic Granville Island. Note that as a circle walk, there are various access points.

Beginning your outing in a counter-clockwise direction from Science World and rounding the end of the inlet, you pass the Plaza of Nations, which is slated for major development in the coming years, and stroll along the edges of Yaletown, Vancouver's trendy, renovated former warehouse district. Next, having passed under the Cambie Street Bridge, you may take a side trip to the Roundhouse Community Centre, which displays artifacts of early rail-roading days, including Engine #374, which pulled the first transcontinental train into the city in 1887. Farther along, a bilingual poem in English and Chinook, a settlement-era trading language, is inscribed on the seawall handrail of David Lam Park. Watch for great blue herons at the water's edge; regenerated habitat in False Creek has attracted the return of these gangly birds. Your next experience is a ride across the water to Granville Island on one of

Looking east across the end of False Creek to Science World.

the mini-ferries that you've seen darting about while you were walking; board one (fare required) at the foot of Hornby Street. See www.theaquabus.com for accessibility information.

To continue your route left from the ferry landing, the most attractive way is the waterside walk past shops and the Sea Village of floating homes to Lookout Hill. Of course, you may want to explore the Granville Island Market and other attractions first. West of Lookout Hill, you cross a footbridge to make your way along the south shore of False Creek, from which your view now takes in the reflective downtown high-rises set against the North Shore mountains.

Continuing along the seawall, you pass residential and light commercial areas, then suddenly notice an old wooden post-and-beam structure at the water's edge, adorned by neon text artwork. This structure marks the site of a shipyard where boats were built for World War I, then later, where steel was fabricated for Vancouver bridges and buildings and for structures all over the world. Next, you may visit Habitat Island, an eco-habitat project designed to be a sanctuary for birds and marine life where a railway yard and lumber mill once stood. Finally, after crossing a contemporary metal bridge as you pass Olympic Village, where the athletes lived during the 2010 Winter Olympic Games, it is but a few minutes back to Science World, your transportation and your exit from this urban wonderland.

GETTING THERE
Transit: Take the SkyTrain to Main Street at Science World or TransLink Buses 3, 8 or 19.
Vehicle: Travel to Science World at Terminal Avenue and Quebec Street. Park in the Science World lot on the west side of Quebec, south of Terminal.

CANADA PLACE
TO BROCKTON POINT

Distance: 12 km (7.5 mi)

Time: 3.5 hours

Surface: paved

Quality: ★★

Difficulty: ●

Season: all year

Car GPS entry: Howe St & Canada Pl

Vancouver, BC

Trailhead (Canada Place): 49°17'15" N
123°06'47" W

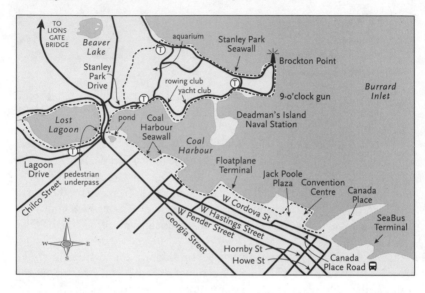

FROM THE seascape-coloured glass towers of downtown to the deep-green forest of Stanley Park, from cruise ships to a historical cannon and lighthouse, from busy floatplane berths to quiet ponds, this walk is a feast for the eyes and the mind. And once in Stanley Park, you could wander at will, then return by bus.

Stanley Park was home to many Indigenous peoples for thousands of years and remains a culturally significant area for the local First Nations people today. Stanley Park is on the territory of the Musqueam, Squamish and Tsleil-Waututh peoples.

From your transportation, walk to the front of Canada Place at the foot of Hornby Street. Adorned with five "sails" symbolizing the area's rich maritime connections, this multi-use facility with an interpretive centre is itself worth exploring. Next, head west and follow the seawalk to stroll around the

Great blue herons nest in Stanley Park and are frequent visitors to Lost Lagoon.

perimeter of the Convention Centre, noting the green-roof system that nourishes indigenous plants. On the centre's west side, climb the steps to Jack Poole Plaza and the impressive cauldron that held the Olympic flame in 2010. Back on the lower level, promenade into history as you travel along the Coal Harbour Seawalk with its historical information boards. Runners jog by, floatplanes come and go and yachts doze in the marinas. After passing Devonian Harbour Park and its pond, you approach the causeway, noting the pedestrian underpass that leads to Lost Lagoon, a diversion for later.

Now, changing direction, you go to your right along the south shore of Stanley Park towards Brockton Point, first passing an information booth, then a naval base on Deadman Island, once a First Nations funerary site. Vancouver's unique nine-o'clock gun, which has been fired almost daily since 1898, sits on the southern "elbow" of Brockton Point. Three hundred metres along stands Brockton Point's iconic, fully functioning, red-and-white lighthouse, built in 1914. From here, wide-ranging views take in the cityscape, ships in the harbour, industrial activities across the water and mountains forming the northern skyline.

The next section stretches 1.3 km (0.8 mi) in view of the Lions Gate Bridge. En route, turn aside to visit the Brockton Point totem poles and learn about their significance and history. Continue on the seawall to Lumberman's Arch, near a waterplay area, where you turn inland. You pass behind the aquarium and make your way to the information booth you passed earlier. Retrace your steps on the seawall to the pedestrian underpass noted previously; this provides access to a pleasant 1.8 km (1.1 mi) circuit of Lost Lagoon Bird Sanctuary. Finally, return through the underpass and back towards the city, perhaps varying your route as you wish.

GETTING THERE

Transit: Take the SkyTrain or SeaBus or TransLink Bus 4, 7, 10 or 50 to Waterfront Station. From there, walk west on Cordova Street to Howe Street, turn right and follow to Canada Place.

Vehicle: Parking downtown may be difficult, and pay parking is in effect throughout Stanley Park.

RENFREW NEIGHBOURHOOD

Distance: 5 km (3.1 mi)

Time: 2 hours

Surface: path, sidewalk

Quality: ★★

Difficulty: ●

Season: all year

Car GPS entry: 3360 Victoria Dr
Vancouver, BC

Trailhead: 49°15'21" N 123°03'56" W

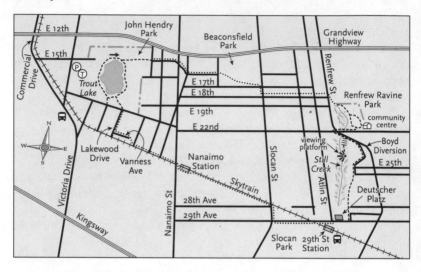

THIS IS a loop walk with two clearly identifiable starting points: 29th Avenue SkyTrain station and John Hendry Park. From the community centre, start your walk in a clockwise direction around Trout Lake, the centrepiece of John Hendry Park, passing through the off-leash dog area. Trout Lake once provided water via a flume for Hastings Sawmill, which was co-owned by John Hendry and located at the foot of Dunlevy Street. At the end of the lake, as you turn to the east, you intersect B.C. Parkway as you walk eastwards away from the lake alongside the baseball diamond to what becomes 15th Avenue. Cross Nanaimo Street and walk along 16th Avenue to the second park of your outing, Beaconsfield. Head diagonally across the park to its southeast corner and another short stretch of residential streets, with 18th Avenue bringing you to a crossing of Renfrew Street and the entrance to the north end of Ravine Park and the Still Creek Loop Trail.

As you descend into the cool twilight and the soundscape of the rushing waters of Still Creek, pause for a moment to reset after your time on the bustling city streets. Now head upstream on the left side until, after ascending

Still Creek flowing through Renfrew Ravine Park.

stairs to the back side of Renfrew Park Community Centre, you rise to a busy intersection where you must cross to the diagonal southwest corner of 22nd Avenue and Renfrew Diversion.

Ahead of you, between the mosaic and yin-yang bench, stairs take you down to a viewing platform on Still Creek. At time of writing, you must return to street level from the platform and go east on the Boyd Diversion, then right on the first lane you encounter. Bear right at intersections to keep the ravine below on your right, first on a lane, then on a trail where you may pause to enjoy the challenge of the labyrinth before emerging on 29th Avenue and the Deutscher Platz, created by Vancouver's German-Canadian community to coincide with Expo 86.

Cross to the 29th Avenue SkyTrain station, the second starting point for the walk, and follow B.C. Parkway, a multi-use path that follows the Sky-Train over much of its length, west to the Nanaimo station. Continue across Nanaimo Street and follow the parkway, gradually descending, but in the process enjoying the sweeping vista of the North Shore mountains. Just before the SkyTrain tracks descend to the surface, your route crosses under the elevated tracks and then parts company with the transit line, joining Vanness Avenue before heading north on Lakewood Drive to John Hendry Park and your starting point.

GETTING THERE

Transit: Take the SkyTrain or TransLink Bus 16, 26, 29 or 33 to 29th Avenue station.

Vehicle: From 12th Avenue/Grandview Highway, go south on Victoria Drive. Just after 17th Avenue, turn left into the Trout Lake Community Centre parking lot.

NEW BRIGHTON PARK/ HASTINGS PARK

Distance: 6.5 km (4 mi)
Time: 2.5 hours
Surface: gravel, paved
Quality: ★★
Difficulty: ●

Season: all year
Car GPS entry: Commissioner St & New Brighton Rd Vancouver, BC
Trailhead: 49°17'22" N 123°02'22" W

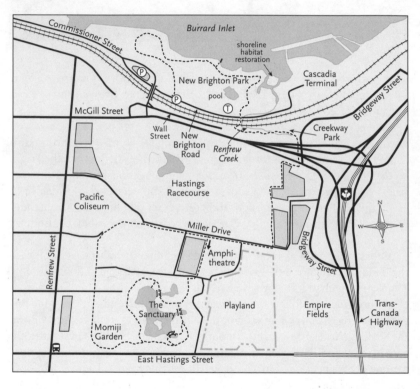

THIS WALK explores three examples of natural habitats that have been restored for all to enjoy. New Brighton Park's shoreline enhancement project restores Renfrew Creek where it meets the inlet and adds a saltwater marsh for juvenile fish and wildlife, including shorebirds, songbirds and waterfowl. The Sanctuary in Hastings Park, once covered by buildings and asphalt, is now a lush wetland habitat of native West Coast vegetation and home to many species of wildlife at different stages of their lives. And between these two is Creekway Park, which preserves a remnant of Renfrew Creek.

Begin your walk at New Brighton Park, taking a few moments to absorb the mountain vista and watch the marine activity in Burrard Inlet before setting off westwards towards the dog off-leash area. Circle the pooch playground clockwise and head back along the shoreline. On the water you may see nimble tugs shepherd-

The rocks, Japanese maple (momiji) trees, flowers and waterfalls in Momiji Garden bring peace and serenity.

ing a freighter into berth at the Cascadia grain terminal. Soon you arrive at the saltwater marsh, where the water level changes with the tide. Although the marsh was completed in 2017, plastic fences remain, temporarily, to protect the young plantings from marauding Canada geese.

Continue past the marsh and across the swimming pool parking lot to enter the pedestrian tunnel under the railway tracks, noting as you do the open culvert that transports Renfrew Creek towards Burrard Inlet. After you exit the tunnel, turn left and ascend to Creekway Park, where Renfrew Creek is being daylighted, allowed to run naturally above ground. When this project is completed, the creek will be exposed from Hastings Street to the inlet.

Follow the path to Bridgeway Street and another tunnel, this time to take you under McGill Street. At the end of the tunnel, cross the McGill Street off-ramp, turn right, walk a short distance beside the parking lot and then go left through an amazing corridor of cedar and cottonwoods to its end at Miller Drive. Follow the yellow planters, keeping Playland and then the amphitheatre on your left, as you approach The Sanctuary. Choose your own way around its gravel paths, perhaps stopping at the boardwalk, the stone terraces or the fishing dock, where urban fisherfolk enjoy their hobby.

To return, find your way through the Momiji Garden, pass beside the PNE Forum, make your way towards the Pacific Coliseum, turn right onto Miller Road and retrace your steps to New Brighton Park.

GETTING THERE

Transit: Take TransLink Bus 14 (Hastings/UBC) or 16 (29th Avenue Station/ Arbutus) to Renfrew Street and East Hastings Street. Begin the walk in reverse, at Momiji Garden.

Vehicle: From Highway 1, take Exit 25 (McGill St) and go west onto McGill Street. Bear right onto Commissioner Street and its overpass to New Brighton Road, where you turn left. Park in the overflow lot or roadside on New Brighton Road.

THE 3-C CIRCUIT

Distance: 5.5 km (3.4 mi)

Time: 1.5 hours

Surface: paved, trail

Quality: ★★★

Difficulty: ●

Season: all year

Car GPS entry: Kerr St & 63rd Ave

Vancouver, BC

Trailhead: 49°12'43" N 123°02'29" W

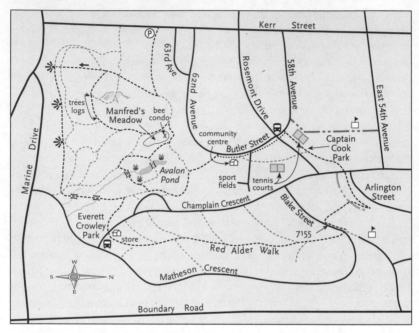

LOCATED IN the southeastern corner of Vancouver, the three Cs are Everett Crowley, Captain Cook and Champlain Heights Parks. Your walk loops through all three, beginning in the first. Note the information kiosk with a map at the parking lot.

Discovering Everett Crowley Park is a happy surprise. Located on slopes overlooking the North Arm of the Fraser River and the farmlands of Richmond, with Mount Baker beyond, this park is one of Vancouver's largest. The site has experienced logging, farming, quarrying and, for 25 years, was a dump for Vancouver's garbage. However, since the park was established in 1987, it has been returning to a more natural state, attractive to birds and wildlife and to people out for a breath of nature.

From your vehicle, walk to the first major intersection, where you turn right on a wide, gravel path. As the path turns east, cross Vista Trail to the narrow, mulched Gary Oak Trail, which offers occasional, brushy viewpoints best enjoyed in the leafless winter. In about 650 m, the trail bends north onto a concrete path (Sunrise Trail) and ascends behind residences to a T-junction. Turn right to reach and cross Champlain Crescent; a few paces to the right, join the Grey Gum Trail, then, at a mini-playground, the Red Alder Trail. Follow this, ignoring side paths, as it rises gently for about 900 m until you exit on Matheson Crescent, opposite a field. Cross at the crosswalk and walk 150 m left to a narrow footpath just past the "Kanata Co-op 7155 Blake Street" sign. Turn right onto this path and then right again briefly, then bend left to join a path paralleling Arlington Street. Cross Champlain Crescent and proceed along a greenway, the woods of Captain Cook Park on your right. Emerging onto Butler Street, turn left and continue past Champlain Heights Park to its end, where your route again leaves the streets to re-enter Everett Crowley Park at its northeast corner.

Avalon Pond is at the heart of Everett Crowley Park.
Photo: Alice Purdey

Bear left when the trail branches and gradually descend, catching glimpses of Avalon Pond below, then turn right to approach the water on a gravel path. The pond was named for Vancouver's last working dairy, owned by the Crowley family and sold in 2011. A footbridge over Kincross Creek at the mouth of the pond provides the best view. Turn right to follow the waterside, mulched Avalon Path, which leads back to the parallel, gravelled Creekside Trail. Now, bearing left and sharp left onto Everett's Loop, watch for Manfred's Meadow with its inviting bench and bee condo. After a pause, retrace a few steps back to Raptors' Way, which takes you right, then right and left back to the parking lot.

GETTING THERE

Transit: Take TransLink Bus 26 (Joyce Station/29th Avenue Station) to Rosemont Drive and Butler Street or to Champlain Crescent and Matheson Crescent. Begin the walk halfway through.

Vehicle: From Kerr Street in southeast Vancouver, park in the lot south of East 63rd Avenue.

VANCOUVER FRASER FORESHORE

Distance: 8 km (5 mi)
Time: 2.5 hours
Surface: trail, paved
Quality: ★★★
Difficulty: ●

Season: all year
Car GPS entry: Boundary Rd & Marine
Way Vancouver, BC
Trailhead: 49°12'05" N 123°01'25" W

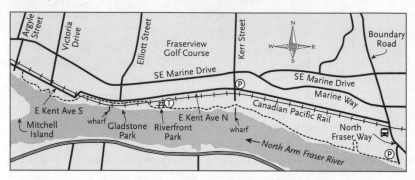

THIS TRAIL, part of a riverside greenway along the north shore of the Fraser River, features log booms, wharves and birdlife on one end; a variety of residential styles and development on the other; and a picnic site and playground halfway along.

Head west from the parking area. (Walk 72 goes east.) The trail begins between a chainlink fence and a string of log booms on the river's edge. This once-busy industrial and log sort area now throbs with the sounds of trucks and diggers relentlessly converting works yards into residential and commercial complexes and manicured grounds. As a diversion, you may follow a paved road from the trail through the developing neighbourhood to Kerr Street, where there is a restaurant, a parking area (an alternative access point), a wharf and a boardwalk. Here, also, the bike and pedestrian paths separate.

Some 700 m later, you arrive at the picnic site and playground, after which the path swings around a works yard and closely parallels the railway tracks, turning back to the water at Gladstone Park. The *Langara II* fishing lodge moors here for the winter; in summer, it is towed to Haida Gwaii for use by sports fisherfolk. A short wharf marks the west end of the narrow Gladstone Park; limited parking is available.

Until now, you will no doubt have noticed the noise and activity on the far side of the Fraser, the traffic running along River Road in Richmond. Beyond that road is a strip of industrial concerns and then farmland. Your next 800 m, however, follow a seawall-like path of paving stones. The path, which wanders

The shoreline along the Fraser River is home to birds and log booms. *Photo: Alice Purdey*

in front of flower gardens, sculpted lawns and attractive townhouses, offers places to sit or lean and watch the river traffic and activities. The river channel here narrows as it splits around Mitchell Island then passes beneath the Knight Street Bridge. The island was originally three separate ones—Mitchell, Eburne and Twigg—divided by channels that have filled in over time and is named for its first pioneer settler and farmer. Alexander Mitchell also advocated successfully for construction of the first Fraser Street Bridge in 1893 to connect Vancouver and Richmond. The bridge was opened for ship traffic with a hand crank. Today, the island is home to industrial activities but also a 0.4 ha (1 ac) park with a fishing pier.

Before you reach the Knight Street Bridge, however, your route ends abruptly and without fanfare at a roadside where you turn to retrace your steps to your starting point.

GETTING THERE

Transit: Take TransLink Bus 116 (Edmonds Station/Metrotown Station) to Boundary Road at Kent Avenue. Walk south on Boundary Road to the trailhead.

Vehicle: From the south end of Boundary Road, which divides Vancouver and Burnaby, cross the railway tracks south of Marine Way. Turn right to stay on Boundary Road where it transitions into North Fraser Way. Park at the end of the road.

IONA ISLAND DUO

Distance (Iona Jetty): 8 km (5 mi)
Time: 2.5 hours
Distance (North Arm Jetty): 6 km (3.7 mi)
Time: 2 hours
Surface: gravel (Iona), sandy beach
(North Arm)

Quality: ★★★★
Difficulty: ●
Season: all year
Car GPS entry: Iona Beach Regional Park
Richmond, BC
Trailhead: 49°13'9" N 123°12'48" W

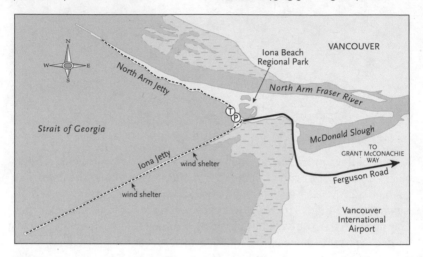

LOCATED ON the Pacific Flyway and the wildlife-rich estuary where the Fraser River meets the Salish Sea, Iona Island offers two walks: North Arm Jetty, with its long beach, rare sand dune plants and gathering place for thousands of migrating birds, and Iona Jetty, a bracing walk in the elements on top of a gigantic sewer pipe where the border between land and sea blurs as you go 4 km (2.4 mi) out to sea. A wind warning is in effect for these two walks.

For the North Arm Jetty, walk through the building, go right and follow the shoreline below the high-tide line to avoid the industrial area on private property to your right. Once past the industrial area, stay on the beach's intertidal zone to minimize your impact on the rare coastal sand ecosystem, where many specialized plants such as sedge, aster, burwood, beach pea and wild rye and creatures such as butterflies, beetles, garter snakes and shorebirds make their homes. In the 1900s, the jetty was built and the mouth of the North Arm dredged to allow boats to enter on any tide and be protected from the wind as they did. The area behind the jetty was known as the booming grounds (and many booms can still be seen today) because it was here that

The Iona Jetty extends into the Strait of Georgia and is a good spot for watching waterbirds.

tugs would pick up logs, tied together in booms, to deliver to the sawmills upstream. Eventually you reach your turnaround point, where the beach narrows and is impassable due to the many logs and pieces of driftwood.

For the Iona Jetty, walk a few paces on the path beside the parking lot and hang a right near the viewing tower onto the jetty. This walk features many unique experiences that unfold as you march along: the intertidal life of herons, soaring eagles, bracing wind, aircraft landing or taking off from YVR, a 360-degree view from Mount Baker to Vancouver Island to the Tantalus Range above Howe Sound to Cypress Bowl to the Golden Ears! Should you need respite from the elements, two wind shelters are provided, at 1.3 km (0.8 mi) and 2.5 km (1.5 mi). Your perseverance in reaching the terminus is rewarded with the opportunity for photos on a platform that projects over the rocks and water below.

After returning from your jetty walk, rest and relax before your journey home by pausing on a bench by the pond to watch the waterfowl and be entertained by the tame red-winged blackbirds.

GETTING THERE

Vehicle: From Highway 99, cross to Sea Island on Grant McConachie Way, turn right on Templeton Street and continue on Ferguson Road. Follow 5.5 km (3.4 mi) to the end and park at Iona Beach Park.

MCDONALD BEACH PARK/ PIRATES COVE

Distance: 6.5 km (4 mi)
Time: 2 hours
Surface: gravel dyke, trail, sandy beach
Quality: ★★★
Difficulty: ●

Season: all year
Car GPS entry: 3500 McDonald Rd Richmond, BC
Trailhead: 49°12'47" N 123°10'07" W

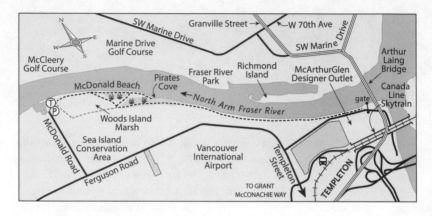

SEA ISLAND is well known as the home of Vancouver International Airport. Less well known is that, in 1995, to compensate for lost fisheries habitat due to a temporary barge-unloading facility where sand and aggregate was delivered for airport construction, an intertidal marsh basin, Woods Island Marsh, was created as a protected area within the Sea Island Conservation Area.

Before you begin, you may want to check tide tables and choose a time other than high tide to ensure you have access to Pirates Cove. From your vehicle, walk upstream on McDonald Beach along the North Arm of the Fraser River amid the dogs and their people in this popular off-leash area. Observe the working boats, yachts and other river activities as you go, watching out for their wakes, which pound the beach with large waves.

Soon, after traversing a rocky causeway that marks an outlet for the marsh, you notice a sandy slope leading to a trail into the forest to which you return soon. Continue along the beach until it bends to the right and terminates at the main outlet channel for the marsh, named by locals as Pirates Cove (haaarrrrggghh!). If you've had enough, return to your starting point from here, for a walk of 45 minutes.

Retrace your steps a short distance to the trail you noted earlier, which you leave the beach to follow, crossing a bridge over a marsh connector creek

Walking along McDonald Beach to the marsh.

as you do and forking left to join the Dyke Road trail, where you go left. For a while, you see the marsh through the trees on your left and then, again, you see diverse boating activities as your route hugs the river. Up ahead midstream on Richmond Island is a large building signed Milltown Drystack, a facility where boats are kept on shelves rather than moored in the water. An orange gate where the trail meets Grauer Road across from the McArthur Glen Designer Outlet mall marks your turnaround point. You may opt to continue 500 m farther towards the Arthur Laing Bridge to visit the location of Eburne, one of the earliest communities in Richmond and a former agricultural hub, though little remains today.

GETTING THERE
Transit: Take the SkyTrain to Templeton Station. Walk north through the parking lot to Grauer Road, then east to where the dyke trail merges with Grauer and do the walk in reverse.

Vehicle: From Highway 99, cross to Sea Island on Grant McConachie Way, turn right on Templeton Street, continue on Ferguson Road and turn right at McDonald Road. Follow 800 m to the end and park at McDonald Beach Park.

LULU ISLAND DYKES

Distance: 18 km (11.2 mi)
Time: 5 hours
Surface: gravel dyke, trail
Quality: ★★★
Difficulty: ■/●

Season: all year
Car GPS entry: 6111 River Rd Richmond, BC
Trailhead (west of Lynas Lane):
49°10'25" N 123°09'50" W
Trailhead (Terra Nova): 49°10'31" N
123°11'42" W

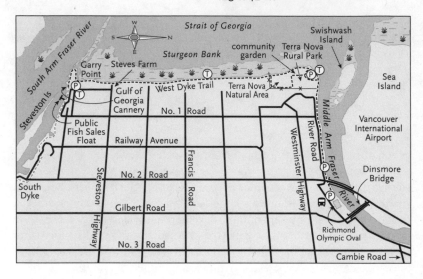

THE WEST end of Richmond's Lulu Island, opposite Vancouver's international airport, is an inviting setting for watching both birds and aircraft. As well, the Terra Nova Rural Park and Natural Area provide a diversion between the dykes on the northern and western banks of Lulu Island. With these options, you can tailor your outing as you wish. (If you prefer not to walk back, either carry bus fare or park a second vehicle in Steveston.)

Beginning near Lynas Lane, climb onto the dyke, pause at the viewing platform overlooking the Middle Arm of the Fraser River, then head downstream. (The walk from the Olympic Oval to Lynas Lane is about 800 m.) An enhanced marshland area with a variety of birds lies close at hand, and Sea Island lies beyond. As you travel westwards, you can see Point Grey, the North Shore mountains and the islands of Howe Sound. Within less than an hour, you arrive at the Terra Nova reclamation projects, on the point where the Fraser River meets the Strait of Georgia (parking available).

Historic Steves Farm preserves land for these Belted Galloway cattle and enhances the area for birds and walkers.

The Terra Nova Rural Park contains historic buildings, community gardens, a picnic area and an adventure playground for children. The Terra Nova Natural Area, separated from the park by the residential end of Westminster Highway, protects former farmland as old field habitat, to maintain the environment required by raptors and other birds and species. (Dogs are not allowed in this area.) A network of trails wanders through the two preserves. The southern trail in the Natural Area meets the west dyke.

The popular West Dyke Trail, with its distant views and occasional benches, stretches from Terra Nova to Garry Point Park. It borders Sturgeon Bank, a rich estuary and an important bird-nesting habitat that is part of the Pacific Flyway. More than 1 million birds migrate through the area annually. Towards the south end of your walk, a line of radar-reflecting towers warns passing ships of the proximity of the mud flats. On the landward side, housing developments have replaced farm crops.

Next, you reach Scotch Pond and Garry Point Park, the end of your walk. However, the "village" of Steveston, reached by following Moncton Street, is worth exploring before you head back. (Walk 47 continues from here.) The #401 bus leaves from Chatham Street east of 2nd Avenue; get off on Westminster Highway at Lynas Lane, walk north to River Road and then to your vehicle, or right to return to the Richmond Oval.

SHORTER OPTION

From the west end of River Road, explore the Terra Nova Rural Park and Natural Area, a looping walk of up to 3 km (1.9 mi).

GETTING THERE

Transit: Take TransLink Bus 414 (Richmond Oval/Brighouse Station) to River Road and Hollybridge Way near the Richmond Olympic Oval. Walk to the dyke and head left, downstream.

Vehicle: Pay parking is available under the Olympic Oval; enter from Oval Way off River Road, just south of the No. 2 Road Bridge. Limited parking is available on River Road west of Lynas Lane.

STEVESTON GREENWAY

Distance: 8 km (5 mi)

Time: 2.5 hours

Surface: paved

Quality: ★★

Difficulty: ●

Season: all year

Car GPS entry: Chatham St & Seventh Ave Richmond, BC

Trailhead: 49°07'31" N 123°11'32" W

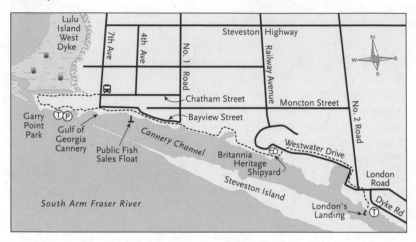

LIFE AND work along this south shore of Richmond's Lulu Island in the first half of the 20th century can only be imagined today through the remaining historical buildings, rotting wooden pilings lining the shoreline and numerous information plaques planted along this route in the village of Steveston.

Go out to Garry Point (links to Walk 46) for a few minutes to see the sculpture of a net-mending needle, a tribute to fishermen who lost their lives at sea, to feel the winds and to look over the waters that once teemed with uncountable quantities of salmon. Now turn back and follow the paved lane heading east from the facilities and leading to the Gulf of Georgia Cannery National Historic Site. Inside, the displays recount the history of the West Coast fisheries and take you through fish processing from catch to canned product. Past the bronze cannery workers out front, angle right to Bayview Street and then, at the foot of No. 1 Road, go right on the waterfront promenade to join the Steveston Greenway. Alternatively, you could stroll along Moncton Street for two or three blocks before jogging over to the waterfront. You might climb the viewing tower at the foot of No. 1 Road and imagine your surroundings as part of a vast wetlands area, harvested by First Nations

Glen Andersen's *Dream of the River* sculpture, a half-built fishing boat with a keel of salmon vertebrae, conveys Steveston's natural and industrial roots.

peoples long before the newcomers' arrival and the construction of the thriving businesses of today.

Other sights along your way include the Britannia Heritage Shipyard, where people once lived and worked in their own ethnically defined zones; the historic Chinese Bunkhouse; and sailboats and working boats at anchor. To bypass the Steveston Harbour Authority facility, your route leaves the waterfront to follow Westwater Drive and Dyke Road to the intersection of No. 2 Road and London Road. Here, you veer right to rejoin a short section of the greenway and, after passing the *Dream of the River* sculpture, arrive at the fishing pier at London's Landing. To extend your outing, consider Walk 48, which begins here. As you retrace your route, you may perhaps wonder what changes will affect this area over the next 100 years.

GETTING THERE

Transit: Take TransLink Bus 410 (22nd Station/Brighouse Station) to 7th Avenue and Chatham Street. Walk west for 150 m into the park.
Vehicle: From Highway 99, take Exit 32 (Steveston Highway) and go west for 8 km (5 mi) to 7th Avenue, then south on 7th to Chatham Street. Park in the lots adjacent to Garry Point Park.

SOUTH DYKE TRAIL

Distance: 8.5 km (5.3 mi)
Time: 2.5 hours
Surface: gravel
Quality: ★★★
Difficulty: ●

Season: all year
Car GPS entry: London Rd & No 2 Rd Richmond, BC
Trailhead: 49°6'56" N 123°9'20" W

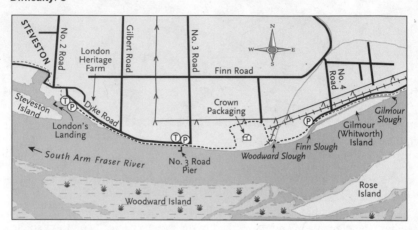

LULU ISLAND'S south dyke upstream from busy Steveston is an inviting setting for watching river traffic and enjoying the sun, wind and rain as you march along.

Beginning near London's Landing, head east (upstream) on the gravel path that runs beside Dyke Road. Soon you pass the London family farm with its 1888 house and gardens open for viewing, leaving the residential and commercial developments behind in favour of open farmland. On the river side, watch for tugs pulling heavy barges and look southeast to see Mount Baker on the horizon. You reach the No. 3 Road fishing pier, enjoyed by fisherfolk in all seasons, to the east of which you pass through an off-leash area for dogs. Your route diverts inland from the river to skirt the large Crown Packaging plant; on its east side, continue straight ahead to the waterfront and the pumphouse at Woodward Slough.

In 5 minutes, you arrive at Dyke Road; this route parallels Gilmour Island, which forms the southern side of Finn Slough, the name referring to the narrow channel of water and to a community that dates from the 1920s, when a group of Finnish fisherfolk settled here. The individualized wooden dwellings on stilts, boardwalks and net sheds that sit amongst the brush and tidal

A house on stilts in Finn Slough.

flats provide a living snapshot into the past and face a tenuous future. Learn more about the Finn Slough community at www.finnslough.com.

From here, retrace your route and perhaps stop to rest at any of the picnic tables and benches along the way.

GETTING THERE
Vehicle: From Highway 99, take Exit 32 (Steveston Highway) and go west for 7 km (4.3 mi) to No. 2 Road, then south on No. 2 Road to London Road. Turn left onto London and then right onto Dyke Road to the parking area.

DEAS ISLAND REGIONAL PARK

Distance: 4.4 km (2.7 mi)
Time: 1.5 hours
Surface: trail
Quality: ★★★
Difficulty: ●

Season: all year
Car GPS entry: Deas Island Rd & River Rd
Delta, BC
Trailhead: 49°07'37" N 123°03'15" W

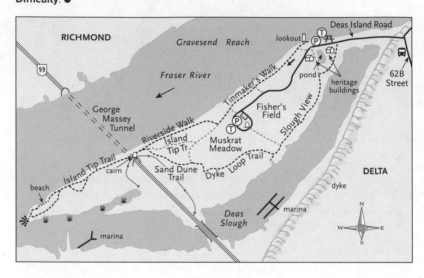

NAMED FOR the tinsmith and cannery owner who purchased the island in 1873, this 120 ha (300 ac) park is now connected to the City of Delta by a causeway small enough not to detract from the land's island status. It is a popular bird-watching destination and features three historic buildings relocated here in the 1980s for preservation. The one-room Inverholme Schoolhouse is near the parking area; next is the Victorian-style Burrvilla, whose attic is a summer nursery for bats; and next again is the Delta Agricultural Hall, now the park's operation centre. To your right, at the Tinmaker's Walk trailhead, are a commemorative tablet and a lookout tower, which mark the site of Deas's long-demolished cannery. The tower provides fine views of activities on the river and, on a clear day, the North Shore mountains with Mamquam Mountain peeking through.

Walking downriver, you pass another parking area and arrive at a fork, the left arm of which, Dyke Loop Trail, takes you back by Deas Slough to your point of departure. By staying right on Riverside Walk, however, you veer closer to the river, being joined in quick succession by Island Tip Trail

Ahhh! The bliss of shade along the Dyke Loop Trail on a hot summer's day.

and Sand Dune Trail, which are combined horse and hiking trails. Soon, you travel over the southern entrance to the George Massey Tunnel, where vehicles emerge from or disappear under the Fraser River on Highway 99. Your trail west stays close to the river now as you make for the island's tip, passing a little beach en route.

From there, you look south across the mouth of Deas Slough, with its marina lying just to the south of Ladner Marsh. Southwest lies Kirkland Island, a navigation beacon marking its shallow waters. North, of course, is the river, and Lulu Island beyond, the shoreline marked by commercial and industrial operations, such as freight terminals and the B.C. Ferries refitting dock.

On your return across the tunnel, go right on Sand Dune Trail, where you experience a sample of dune ecology, then join Dyke Loop Trail. Where it meets Slough View Trail, you have views across Deas Slough, a popular site for rowing and, in the summer, wake-boarding. To complete your circular tour of the park, stay right on Slough View Trail, where a left fork leads to the picnic area at Fisher's Field. Continue along the sandy route until, just behind Burrvilla, you keep right again and cross the bridge on Tidal Pond Trail, the pond replete with vegetation and a blaze of colour in summer. All too soon, you emerge at the picnic area near where you began your outing.

GETTING THERE

Transit: Take TransLink Bus 640 (Ladner Exchange/Scott Road Station) to River Road at Deas Island Road. Walk west for 350 m on Deas Island Road to the park.

Vehicle: From Highway 99, take Exit 28 (Ladner/River Road) and go east on Highway 17A, which becomes 62B Street and then River Road. At Deas Island Road, beside a gravel business, go left (west) and drive along the dirt causeway to a parking lot.

BRUNSWICK POINT

Distance: 10 km (6.2 mi)
Time: 2.5 hours
Surface: gravel
Quality: ★★★★
Difficulty: ●

Season: all year
Car GPS entry: River Rd W & Westham
Island Rd Delta, BC
Trailhead: 49°04'29" N 123°07'51" W

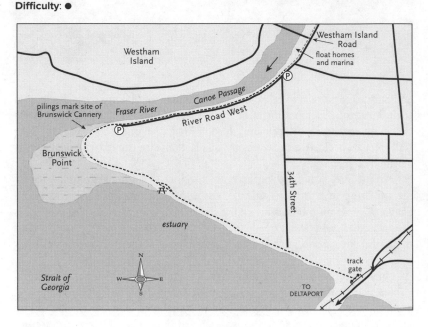

THIS OUTING takes you along a dyke that separates rich delta marshland abundant with plants and birds from rich agricultural land nourished by its deltaic under-burden. It also contrasts reminders of the one-time cannery industry at Brunswick Point with the modern-day coal and container terminals at Deltaport. Be sure to take your binoculars, and be prepared for brisk winds.

Your walk begins on the shore of Canoe Passage, the southernmost arm of the Fraser River and part of the immense Fraser River Estuary. (The far banks are on Westham Island, which adjoins Reifel Island, home of the George C. Reifel Migratory Bird Sanctuary. Part of the Pacific Flyway, the estuary is a key stopover for more than 1 million migrating birds.) About 1.7 km (1 mi) along the dyke, you reach the end of the road, an alternate place to park. Ahead, look for an eagle nest in a line of trees planted as a windbreak.

Looking towards the North Shore mountains from Delta's fertile fields.

A few minutes later, you find a "garden" of ragged-top pilings, often occupied by cormorants drying their outspread wings. The Brunswick Cannery, one of many that existed along the Fraser River Delta, operated here from 1897 to 1930, after which the premises were used for other fishing-related purposes until its demolition in 1983.

Continuing around the point, you pass two sets of benches, beyond which a track drops off the dyke and enters high brush. Hidden in here is a sheltered picnic table, about midway to your turnaround point. If you were an eagle soaring overhead, you would see how the powerful Fraser River continuously reshapes the underwater landscape. Its burden of silt fills in channels and adds to the flats, which extend seawards for about 6 km (3.7 mi) before dropping off into deep waters in the Strait of Georgia. Watch for large flocks of dunlins, which overwinter here, their white bellies and dark backs alternately contrasting as they swoop and swarm over the marshlands to confuse their predators.

The towering cranes of Deltaport loom larger on the horizon as you approach 34th Street, unfortunately separated from the dyke by a deep ditch. This makes a good turnaround point, or you could continue to a gate 700 m farther. Your return walk rewards you with an unobstructed 360-degree view of the mountains surrounding the Lower Mainland, from southern Vancouver Island to Mount Baker and the Fraser Valley and around to the North Shore and the Sunshine Coast, with high-rises on Kingsway Ridge in the foreground.

GETTING THERE

Vehicle: From Highway 99, take Exit 28 (Ladner/River Road) and go west on River Road through Ladner. Continue for 7 km (4.3 mi) until you reach Westham Island Road. Some 600 m beyond this turnoff to the Reifel Migratory Bird Sanctuary, find a small parking area on the dyke opposite 34th Street.

BOUNDARY BAY DUO

Distance: (north section): 8.5 km (5.3 mi)
Time: 3 hours
Distance: (south section): 4.5 km (2.8 mi)
Time: 1.5 hours
Surface: gravel dyke, sandy trail
Quality: ★★★
Difficulty: ●

Season: all year
Car GPS entry: 72 St & Ladner Trunk Rd
Delta, BC
Trailhead (72 Street): 49°03'35" N
123°01'27" W
Car GPS entry: 12 Ave & 56 St Delta, BC
Trailhead (12 Avenue lot): 49°01'28" N
123°03'29" W

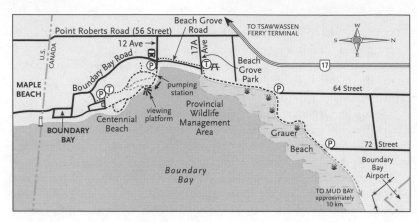

BOUNDARY BAY is of international importance to migrating and wintering birds. Waterfowl and shorebirds are common; hawks and eagles hunt small mammals; and in winter, you might spot a snowy owl. Fabulous marine and mountain views are an added attraction. The north section is a straightforward multi-use dyke walk at the edge of farmland; the south section includes Centennial Beach, a wildlife reserve and several trails.

To walk the north section, turn right onto the dyke, which hugs the shoreline of Boundary Bay, its daily character determined by weather and tide, before it arrives at the beginning of housing. Here the trail follows a short lane to the corner of 17A Avenue and Beach Grove Road. A few steps farther up 17A, there is a park with picnic tables and facilities, a nice place to relax before your return. However, if you are keen to continue to the south section, follow Beach Grove Road for 15 minutes to the entrance to Dyke Trail, remembering that this diversion will add considerably to your return distance.

To walk the south section, from the 12 Avenue lot, walk on the Dyke Trail towards the water, noting a pumping station on your right. As you continue

Yarrow thrives along the dyke trail beside Boundary Bay.

past the viewing tower, the dyke becomes indistinguishable from the beach and a trail veers inland, heading towards the facilities at Centennial Beach. An optional loop on the left provides information on dune ecology. To vary your return and enjoy some undeveloped marshland, head towards the three-way-stop intersection at the park entrance. From here, follow a rough track just outside the park boundary and work north, a ditch to your left and a narrow strip of bush separating you from the parking lot on your right (accessed from Boundary Bay Road). Soon, you join the Savannah Trail that leads back to the main Raptor Trail. Thereafter, keep left until, close to the main dyke, you veer right to meet it by the pumping station you noted earlier. (The maze of trails available to explore will not lead you too far astray.) From the pumping station, proceed to your vehicle.

GETTING THERE

Vehicle (north section): From Highway 99, take Exit 28 (Ladner/River Road) south to Highway 10 (Ladner Trunk Road). Go east to 72 Street or, to halve the distance of your walk, to 64 Street. Drive south to the end of the road.

Transit (south section): Take TransLink Bus 614 (English Bluff/South Delta Exchange) to Beach Grove Road and 12 Avenue.

Vehicle (south section): From Highway 99 or the South Fraser Perimeter Road (Highway 17), go south to 56 Street (Point Roberts Road) in Tsawwassen and then east on 12 Avenue to a small parking lot at road's end.

WATERSHED PARK TO MUD BAY

Distance: 14 km (8.7 mi)

Time: 4 hours

Surface: trail, paved

Quality: ★★

Difficulty: ■

Season: all year

Car GPS entry: 11200 Kittson Pkwy
Delta, BC

Trailhead: 49°07'08" N 122°54'57" W

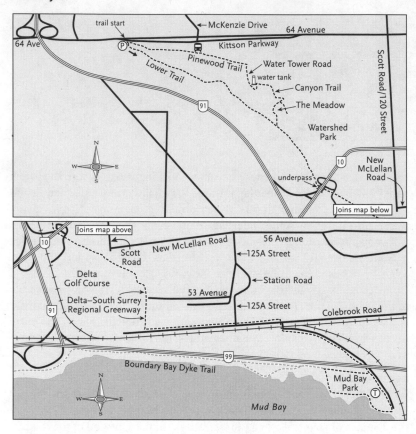

IF YOU like both forest and shoreline, then this walk is for you. Beginning in Watershed Park, you travel through second-growth coniferous forest, through swampland with its largely unseen creature activities, past overgrown pastureland and along a road between railway tracks and blueberry fields, before you arrive at Mud Bay with its abundant birdlife.

There are several park entrances off Kittson Parkway; this walk begins at the westernmost one, a few paces west from the information board where

Mud Bay provides important habitat for migrating birds.

a narrow trail descends to a T-junction with the Lower Trail onto which you turn left. This you follow past various small trail and road diversions used by mountain bikers, runners and dog walkers. After 2 km (1.2 mi), you pass under Highway 10 to join the Delta–South Surrey Regional Greenway, which continues between neglected pastureland and steep slopes until, at a high chain-link fence, you are directed south. Here, a raised path, bounded by scrubby trees, leads through swampland; the views and bird watching are best when the trees are leafless. Your arrival at Colebrook Road (go left) marks the beginning of a 2 km (1.2 mi) roadside trek past agricultural land until you cross the railway tracks and pass under Highway 99 to arrive at Mud Bay Park. As you cross the tracks, note that the rails from the United States join the Canadian line here.

An extension of Boundary Bay, Mud Bay is a delta formed by the Serpentine and Nicomekl Rivers. The tidal marshes and eelgrass beds support millions of migratory birds that stop or overwinter here, making it a birder's paradise. A looped dyke trail, with inviting benches, looks across the bay to Blackie Spit close in and to Point Roberts and Tsawwassen in the distance to the right.

Well rested, you must retrace your steps to Watershed Park, but from there you can vary your return. Six hundred metres beyond the Highway 10 underpass, turn right up a wide stony road. Very soon, you arrive at the Meadow, a gently sloping grassland with benches and a viewpoint overlooking Mud Bay, where you just were. From the north side of the Meadow, follow woodsy Gravity Bowl Trail for a few paces, then go left onto Canyon Trail. This contours the hillside until it exits onto Water Tower Road near a water tank and, 150 m up the hill, surprise! An artesian water supply, cool and refreshing, flows almost magically from a tap in a boulder. From here, follow the Pinewood Trail for the final 900 m back to the start.

GETTING THERE

Transit: Take TransLink Bus 340 (Scottsdale/22nd Station) to Kittson Parkway at McKenzie Drive (in Delta), then walk 400 m west to the trailhead.
Vehicle: From Highway 91, take Exit 4 (64th Avenue) and go east along the northern boundary of Watershed Park. As the road becomes Kittson Parkway, follow it to the westernmost Watershed Park sign, 800 m east of Highway 91, or 1.8 km (1.1 mi) west of Scott Road. Park off the road on the south side.

BARNSTON ISLAND

Distance: 10 km (6.2 mi)
Time: 2.5 hours
Surface: paved road, trail
Quality: ★★
Difficulty: ●

Season: all year
Car GPS entry: SFPR & 104 Ave
Surrey, BC
Trailhead: 49°11'30" N 122°43'35" W

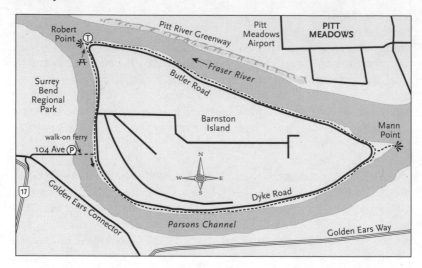

YOUR FIRST steps on this little adventure are onto a tugboat/barge-combo ferry for a free 5-minute ride to Barnston Island, which sits in the middle of the Fraser River between Surrey and Pitt Meadows. Your remaining steps follow a paved country road that circuits the island between operations of two of B.C.'s economic foundations—agriculture and forestry—and passes through part of Katzie First Nation Reserve, though the entire island is within Katzie traditional territory. There are no stores on the island.

Once off the ferry, turn right to make the circuit counter-clockwise. Then, when you reach the picnic site at the northwest corner of the island, you will be ready for a rest; there are no other resting spots en route. Initial impressions of prosperity are followed by mixed impressions at the sight of abandoned homes, now being reclaimed by nature's brambly arms. However, on the rest of your walk, you see cattle, sheep, even a couple of llamas and other farming activities. Across the river in Port Kells are the busy lumber mills and their resulting mountains of woodchips. Watch for eagles overhead and listen for the prehistoric squawk of the heron.

View northeast from near Robert Point to the Goldén Ears group.

About 4 km (2.5 mi) from the start, the road curves as it reaches the east end of the island. Look for a signpost off the road beside a narrow trail leading to Mann Point. If, however, it appears too brambly, walk another 100 m along the road to a rough off-road vehicle track through the woods to the point. Here, on a sandy beach, you see river and birdlife and a close-up view of the Golden Ears Bridge and the mountains beyond.

Back on the pavement, you next see Pitt Meadows on the opposite shore with its little airport, busy with the comings and goings of small aircraft. The sight of log booms at anchor, barges in tow and fishboats continues in this stretch of the river. On land, you pass colourful acres of cranberries. Other products of this small island are hay, herbs, beef and organic dairy products. Finally, Robert Point lies ahead, 4 km (2.5 mi) from Mann Point. The secluded picnic setting is an attractive place to rest and watch the river scene.

The last leg of your stroll, about 2 km (1.2 mi), takes you back to the ferry and a peaceful return across the water to your vehicle.

GETTING THERE

Vehicle: From Highway 1, take Exit 53 to Highway 17 north. As you near the bottom of the hill, exit right for 104 Avenue East. At the intersection, go right and then left onto 104 Avenue. Follow to the parking lot at the end of the road.

SURREY BEND

Distance: 5 km (3.1 mi)
Time: 2 hours
Surface: trail, gravel, subject to seasonal flooding

Quality: ★★★★
Difficulty: ●
Season: all year
Car GPS entry: SFPR & 104 Ave Surrey, BC
Trailhead: 49°11'38" N 122°43'45" W

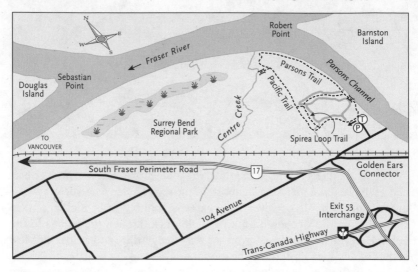

SURREY BEND Regional Park protects one of the few remaining undyked and undisturbed natural floodplains along the lower Fraser River. The natural ebb and flow of the water, tidal flow and seasonal flooding in May and June provide a refuge for birds, fish and mammals and maintain a floodplain forest dominated by giant cottonwoods and spruce trees, red alder, marshes, bogs and thickets.

From the parking lot, take the Spirea Loop Trail as it follows berms that were established to create tidal channels for young fish. At the trail marker, turn north (right) to continue parallel with the channel. From the T-junction with the Spirea Loop Trail, go left to continue on the Pacific Trail, once a service road. On your left is the vast grassland of the Centre Creek floodplain and bog. Depending on the season, it is lush, green and tall or flattened and russet brown. As you walk, you see, approaching from the distance, the tall stands of the floodplain forest with a view of mountains in the distance.

On reaching the junction with the Parsons Trail, go left for a short distance to the bridge over Centre Creek where you can enjoy a view back across

Looking over the Centre Creek floodplain from the bridge.

the floodplain. Returning to continue on the much narrower and rougher Parsons Trail, you enter the forest. Black cottonwood giants live here, their grey deeply furrowed bark attesting to their age. In spring, their smooth green fruit split, releasing seeds covered with fluffy white cotton-like hairs that float on the air and disperse over wide distances. Also present are mature Sitka spruce trees with their scaly bark and prickly needles.

Soon, a branch in the trail leads to a viewpoint at the mouth of Centre Creek near where Parsons Channel meets the Fraser. Here you catch a glimpse of the industrial activity that takes place along the river and, in the distance, a panorama from Mount Seymour to the Golden Ears. Return to the main Parsons Trail and follow its meanderings as you enjoy the variety of natural forest growth. Too soon, the trail emerges from the forest at a bridge crossing Spirea Channel and a viewpoint over Parsons Channel to Barnston Island. Next, a trail junction presents you with a choice: continue directly back to the park entrance or take the longer way back by following the Spirea Loop Trail.

GETTING THERE
Vehicle: From Highway 1, take Exit 53 to Highway 17 north. As you near the bottom of the hill, exit right for 104 Avenue East. At the intersection, go right and then left onto 104 Avenue. Follow 104 Avenue and take the turnoff for Surrey Bend Regional Park and its parking lot.

TYNEHEAD REGIONAL PARK

Distance: 5.5 km (3.4 mi)
Time: 2 hours
Surface: trail
Quality: ★★★
Difficulty: ●

Season: all year
Car GPS entry: 168 St & 96 Ave Surrey, BC
Trailhead (hatchery parking): 49°10'40"
N 122°45'42" W

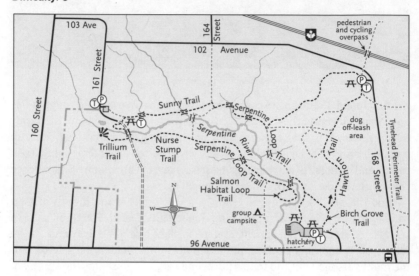

THE PROXIMITY of this trail to the Serpentine River and its many feeder streams, and the impressive number of enormous nurse stumps that nourish large second-growth trees in this area, are two of the highlights along this pleasant, winding walk.

At the hatchery entrance, pick up a brochure at the information kiosk and then head north on the Birch Grove Trail, which very soon divides. The right fork, the aptly named Hawthorn Trail for the many hawthorn trees, takes you through dog heaven, an unfenced off-leash area that traverses one-time farmland to the northeast entrance on 168 Street, an alternate access to this walk. Nearby, a footbridge arches over Highway 1. Next, bearing west through a tunnel of hawthorn trees and then bearing southwest, you meet the northern loop of the Serpentine Loop Trail, where you go right, passing some intriguing nurse stumps en route. Successive crossings of headwater tributaries are particularly attractive in spring. At another fork, left leads to a bridge over the main waterway, so keep right, ignoring the trail out to 102 Avenue. Make your way along the southern edge of a meadow via Sunny Trail, beyond which

Two of Tynehead's Sitka spruce trees are more than 150 years old!

you come to a picnic area with tracks going off in various directions; cross the bridge at the bottom of the meadow then go right on Trillium Trail. This route takes you past more fascinating nurse stumps and up a 5-minute ascent ending at a viewpoint that overlooks rearing habitat for coho and steelhead fry.

After descending, you follow the Nurse Stump Trail downstream to rejoin the Serpentine Loop Trail. Signage along the way reminds you that these trails wind through sensitive habitat for the fish that live here throughout the year, in all their life's stages. Both humans and dogs, therefore, need to avoid temptations to play in the water. The Serpentine Loop Trail ends in a 10-minute interpretive loop just before an arching bridge. Cross this and keep right for the final lap back to your vehicle and a possible visit to the hatchery.

LONGER OPTION
Tynehead Park also features the Perimeter Trail, a multi-use interpretive trail on the Tynehead Greenway. The 4.8 km (3 mi) rolling circuit, which includes some long uphill sections, requires about 90 minutes to complete. This trail lies to the east of 168 Street and may be accessed from both the hatchery and Serpentine parking lots, the latter off the north end of 168 Street.

GETTING THERE
Transit: Take TransLink Bus 388 (22nd Station/Carvolth Exchange) to 96 Avenue at 168 Street and follow the directions as below.
Vehicle: From Highway 1, take Exit 50 (160th Street) and go south to 96 Avenue. Turn left (east) until you reach the parking lot entrance 100 m west of 168 Street on the north side of 96 Avenue.

GREEN TIMBERS URBAN FOREST

Distance: North and Centre sections:
3 km each (1.9 mi)
Time: 1 hour each
Distance: South section: 5 km (3.1 mi)
Time: 1.5 hours
Surface: trail, gravel

Quality: ★★★
Difficulty: ●
Season: all year
Car GPS entry: 100 Ave & 144 St
Surrey, BC
Trailhead: 49°10'59" N 122°49'14" W

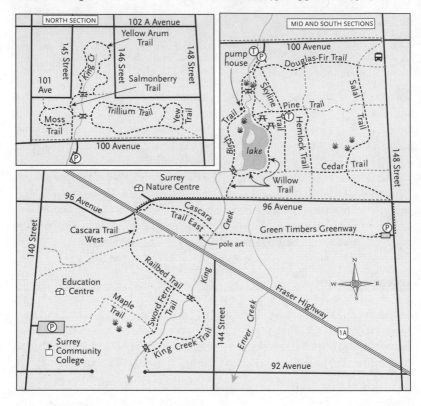

SURROUNDED BY urban development, this forested oasis owes its existence to the efforts of the Green Timbers Heritage Society. After it was logged against protest in 1930, reforestation, then a pioneering concept, began immediately. Today this forest is a mix of logging survivors and natural regeneration, but unfortunately is divided into three sections by 100 and 96 Avenues.

To walk the north section, from the parking lot cross 100 Avenue at the pedestrian-controlled crosswalk and look for the trailhead a few paces left. Salmonberry Trail, a one-time logging railway, connects three loops: Moss

Loop, which was an experimental Scotch pine plantation; Yellow Arum Loop, which edges the marsh that forms the headwaters of King Creek; and the Trillium-Yew Loop, which leads you through a fine stand of Douglas-fir that survived the logging of the 1920s as young trees.

Green Timbers Lake makes a good picnic spot.

Back at the parking lot, you can now do a horseshoe-shaped loop of the mid-section. At the information board, take the left-most trail, the Douglas-Fir Trail, to Salal Trail, where you turn right, cross Pine Trail and continue to Cedar Trail, where you turn right again. This large wet area supports alder, maple and cottonwood trees and ferns, salal and huckleberry bushes, amongst others. Turn right yet again onto Skyline Trail, where you leave the forest and pass through meadows with the lake to your left. At the intersection with Pine Trail, go left and descend past the picnic sites to Green Timbers Lake, where again you go left to circle the lake clockwise on Willow Trail and Birch Trail, enjoying the waterfowl and scenery until you are back at your vehicle.

For the south section walk, you may extend your mid-section walk by exiting onto 96 Avenue at 148 Street from the Salal Trail south of Cedar Trail and then crossing to the Green Timbers Greenway a few paces south on 148 Street. Alternatively, you may park in the B.C. Hydro lot south of 96 Avenue on the west side of 148 Street. From 148 Street, follow the multi-use, paved Green Timbers Greenway west to Cascara Trail East (where there are some rare yew trees), cross Fraser Highway at the lights and re-enter the forest on Cascara Trail West. The aptly named Railbed Trail crosses King Creek, the first trickle of which you saw on the north section's Yellow Arum Trail, then becomes King Creek Trail, where the reforestation was most successful. Next, keep right on Sword Fern Trail, where there are lots of overarching vine maple trees and ferns, until you meet Railbed Trail, from where you retrace your path. A brief diversion off Sword Fern Trail onto Maple Trail passes through wetlands with a variety of deciduous trees and some nice Douglas-firs. From your turnaround point, retrace your steps to return to your starting point.

GETTING THERE

Transit: Take TransLink Bus 341 (Guildford/Newton Exchange) to 148 Street at 100 Avenue. Walk east on 100 Avenue to the trailhead.

Vehicle: From Highway 1, take Exit 50 (160 Street) and go south to 100 Avenue. Turn right and find the parking lot on the south side of 100 Avenue, between 144 and 148 Streets.

SURREY LAKE/FLEETWOOD PARK

Distance: 7 km (4.3 mi)
Time: 2.5 hours
Surface: gravel, trail
Quality: ★★★★
Difficulty: ●

Season: all year
Car GPS entry: 72 Ave & 152 St
Surrey, BC
Trailhead: 49°08'22" N 122°48'01" W

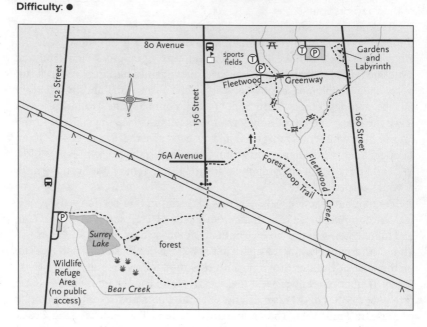

THIS WALK explores two wonderful natural parks that include a lake with waterfowl, an ideal path for forest bathing, sculptures and a labyrinth.

Begin by crossing the bridge over Bear Creek to arrive at the lakeshore. Artificial Surrey Lake, completed in 2002, provides food control for farmers and wetland wildlife habitat and forest sanctuary for amphibians, fish, birds and mammals. As you walk along the water's edge you may see waterfowl such as bufflehead, golden eye, mallard and Canada goose. At the junction go left to ascend through the forest to your next junction, where you go left again, and under the power lines to 156 Street. Hang a right at 76A Avenue, follow it to its end and continue on a gravel-topped trail entering Fleetwood Park.

After ignoring a trail that joins on the left, you arrive at a T-junction with Forest Loop Trail (unsigned). Go left on this broad, well-maintained trail until you reach a junction with the paved Fleetwood Greenway and a kiosk. Back-track about 20 paces and take the narrow, earthen track into the interior of

Rest awaits where the trail crosses Fleetwood Creek ravine.

Fleetwood forest. Turn off your phone, put away your camera, slow down and enjoy shinrin-yoku on this rudimentary track as it winds amongst large cottonwood, bigleaf maple and occasional cedar trees and where you meet Fleetwood Creek.

Too soon, you rejoin the main trail where you take a left turn to continue to your next objective. The trail exits the park briefly onto 160 Street where you walk on the side of the road, passing the paved Fleetwood Greenway and re-entering the park at Fleetwood Gardens. Let your curiosity guide you amongst the paths of this garden mosaic, quiet your mind in the seven-circuit labyrinth and discover the stone sculptures in the woodland area.

Begin your return by retracing the route on 160 Street and entering the forest where you earlier emerged. Stay on the broad, gravel trail, passing as you do the narrow track previously used. As the trail curves to the right, pause to enjoy Fleetwood Creek, now in a ravine overlooked by mature cedars, before ascending to the junction with your outbound trail where you go left to come out at 76A Avenue. After passing under the power lines and entering Surrey Lake Park, you may choose left or right; both trails return you to the parking lot via the lakeshore.

GETTING THERE

Transit: Take TransLink Bus 335 (Newton/Surrey Central Station) or 375 (White Rock/Guildford) to 152 Street at 76 Avenue. Walk south to the Surrey Lake Park entrance.

Vehicle: From Highway 1, take Exit 50 (160 Street) south to 88 Street. Turn right and go west to 144 Street, then turn left and go south to 72 Avenue. Turn left and go east to 152 Street. Turn left, continue north on 152 Street and turn right at the Surrey Lake Park sign into the parking lot.

ELGIN HERITAGE TRAIL

Distance: 7 km (4.3 mi)
Time: 2 hours
Surface: trail, gravel
Quality: ★★★
Difficulty: ●

Season: all year
Car GPS entry: Crescent Rd & 142a St
Surrey, BC
Trailhead: 49°04'02" N 122°49'38" W

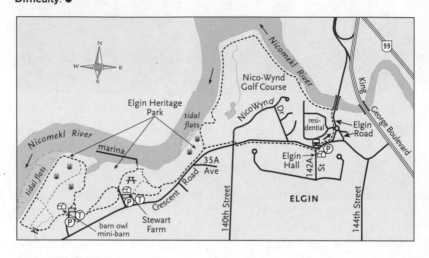

THIS PLEASANT stroll winds along the calm waters of the narrow Nicomekl River, around a golf course, through a historic farmyard, past tidal flats and marshes and through an inviting second-growth forest.

After parking at the community hall, go right along Crescent Road and cross to its north side at Elgin Road. Continue on Elgin Road until you see a cairn marking the trail's beginning (49°04'07" N 122°49'32" W). Here, a paved path fronts colourful townhouses; look for an eagle's nest not too far along and pause at the various information boards. Soon, you'll have to be alert for flying golf balls, but this is also a great area for bird watching as you stroll past the tidal flats beyond the golf course.

Next, at a fork in the trail, bear right to the riverside lawns that mark the beginning of Elgin Heritage Park. This area is located along the Pacific Flyway, an invisible aerial highway that migrating birds follow. In spring and fall, visiting birds rest and feed on the mud flats. Note the buildings of a historic farm and its restored 1894 Victorian mansion. The Stewart family settled here in the late 19th century and developed a productive hay farm. Leaving the buildings for closer examination later, continue past the parking lot through a forested area with many large native trees and some remnant

A barn for barn owls!

stumps. Beyond a second parking lot, your route follows dykes and board-walks around marshes and across tidal sloughs, habitat for a variety of birds from the patient great blue heron and majestic bald eagle to the swallow, red-winged blackbird and tiny wren. Across one wet meadow, you spot an intriguing building on a pole, a wee barn to house barn owls that no longer have access to real barns for nesting.

Finally, your path takes you back to the heart of Elgin Heritage Park: the Stewart Farm, where tours are available in season. Guides in Victorian costume provide tours of the house and grounds, including agricultural tools and machinery displays. Once your curiosity is satisfied, make your way back to your vehicle, following the trail that parallels the highway until it swings away, at which point you emerge onto Crescent Road for the 7- or 8-minute walk to Elgin Hall.

SHORTER OPTION
If you prefer a shorter loop, you could park at Stewart House (or in the lot just west) and from there content yourself with a walk of about 3 km (1.9 mi) within the park.

GETTING THERE
Transit: Take TransLink Bus 352 (Ocean Park/Bridgeport) to Crescent Road at 142A Street.
Vehicle: From Highway 99, take Exit 10 (King George Boulevard) and go south to Crescent Road. Turn right (west) and park at the old Elgin Hall at 142A Street, noting the time restrictions.

SOUTH SURREY URBAN FORESTS

Distance: Sunnyside Acres 3 km (1.9 mi)
Time: 1.5 hours
Distance: Crescent Park 3 km (1.9 mi)
Time: 1.5 hours
Surface: trail
Quality: ★★★
Difficulty: ●

Season: all year
Car GPS entry: 144 St & 24 Ave Surrey, BC
Trailhead: 49°02'46" N 122°49'17" W
Car GPS entry: 132 St & 28 Ave Surrey, BC
Trailhead: 49°03'10" N 122°51'51" W

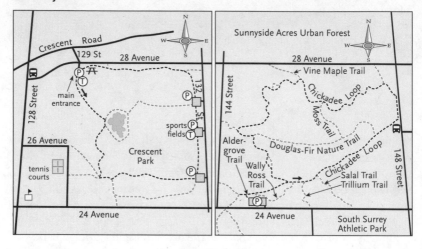

LOOKING FOR a shady walk on a hot summer's day? Consider these little oases, which are similar yet different in character. Sunnyside Acres is a natural second-growth forest rescued from development by the local heritage society; Crescent Park has picnic and sports facilities as well as trails.

Starting with Sunnyside Acres, at the information kiosk look for the Interpretive Trail Map and a guide to numbered stops, and begin on the Stellar's Jay Trail. Go right on Alder-grove, noting in passing the short, wide Wally Ross Trail to your right. Next, you come to a junction with Chickadee Loop Trail, which you join, going right. Keeping left (side trails to the right lead to streets), and enjoying the shade of Douglas-fir trees, you very soon pass the Douglas-Fir Nature Trail, a little track that disappears into the trees on your left (ideal for shinrin-yoku). Then you enter an area with a more open canopy and an abundance of shrubs. When your path emerges onto busy 148 Street, you go left for a minute or two before re-entering the forest. Keeping left at main intersections and ignoring all unofficial tracks, make your way past windfalls—some old, some recent—and great cedar stumps, relics of the

A tunnel of arched vine maples on Alder-grove Trail.

forest logged a century ago. Then the western end of the Douglas-Fir Nature Trail emerges on your left as you continue and, finally, back at the Chickadee Loop–Alder-grove Trail T-junction, go right, retracing your outward route the short distance back to your car.

For a short stroll to the heart of Crescent Park from the main entrance, take the path to the right behind the washrooms. This leads through a wide clearing and picnic area and to a little pond with waterfowl, circled by several trails. For a ramble round the perimeter of the park, go left at the entrance on a bridle trail through fine second-growth forest, until you emerge to pass several sports fields and their associated parking lots along 132 Street. At the third of these, the walkway leads westwards; keep right at forks and continue to the central pond and its picturesque little bridge, on the near side of which lies the return path to your vehicle.

GETTING THERE

Transit (Sunnyside Acres): Take TransLink Bus 352 (Ocean Park/Bridgeport) to 148 Street at 26 Avenue. Begin the walk halfway through at the nearby entrance.

Vehicle (Sunnyside Acres): From Highway 99, take Exit 10 (King George Boulevard) and drive south to 24 Avenue in South Surrey. Turn right (west) and drive to the Sunnyside Acres parking lot on the north side, between 148 and 144 Streets.

Transit (Crescent Park): Take TransLink Bus 351 (Crescent Beach/Bridgeport Station) or 360 (Ocean Park/Peace Arch Hospital) to 128 Street at 26B Avenue.

Vehicle (Crescent Park): From Highway 99, take Exit 10 (King George Boulevard) and drive south to 24 Avenue in South Surrey. Turn right (west) to 132 Street and then go right (north) to 28 Avenue and left (west) on 28 Avenue to Crescent Park's main entrance.

REDWOOD PARK

Distance: 4.5 km (2.8 mi) or less
Time: 1.5 hours
Surface: trail, paved
Quality: ★★★★
Difficulty: ●

Season: all year
Car GPS entry: 180 St & 20 Ave
Surrey, BC
Trailhead: 49°02'09" N 122°43'31" W

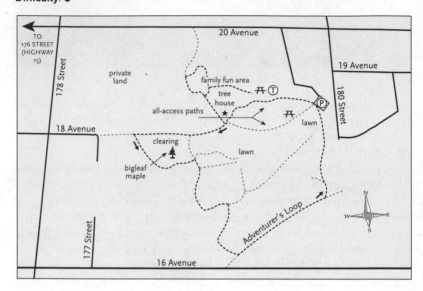

ALTHOUGH SMALL at only 26 ha (64 ac), Redwood Park has something of interest for the whole family. At the parking lot, check the information board and pick up a pamphlet to help with your planning. You have a choice of three main trails: the 1.5 km (0.9 mi) Adventurer's Loop footpath, which winds amongst groves of exotic trees; the paved 650 m universal-access path; and the 1.3 km (0.8 mi) Family Fun footpath.

Exotic trees? How did these come to be here? They are the result of a passion by twin brothers, David and Peter Brown. Their father, who homesteaded and logged this sloping, wooded hill in the late 19th century, gave each brother 16 ha (40 ac) on their 21st birthday. The brothers then began to plant the area with seeds of 32 species of exotic trees collected from around the world, including Europe, Asia and North Africa. Amongst these are California redwoods, giant sequoia, European beech and Chinese chestnut, and the brothers included native conifers, Pacific dogwood and maples as well. (The Meet the Trees of Redwood Park brochure is available on the City of Surrey website.)

Follow the Family Fun Loop to see the many limbs of the bigleaf maple.

The Family Fun footpath takes you past the treehouse where the Brown brothers lived for several decades until the 1950s, though this is a contemporary model built to replace previous structures. A signboard gives a short account of its history. Elsewhere on this trail, to the north of the treehouse, look for fairy houses and wee troll-house doors at the base of trees, a fun project begun by the Girl Guides many years ago.

Although you may wander the network of trails at random—and not all are marked on the map—the Adventurer's Loop covers most of the features. As you pass through clearings, try to catch a view out to the San Juan Islands. The trail takes you west from the treehouse to a fence marking private property, south on a downhill slope to a swampy area and an old railroad grade by a small canal, then left and northeastwards up a gentle slope to a lawn and the parking lot.

The City of Surrey has been making improvements to the trail and picnic facilities to meet universal access standards. The many covered tables near the parking lot are ideal for large groups, and a good playground and grassy area are nearby.

GETTING THERE

Vehicle: From Highway 99, take Exit 4 (16 Avenue) and drive east to Highway 15 (176 Street). Go left (north) to 20 Avenue, where you turn east (right) again. Continue to the Redwood Park sign on the south side, 250 m past 178 Street, and then drive 300 m through the woods to the parking lot.

SEMIAHMOO TRAIL

Distance: 8 km (5 mi)
Time: 3 hours
Surface: trail, paved road
Elevation: 110 m (361 ft)
Quality: ★★★
Difficulty: ●

Season: all year
Car GPS entry: 20 Ave & 151A St
Surrey, BC
Trailhead: 49°02'23" N 122°48'09" W

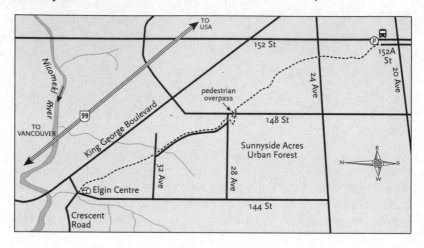

THE SEMIAHMOO Trail takes its name from the Indigenous peoples who originally lived in the region and preserves a portion of a historical route that once connected their settlements at Boundary Bay to the Nicomekl River, which was used for trading and communication inland. By the late 1800s, settlers had begun logging the area's dense fir, cedar and hemlock forests and clearing the land for small farms. The Semiahmoo Trail became a road that ran approximately 40 km (25 mi) from Brown's Landing, present-day Brownsville Bar, on the Fraser River to the U.S. border at the settlement of Semiahmoo, now Blaine. This walk takes you along 4 km (2.4 mi) of this heritage trail that traverses urban South Surrey.

Begin in the cul-de-sac at the end of 151A Street, where a gravel path enters a narrow band of forest between residences. The trail crosses 23 Avenue and then 24 Avenue at a pedestrian-controlled crossing and here begins a section that provides a glimpse of what the road may originally have been like. The trail passes through a forest of mature cedar, western hemlock and tall Douglas-fir trees with a canopy of curving vine maple trees providing a shaded archway. Cross 148 Street via an overpass and follow the trail as it

Large cottonwoods and Douglas-firs guide walkers along the trail.

curves to the right and descends to arrive at 28 Avenue. Cross 28 Avenue and continue your walk on the paved road ahead of you. Remain on the road for some distance, passing as you do a pond where you may decide to pause and relax to watch ducks go about their lives.

The paved section ends at 32 Avenue where you cross and re-enter the greenway. Another pedestrian crossing at 34 Avenue takes you to the final section of the trail that ends at the Elgin Centre, built in 1921 and preserved today as a heritage site.

To enjoy a rest on a bench overlooking the banks of the Nicomekl River before you begin your uphill return walk, go 300 m west on Crescent Road, cross to Elgin Road and follow it to the Nicomekl River. From there, retrace your steps to your starting point.

GETTING THERE
Transit: Take TransLink Bus 351 (Crescent Beach/Bridgeport Station) or 375 (White Rock/Guildford) to 152 Street and 20 Avenue, then continue as below.
Vehicle: From Highway 99, take Exit 4 (16 Avenue) and go west to 152 Street where you go right (north) to 20 Avenue. Turn left (west) onto 20 Avenue and then right (north) onto 151A Street, where you park.

BLACKIE SPIT/CRESCENT BEACH

Distance: 5.5 km (3.4 mi)
Time: 1.5 hours
Surface: gravel, paved road
Quality: ★★★
Difficulty: ●

Season: all year
Car GPS entry: 3140 McBride Ave
Surrey, BC
Trailhead: 49°03'37" N 122°52'46" W

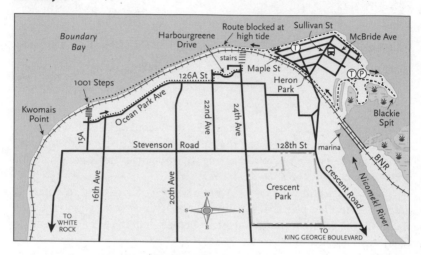

CRESCENT BEACH, a beachfront community popular with bathers, birders and walkers, offers walks that combine a sweeping ocean coastline with panoramic views of Boundary Bay and the Coast Mountains, and tidal marshes with their resident and visiting waterfowl and shorebirds.

From the parking area, walk the short distance to the entrance to Blackie Spit with its kiosk (Walter Blackie was New Westminster's first blacksmith). Follow the path down the middle of the spit to its end, where waterfowl and shorebirds linger and dive before you and from which you view, silhouetted in the distance, the North Shore and Fraser Valley mountains. Retrace your steps to the spit entrance and go left on the track that borders the tidal marshes, which in fall and winter are home to visiting waterfowl in numbers. Soon, on your left, is the entrance to the Savenye Environmentally Sensitive Area, whose short loop trail takes you for a close-up view of the tidal marsh. Notice the many old pilings, remnants of a dock and bunkhouse that once belonged to the Crescent Oyster Company. Continue on the track around a wide lagoon and keep left on a narrow dyke with sloughs on either side. Go right past the pump station to join Maple Street, a gravel road, and then, passing Dunsmuir Community Garden, you meet Beecher Street.

Tide lines on Blackie Spit.

Cross at the crosswalk and pick up a path that takes you through Heron Park to lane-like Maple Street on which you stay as you head for the seafront. A right turn onto the esplanade, an elevated dyke that protects Crescent Beach from winter storms, with its dramatic view of Boundary Bay and Tsawwassen, leads you back to your starting point.

LONGER OPTION
Check the tide before you embark on this extension, since it is impassable at high tide. Also note that this section is popular with nude sunbathers in the summer months. To add 5 km (3.1 mi) and 2 hours to your walk, turn left when you reach the esplanade and continue along the beach, pebbly and rocky as it is, with the BNSF Railway running between you and the cliff. After about an hour, you reach the 1001 steps (although there are not really 1001 steps, there are a lot!). From the top of the steps, begin your walk back from 15A Avenue. Turn left and follow Ocean Park Drive to 22 Avenue, where you go left for one block and then continue right on Harbourgreene Drive to 24 Avenue—a total distance on roads of 2.2 km (1.4 mi). At 24 Avenue, a left turn takes you to steps down the cliff and your return north to Crescent Beach.

GETTING THERE
Transit: Take TransLink Bus 351 (Crescent Beach/Bridgeport Station) to McBride Avenue at Sullivan Street. Continue northeast on McBride for 500 m to reach the trailhead.
Vehicle: From Highway 99, take Exit 10 (King George Boulevard) in South Surrey and go south to Crescent Road. Follow Crescent Road west, turn right at Sullivan Street and go right on McBride to a parking area.

CONFEDERATION PARK/ CAPITOL HILL

Distance: 6.2 km (3.9 mi)
Time: 2.5 hours
Surface: trail, paved roads
Elevation gain: 150 m (492 ft)
Quality: ★★★

Difficulty: ■
Season: most of the year
Car GPS entry: Hastings St & Beta Ave
Burnaby, BC
Trailhead: 49°17'02" N 122°59'51" W

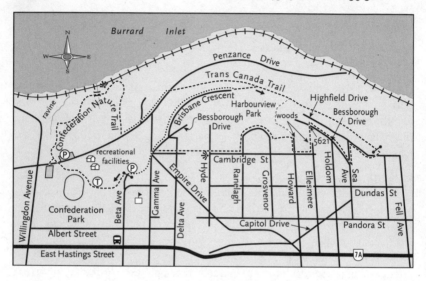

THIS EXCURSION explores the wilderness retreat that is hidden between bustling Hastings Street and the waters of Burrard Inlet. It begins in the "civilized" part of Confederation Park, descends through its wild side to sea level, then finishes with the ascent of Capitol Hill 200 m above, providing a good workout. The plentiful, ever-changing vistas make it all worthwhile.

Start by passing through the gate in the parking lot. Walk beside the fence abutting the picnic grounds and play park, then go right at the sports track. Straight past the skateboard park, cross Penzance Drive and find the Confederation (Penzance) Nature Trail loop at the left edge of the parking lot. The trail begins with a sustained descent through forest. Keep right at a fork and cross the footbridge, then follow the trail as it bends around and rises stiffly back to Penzance Drive. (For a shorter route, turn back at the road, or, to ascend Capitol Hill only, begin here.)

The Capitol Hill (Trans Canada) Trail (TCT) begins 330 m to your left along Penzance Drive at a pedestrian crossing. Rising gently, it skirts Capitol

View of Burrard Inlet from Capitol Hill, with Bowen Island in the distance.

Hill and then exits at a gate onto Cambridge Street, where you turn sharp right. Now begins a sustained ascent to the summit of Capitol Hill. Ascend to, and go right on, Highland Drive and walk left on North Sea Avenue, then sharp right on Bessborough Drive, enjoying the views over Burrard Inlet as you rise. Opposite house number 5621, enter the forest. Immediately go left and uphill on a track that exits onto Ellesmere Avenue. Turn right onto Cambridge, then right again onto North Howard Avenue, where you'll find a pleasant track leading through the woods to Harbourview Park, the summit of Capitol Hill.

After pausing to celebrate your ascent, continue round the curved Grosvenor Crescent to again turn west on Cambridge. Now you may enjoy expansive views south and west as you descend steeply (avoid when slippery), cutting through a tiny park atop a reservoir and arriving at Gamma Avenue. Here, jog left then right to descend diagonally through woodland and past a few picnic tables to arrive at your parking lot. If you haven't already, you might want to check out the variety of facilities available in Confederation Park.

SHORTER OPTIONS

For a walk of 1 hour and 2.7 km (1.7 mi) on the nature loop, go right on Penzance Drive to return to your starting point. Or, for a walk of 1.5 hours and 5 km (3.1 mi), make your way through Confederation Park and turn right on Penzance Drive to join the described walk to Capitol Hill.

GETTING THERE

Transit: Take TransLink Bus 129 (Patterson Station/Holdom Station) or 160 (Port Coquitlam/Kootenay Loop) to Hastings Street at Beta Avenue. Walk 300 m north on Beta to the park.

Vehicle: From Highway 1, take Exit 26 and go east on Hastings Street for 3 km (1.9 mi) to Beta Avenue. Turn left (north) and drive to the parking lot at the end.

BURNABY MOUNTAIN/SFU

Distance: 8.5 km (5.3 mi)
Time: 3 hours
Surface: trail, paved road
Elevation gain: 180 m (590 ft)
High point: 340 m (1115 ft)

Quality: ★★★
Difficulty: ● to ■
Season: most of the year
Car GPS entry: Duthie Ave & Hastings St
Burnaby, BC
Trailhead: 49°16'49" N 122°56'58" W

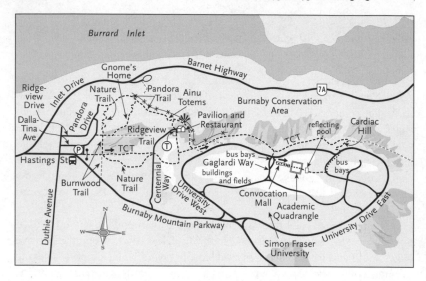

SET IN the midst of the Burnaby Mountain Conservation Area, Burnaby Mountain is a popular destination because of its spectacular views, its network of trails through second-growth forest and its proximity to the mountaintop Simon Fraser University (SFU) campus.

On foot from the gate at Dalla-Tina Avenue, walk up the incline—where you'll find lots of berries in season—to a Trans Canada Trail (TCT) sign, just past the Burnwood Trail crossing. Here, you may either continue directly up the multi-purpose pathway or take the more interesting nature trail to the right and ascend through forest to Centennial Way. Across the road, continue on the TCT past a towering rock with a plaque commemorating the 1967 Confederation Centennial plantation of rhododendrons, now unfortunately overshadowed by trees. A rising, wide sweep takes you to the TCT pavilion, your point of decision.

For the shorter walk, head north through open lawns and picnic sites towards the Horizons Restaurant and the lovely rose garden beyond. Enjoy

Spring blossoms and Ainu totems on Burnaby Mountain.
Photo: Alice Purdey

the views along Indian Arm and Burrard Inlet and note the Kamui Mintara, the Ainu totems that commemorate Burnaby's friendship with its sister city, Kushiro, Japan. Follow the gravel path that loops below the totems to join the fence-side Pandora Trail into the woods. In about 10 minutes, you reach the junction where Gnome's Home branches left. This will lead you to the Ridgeview and Burnwood Trails and down to your starting point.

For the longer walk to the SFU campus, head uphill from the TCT pavilion kiosk. Just past a water tank, at an information kiosk and fork, continue straight. This leads to University Drive, where you continue on the roadside pathway to the T-junction with Gaglardi Way, a bus hub. Cross here, bear left and climb a broad stairway to a courtyard with a fountain. Convocation Mall draws you in under its glass and trussed roof, thence more stairs lead to the Academic Quadrangle, a large reflecting pool and other points of interest and finally to the bus loop opposite a pleasant cascade of waterfalls. From here, descend East Campus Road beyond University Drive and walk 2 minutes right to an information kiosk and the top of the steep, popular Cardiac Hill, which you descend to meet the TCT. Go left to return to the restaurant area, head towards the totems and proceed as for the shorter outing.

SHORTER OPTION

For a 2-hour walk of 5 km (3.1 mi) on easy terrain, head north at the TCT pavilion through open lawns and picnic sites, as described.

GETTING THERE

Transit: Take TransLink Bus 95 (SFU/Burrard Station—B-Line) or 144 (SFU/ Metrotown Station) to Hastings Street at Duthie Avenue. Walk 250 m east on Hastings to the gated road.

Vehicle: From Highway 7A, follow Hastings Street east where it diverges from Highway 7A. At the east end of the curve where Hastings and Burnaby Mountain Parkway blend, turn north onto Dalla-Tina Avenue and then immediately right. Park near a gate at the corner.

BURNABY MOUNTAIN SOUTH

Distance: 6.8 km (4.2 mi)
Time: 2 hours
Surface: trail
Quality: ★★★
Difficulty: ●

Season: all year
Car GPS entry: Burnwood Dr & Greystone
Dr Burnaby, BC
Trailhead: 49°16'04" N 122°56'35" W

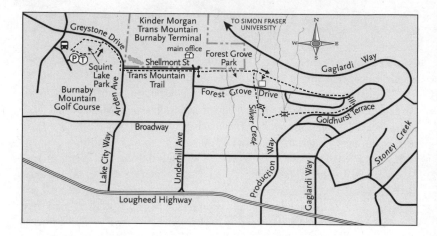

THIS OUTING treads the southeastern slopes of Burnaby Mountain on a ramble along nature trails through residential and recreational areas that, although sandwiched between intellectual activity (Simon Fraser University) and industrial activity, preserve for your enjoyment forested areas and the creeks and ravines that intersect them.

From the parking lot, walk past the children's playground on the trail between the park and the golf course. Just before you reach Greystone Drive, note a junction that offers an alternative return route. Take the trail that parallels Greystone Drive to the intersection with Shellmont Street, where you cross and find the Trans Mountain Trail. Continue past an oil-tank farm to the main entrance of the Kinder Morgan facility, marked by a totem pole carved by Mike Antone of the Squamish First Nation and, a few paces beyond, a gated gravel road.

About 500 m beyond the gate, past the playing areas, you come to a fork. Ignore the narrow path into the bush and walk straight ahead on the Trans Mountain Trail. At Ash Grove Crescent, cross onto a path below townhouses; this leads to Forest Grove Drive opposite Maple Grove Crescent. Cross Forest Grove and descend the wide stairway to a path just above the road's parallel

The totem pole carved by Mike Antone of the Squamish First Nation.

lower section. Now, turn back west on this trail, which combines successive paths and stairs, as it gently ascends. Soon the trail crosses a pedestrian bridge high above a ravine of cedar, hemlock and bigleaf maple and continues to a T-junction. Turn right and walk with another ravine to your left before crossing it on a bridge. Go right to Forest Grove Drive where you cross over to Forest Grove Park. A path through the park beside the playground leads to your outward route, where you go left and retrace your steps to Squint Lake Park. To extend your return walk by going around the park, go right on the previously noted trail just after you enter the park from your march along the trail beside Greystone Drive.

And where is Squint Lake? It's located not in the park, but farther down Halifax Street next to the golf course parking lot.

GETTING THERE
Transit: Take TransLink Bus 136 (Lougheed Station/Brentwood Station) to Burnwood Drive at Woodbrook Place. Walk south along Burnwood to Halifax Street and the trailhead, as below.
Vehicle: From Highway 7 (Lougheed Highway), take the Lake City Way exit. Heading north, cross Broadway onto Arden Avenue, which becomes Greystone Drive. Turn left (south) at Burnwood Drive and left again (east) at the sign for Squint Lake Park (Halifax Street). Turn left to the parking lot before you reach the golf course parking.

STONEY CREEK/SFU

Distance: 8 km (5 mi) one way
Time: 3 hours one way
Surface: trails, paved road
Elevation gain: 330 m (1082 ft)
High point: 360 m (1180 ft)

Quality: ★★★
Difficulty: ◆
Season: most of the year
Car GPS entry: Gatineau Pl & Austin Rd
Burnaby, BC
Trailhead: 49°15'00" N 122°53'54" W

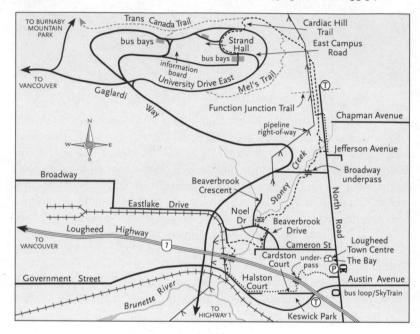

THIS WALK provides something of a workout; it takes you uphill all the way from a busy shopping centre and along greenway paths to Simon Fraser University on the summit of Burnaby Mountain. There, you may explore as you wish before walking down or riding the bus (take a #145 bus to Production Way, then hop onto the SkyTrain to travel one stop east to Lougheed Town Centre). The time, distance and directions given are for a one-way walk.

Begin your trek at the crosswalk at a bend in the parking lot's perimeter road west of The Bay. A few steps take you to a sidewalk (turn left), a pedestrian tunnel under Highway 7 (Lougheed Highway) and a winding path between apartment complexes that leads to a street named Cardston Court and, across from you, Keswick Park. Turn right on Cardston Court, which

Cardiac Hill Trail leads to the high point of the walk.

soon becomes Halston Court. Turn right onto Government Street for about 300 m, then right into the trees and onto the wide, more tranquil path of the Brunette–Fraser Regional Greenway, here running alongside Stoney Creek, with its restored fish habitat (see scec.ca). You pass under Highway 7 again before exiting onto the end of Eastlake Drive to turn right. Now, in short order, pass a ball field and cross a bridge to Keswick Avenue, go left on Keswick, turn right onto Cameron Street, left again onto Noel Drive, then across and left on Beaverbrook Drive to its meeting with Beaverbrook Crescent. Here, you leave the streets for the last time until arriving at your destination.

Your track enters the trees at the street corner, where you drop to the creek and a bridge. Stay with the path beneath two overpasses, the second being Broadway; curve around a residential area and then go left onto North Road just long enough to cross the bridge and dive back into the woods, now onto the dual-use North Road Trail. After walking for about 10 minutes and 500 m uphill, you arrive at a small pipeline building; jog left and then immediately right onto the Powerline Trail. Surprisingly, about 650 m up the road, is a convenient outhouse. Next, you bear left at a fork with a kiosk to join Trans Canada Trail (TCT) West and re-enter the trees.

Continue your relentless pace, pass the turnoff for Mel's Trail and head up the challenging Cardiac Hill Trail. Once at the top, your track almost flattens, or so it seems, as you make your way along University Drive East and East Campus Road to the bus loop. Here, you may rest, visit a café or further explore the campus (Walk 64) before making your way back down to your transport, by bus or by foot.

GETTING THERE
Transit: Take the SkyTrain or TransLink Bus 101, 109, 110, 136, 152, 156, 157, 180 or 555 to Lougheed Town Centre.
Vehicle: From Highway 7 (Lougheed Highway), take the North Road exit north to the Austin Road entrance on the south side of Lougheed Town Centre. Park near the southwest corner of The Bay (4 hours free).

BURNABY LAKE

Distance: 10 km (6.2 mi)
Time: 2.5 hours
Surface: trail
Quality: ★★★
Difficulty: ●

Season: all year
Car GPS entry: Avalon Ave & Cariboo Rd
Burnaby, BC
Trailhead: 49°14'49" N 122°55'06" W

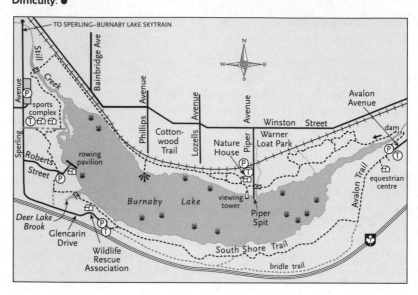

AN OASIS of nature, the long, narrow Burnaby Lake is home to more than 200 species of resident or visiting birds as well as animals—look for trees gnawed by beavers. The park attracts runners, walkers, bird watchers and families who enjoy feeding the ducks and geese. The most interesting section for a short outing lies between the Avalon parking lot and the Piper Spit area. Information kiosks are located at parking lots and trailheads.

Circling the lake in a counter-clockwise direction gives you the choice of doing either the short or long loop. Heading right (north) from the Avalon parking lot, you'll soon cross the Brunette River (Walk 68) on the Cariboo Dam, which was built to control waterflow from the lake while managing fish access. Prior to dam construction in 1915, logs were floated along the lake and downstream to the Fraser River. A few minutes beyond the dam, there are two side loops to explore before you arrive at Piper Spit. Here, a wharf extends out to a beaver lodge, wild iris and other marshland plants thrive and a variety of noisy waterfowl provide entertainment. If you want to feed the

Waterfowl at rest by Piper Spit.

birds, bring grains, which are better for them than bread. Near the spit are the Nature House, a butterfly garden, a viewing tower and one more loop, where a sawmill once operated. (Limited parking is available at Piper Spit.)

The next leg of the trail stretches ahead for 2.3 km (1.4 mi), squeezed between railway tracks and lakeshore greenery, then makes a sharp turn to cross Still Creek before traversing the parking lot (an alternative starting point) and playing fields at the Burnaby Sports Complex. Continue south, cross the rowing pavilion parking lot, then regain your trail amongst blackberry bushes and shrubbery. Pause on the Deer Lake Brook bridge and, in warm weather, look for turtles basking on logs. The next 3.5 km (2.2 mi) along the Southshore Trail lie between the lake, near which farms once thrived, and the highway, where an electric tram once travelled. Boardwalks traverse swampy sections made brilliant by the yellow swamp lanterns (skunk cabbage) in spring. Eventually arriving at a T-junction, go left on the broad multi-use Avalon Trail—where you may meet horseback riders from the equestrian centre—and so back to your starting point.

SHORTER OPTION
For a walk of 1.5 hours and 5 km (3.1 mi) or less, retrace your steps to the starting point after exploring Piper Spit.

GETTING THERE
Transit: Take TransLink Bus 101 (Lougheed Station/22nd Station) to Cariboo Road and Avalon Avenue.
Vehicle: From Highway 7 (Lougheed Highway), travel south on Brighton Avenue, east on Government Street, south on Cariboo Road, then west on Avalon Avenue to a parking lot at the east end of Burnaby Lake.

BRUNETTE RIVER

Distance: 6 km (3.7 mi)
Time: 2 hours
Surface: trail, paved
Quality: ★★★
Difficulty: ●
Season: all year

Car GPS entry: E Columbia St & Holmes
St New Westminster, BC
Trailhead: 49°14'19" N 122°53'33" W
Car GPS entry: Avalon Ave & Cariboo Rd
Burnaby, BC
Trailhead: 49°14'49" N 122°55'06" W

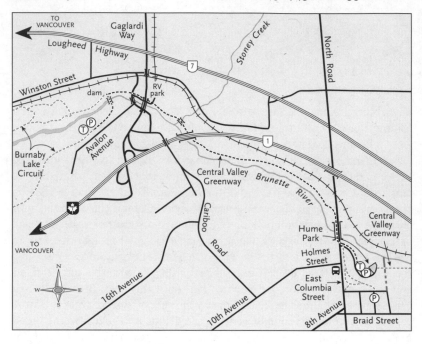

THE BRUNETTE River, so named for the brown colour derived from the peaty soil with which its waters mix, flows from Burnaby Lake to the Fraser River. This attractive walk follows the banks of the river upstream from Hume Park, though you could also do the walk in reverse from Burnaby Lake.

From Lower Hume Park, walk to East Columbia Street, cross at the pedestrian light, then head north over the bridge (where Columbia Street becomes North Road) to the service road on your left, the beginning of your excursion. The river banks are thick with a variety of shrubs and other greenery, planted to assist in restoring fish-spawning and -rearing habitat, and riparian and wildlife habitat. Keep an eye open for birdlife along the river, particularly for the great blue herons and the common kingfishers that frequent the area

Stacked stones standing silently over a riffle in the Brunette River.

looking for lunch. Seasonal water levels vary from a gentle flow, with tiny cascades over the two weirs, to swollen and rapid currents. As you stroll along, the sounds of nature compete for your attention with the dull drone of traffic. Compare this with the environment in 1859, when Robert Burnaby explored the river in its wilderness state, finding it tortuous, shallow and tangled with blowdowns.

After passing under the highway bridge, you come to Stoney Creek, where, thanks to the diligent efforts of volunteer streamkeepers, salmon return to spawn. (Dogs, of course, have to rely on their owners to keep them out of the fish habitat areas, no matter how inviting a nice splash may be.) Next, you pass the entrance to an RV park, follow the access road (Cariboo Place) to a crossing of Cariboo Road, then walk 250 m to the Cariboo Dam, with its fish ladder and nearby rest area. From here, you may continue up the right side of the water to the short loop on the Burnaby Lake walk (Walk 67), or you may return the way you came, enjoying the view from the opposite direction.

GETTING THERE

Transit: Take TransLink Bus 109 (New Westminster Station/Lougheed Station) to East Columbia Street at Holmes Street, enter Hume Park and follow the Central Valley Greenway signs south and east to the Brunette River. Or, from the bus loop at Braid SkyTrain station, find a passage through the fence opposite, which takes you across railway tracks and onto a path, the Central Valley Greenway. Go left to arrive at Lower Hume Park in about 15 minutes. This adds 900 m each way to your walk.

Vehicle: From Highway 1, take Exit 40 (Brunette Avenue) and go south. Turn right (west) onto Braid Street, then right again (north) onto East Columbia Street and drive 500 m to the park. Pass park facilities to reach a small parking lot. Or use the parking lot for Walk 67, walk 200 m north (right) to cross the Brunette River on the Cariboo Dam and meet the route of the upstream walkers.

DEER LAKE PARK

Distance: 7 km (4.3 mi)
Time: 2.5 hours
Surface: trail
Quality: ★★★
Difficulty: ●

Season: all year
Car GPS entry: Buxton St & Royal Oak
Ave Burnaby, BC
Trailhead: 49°14'18" N 122°59'19" W

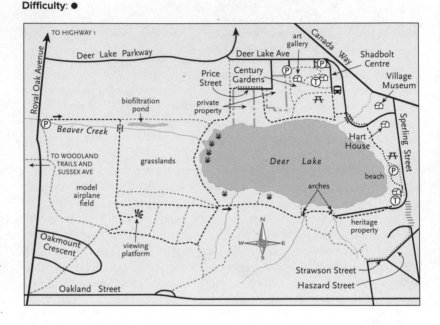

DEER LAKE Park offers walking trails, a beach and water-recreation facilities, broad views of the Lower Mainland's mountains and easy access to the beautiful Century Gardens and Burnaby's cultural hub.

Beginning your outing at Royal Oak, walk east beside Beaver Creek, the major feeder stream for Deer Lake, to the first junction, where you turn right onto a straight path. Immediately on your left is a side path with an information board explaining the nearby biofiltration pond; a few steps along on your right is a meadow for model airplanes. Surrounding grasslands were once the site of a farm worked by inmates of Oakalla Prison Farm, which sat on the slope ahead, now occupied by housing. Continue walking up a rise, past two trails to your left, to a platform offering a wide view of the Burnaby and Golden Ears mountains, with Deer Lake as foreground.

Just above the platform, turn left and stay high until you reach a T-junction, where you turn downhill to meet the lakeside trail. Go right to travel along the south shore, where you'll traverse the edge of marshlands, walk under two arches on a boardwalk and pass in front of two city-owned heritage properties, the Eagles Estate and Baldwin House, before turning left at an information board to reach the beach area with its many facilities. (To park and

Deer Lake seen from its grassy southern slopes.

begin your outing here, turn south off Canada Way onto Sperling Avenue.) Some 300 m beyond the beach, the trail swings "inland" to cross a small creek on a bridge on Deer Lake Avenue and then immediately angles back towards the lakeshore.

Much of the north-side trail is on boardwalk with occasional benches. You may choose to make a side trip to explore Century Gardens, the Burnaby Art Gallery and the Shadbolt Centre grounds before you have to detour around private property. On a signed route, the trail makes a sharp turn north for 200 m to Price Street, travels 150 m west along Price, then heads south to rejoin the lake at its west end. Now, follow the boardwalk south through marshland to the junction of trails you crossed earlier. Here, for a variation on your return, choose one of the two lower trails heading west, turn uphill at its end, pass the viewing platform, continue uphill and right, then finally turn downhill, Royal Oak Avenue on your left.

Back on the flats, you may choose to extend your outing by passing under the roadway and wandering around woodland trails on the far side. Or you may choose to continue north back to your starting point.

GETTING THERE

Transit: Take TransLink Bus 123 (New Westminster Station/Brentwood Station) or 144 (SFU/Metrotown Station) to Deer Lake Avenue at Shadbolt Centre; join the trail at the lake.

Vehicle: From Highway 1, take Exit 29 (Willingdon Avenue) south to Grange Street. Turn left (east) on Grange, which becomes Dover Street, to Royal Oak Avenue. Or, take Exit 33 (Kensington) south to Canada Way and then southeast to Burris Street. Turn right (west) and continue, as Burris becomes Oakland Street, to Royal Oak. Go north on Royal Oak Avenue, watching carefully for the entrance (right turn only) into a small lot at the bottom of the long hill.

BYRNE CREEK RAVINE PARK

Distance: 3.5 km (2.2 mi)
Time: 1.5 hours
Surface: trail
Quality: ★★★
Difficulty: ●

Season: all year
Car GPS entry: Rumble St & Hedley Ave
Burnaby, BC
Trailhead: 49°12'42" N 122°58'06" W

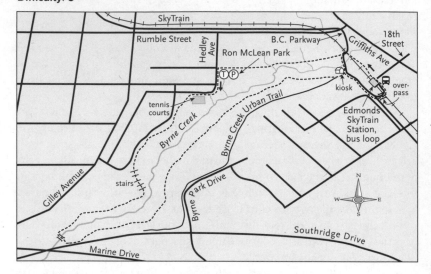

BYRNE CREEK Ravine Park, the "wilderness" portion of an urbanized watershed, provides a quiet oasis and pleasant escape from its busy surroundings, particularly on a hot day.

By transit, from the entrance of Edmonds SkyTrain station, turn left and go through the parking lot by the bus loop to a path underneath the SkyTrain. Follow the path parallel to abandoned railway tracks, cross these to go left at a wide junction signed B.C. Parkway, then immediately go right and walk between woods and townhouses for 500 m to the Ron McLean Park parking lot.

From the parking lot, walk downhill to the end of Hedley Avenue and turn right; the Byrne Creek Ravine Trail begins just beyond the tennis courts. Initially, the trail is level and bordered by deciduous shrubs and bigleaf maples, but then it drops about 75 m down dozens of steps to creekside. The creek water you see is collected by drains in the watershed and carried underground to the head of the ravine, where it is "freed" for a brief run. After flowing through more pipes, it winds up in the lowlands and artificial

The muscular roots of a red cedar clinging to the slopes of the ravine.

spawning grounds near the Fraser River (Walk 72). Today, Byrne Creek is cared for by streamkeepers who nourish salmon-spawning habitat. (Dogs who frolic in the water do unseen damage to this fragile resource.) In the 1870s, prime timber for ship masts was cut in the area and then floated downstream to the Fraser River.

After crossing the creek on a footbridge, ascend to reach Southridge Drive, a noisy but brief interruption to your peace. Walk 10 m left to a short, steep embankment, which you climb to regain your trail. This path now braids its way along, well above the ravine, with views down the steep, forested slopes, until you arrive at cement-and-stone foundations and large walnut trees. You could wander around here and try to picture what life might have been like before our population density forged the current environment: residential towers that you glimpse through the trees. Continue straight ahead, the towers and the paved Byrne Creek Urban Trail to your right, until you meet a T-junction with an information kiosk. Look downstream from beside the kiosk to see the side channel–type fish ladder, built by streamkeepers to help juvenile fish on their upstream journey.

To return to Edmonds station, turn right and follow a paved path for about 175 m to meet stairs leading up and over the SkyTrain tracks, then go left to the station. To return to Ron McLean Park, turn left at the kiosk and continue on paved path for about 80 m, then veer left onto a gravel path between woods and townhouses.

GETTING THERE
Transit: Take the SkyTrain or TransLink Bus 106, 112, 119, 133, 147 or 148 to Edmonds station.
Vehicle: From Highway 1, take Exit 33 (Kensington Avenue) to Canada Way, turn left (east) and go east to Imperial Street. Follow Imperial and turn left (south) on Griffiths to Rumble. Or, from Highway 91A (Queensborough Connector), take the 20th Street exit and go north, staying with it as it becomes Griffiths, to Rumble. Go west on Rumble until you reach Hedley Avenue. Drive two blocks south to the Ron McLean Park parking lot.

ROBERT BURNABY PARK

Distance: 5.7 km (3.5 mi)

Time: 2 hours

Surface: gravel, trails

Quality: ★★★

Difficulty: ●

Season: all year

Car GPS entry: Canada Way & Edmonds St Burnaby, BC

Trailhead: 49°13'51" N 122°56'10" W

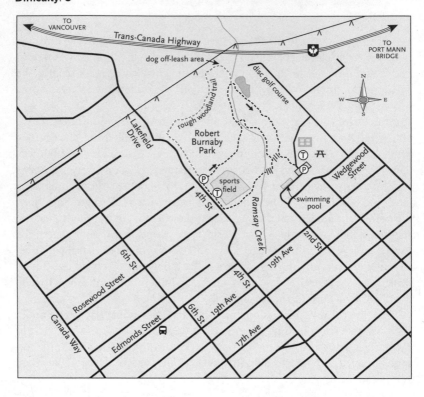

THIS LITTLE gem of a park is popular with locals but otherwise largely unknown, despite its proximity to Burnaby Lake (Walk 67) and Highway 1. The reason may be that there is no direct access from the highway, but it's well worth a visit for quiet walks on wooded ravine and forest trails, restful reflection on secluded benches alongside the creek and family picnics in grassy glades. Built during the Great Depression, the park was named for a merchant and provincial politician who explored the region around Burnaby Lake in 1859.

White trilliums are abundant in the park in spring.

This park has its mild side and its wild side: the trails on the mild side are smooth, well-groomed gravel while those on the wild side are rough and rooty. To begin, walk directly downhill beside the sports field on the main mild-side trail and bear right to descend towards Highway 1. Look for a path leading to a pair of benches tucked away near a tributary creek on your right.

As you reach the park's low point, you can visit the wild side via the dog off-leash area by turning west and walking uphill (before you reach the power line) into the undeveloped part of the park, where woodland trails lead through hemlock, cedar and Douglas-fir forest and over several creek-crossings before looping back around to the parking lot where you began.

Alternatively, to remain on the mild side, turn right and walk uphill past the disc golf fields to a junction, where you go right to descend stairs into the Ramsay Creek ravine and the middle section of the park. Follow your inclination and explore the trails that lead you amongst the small ravines and tributary creeks in this area of the park. When it is time to end your explorations, ascend to the opposite side of the sports field and return to your starting point.

GETTING THERE
Transit: Take TransLink Bus 106 (New Westminster Station/Edmonds Station) to Edmonds Street at 6th Street. Walk northwest for 250 m on Edmonds to 4th Street and enter the park by the sports field.
Vehicle: From Highway 1, take Exit 33 (Kensington Avenue) south and turn left (east) onto Canada Way. Drive to Edmonds Street, where you turn left. Soon after, turn right onto 6th Street then left onto 17th Avenue (or 16th Avenue). At 4th Street, turn left and park in the lot at the Robert Burnaby Park sports field.

BURNABY FRASER
FORESHORE PARK

Distance: 8 km (5 mi)

Time: 2.5 hours

Surface: trail, paved

Quality: ★★★

Difficulty: ●

Season: all year

Car GPS entry: Boundary Rd & Marine Way Burnaby, BC

Trailhead: 49°12'05" N 123°01'24" W

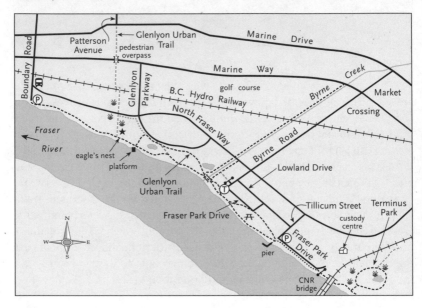

THIS PLEASANT stroll along the North Arm of the Fraser River offers places to watch activities on the river, an ecological reserve and play and picnic areas.

From your vehicle, approach the river and turn left (Walk 50 goes right) on the dyke trail that lies between light industrial businesses sitting on ancient peat bog on one side and the Fraser River on the other. Look for an eagles' nest high in a cottonwood tree up a side trail at the end of the buildings and elsewhere along the route. Near the Glenlyon Creek dam, a viewing platform invites you to a closer view of log booms and activities on the busy Fraser. Soon thereafter, at Byrne Creek, a mounted picture frame outlines the scene.

Here you may take a diversion. Turn upstream on the east side of the creek to reach a footbridge. (The west side will eventually reopen after upgrading.) You may cross to the picturesque Glenlyon Urban Trail, which wanders past

The wooden archway reflects the long history of logging along the Fraser River and its foreshore. *Photo: Alice Purdey*

attractive little ponds back to the main trail, or you may cross North Fraser Way and continue northwards to end at Marine Way. Placid Byrne Creek provides habitat for salmon spawn and fry under the guardianship of the Byrne Creek Streamkeepers.

Continuing west on the main trail, you pass scattered picnic tables, extensive grassy fields between footpath and bike path, toilets, a small play area and exercise stations before arriving at a spacious platform ideal for relaxing and viewing. Shortly thereafter, you reach the archway at Tillicum Street. (Parking is available both at the picnic site, located near Fraser Park Drive off Byrne Road, and near the archway on Fraser Park Drive.) Now, walk along the gravel path to a gated, riverside trail. Within 5 minutes, you pass under the Canadian National Railway (CNR) bridge, with its centre span left open for river traffic, and arrive at the wide, unmarked junction to the Estuary Nature Area of the Fraser Foreshore Park, also known as Terminus Park. Here there are more than 2 km (1.2 mi) of trails through a diversity of habitats, including restored wetlands and an old-field meadow.

Back on the main trail, continuing east for 500 m leads to an abrupt end at a waterworks bunker and shore access. Now return the way you have come, enjoying the general atmosphere and perhaps wandering up some of the side trails. Note that during winter rains, high tides on the Fraser—yes, ocean tides stretch up here—flood some of the low-lying trails. These can be skirted on higher paths.

GETTING THERE

Transit: Take TransLink Bus 116 (Edmonds Station/Metrotown Station) to Boundary Road at Kent Avenue. Walk south on Boundary Road to the trailhead.

Vehicle: From the south end of Boundary Road, which divides Vancouver and Burnaby, cross the railway tracks south of Marine Way. Turn right to stay on Boundary Road where it transitions into North Fraser Way. Park at the end of the road.

EDMONDS/NEW WESTMINSTER QUAY

Distance: one way from Edmonds
Station: 7 km (4.3 mi)
Time: 2.5 hours
Surface: paved
Quality: ★
Difficulty: ●

Season: all year
Car GPS entry: Station Hill Dr Burnaby, BC
Trailhead (Edmonds station): 49°12'42"
N 122°57'32" W

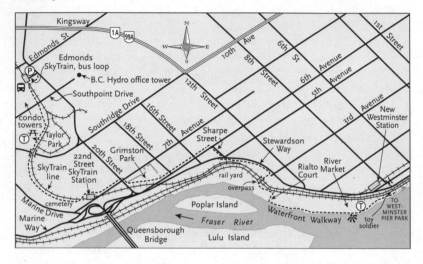

B.C. PARKWAY is a 26 km (16.2 mi) multi-use pathway that roughly parallels the SkyTrain's Expo Line. This outing, along a portion of the parkway, follows a decommissioned railway line, passes through a variety of residential and industrial environments and ends at an urban esplanade and quayside market on the banks of the Fraser River in New Westminster. You may, in fact, begin this circuit anywhere along the route, return to Edmonds station on the SkyTrain after visiting the quay, then stroll back to your vehicle on the pathway to complete your walk.

As you exit the Edmonds station, turn right, walk less than 100 m to an overpass on which you cross the tracks, then, across from the condo towers, turn left to join a wide, paved path, which is the B.C. Parkway (going right leads to Walk 70). Follow the path across Southpoint Drive and past townhouses until, within 600 m, you reach Taylor Park. Once a landfill, the area has been transformed into a large multi-use attraction that is worth exploring. Visit the butterfly meadows near the bike park, and, in season, bring a pail to collect blackberries from the bushes that line the B.C. Parkway.

Waterfront Walkway along the Fraser River.

Next, cross Southridge Drive on an overpass and skirt the cemetery that lies tucked behind a cedar hedge, making a wide curve before arriving at the 22nd Street SkyTrain station. Pass this on the uphill side and follow 7th Avenue to 20th Street, cross 20th and go right, then turn left just before passing under the SkyTrain to reach Grimston Park. (As you make your way along, take the opportunity to look for views down the side streets.) Follow the path until you are blocked by Stewardson Way.

To continue, walk along 6th Avenue, past 16th Street, to Sharpe Street, where you turn right. Where Sharpe Street meets 5th Avenue on a bend, descend a ramp to Stewardson Way and then go right 50 m to a controlled pedestrian crossing. Cross, then go left. Follow the sidewalk past industrial properties, where you regain the B.C. Parkway, then turn right on 3rd Avenue. Cross the tracks on the overpass and continue as you descend onto Quayside Drive to meet Rialto Court, onto which you turn right to reach the riverside.

Here, the whole atmosphere changes. Now you may stroll at leisure for about 1.5 km (0.9 mi) to River Market along an esplanade lined with condos, information plaques, views and piers for fisherfolk. From its beginnings as a farmers' market in 1892, River Market has evolved—and continues to do so—into a family destination with a variety of diversions, eateries and shops.

Finally, at a children's play area overseen by a 9.8 m (32 ft) tin soldier (modelled on the Royal Engineers who founded New Westminster), cross the SkyBridge to the SkyTrain station, which is just beyond Columbia Street, for your return journey to Edmonds station.

LONGER OPTION

Continue your waterfront walk from the tin soldier for 400 m (0.25 mi) to Westminster Pier Park. The 600 m boardwalk along the waterfront features more views over the Fraser River plus picnic tables and public art. A leisurely stroll of 20 to 30 minutes will take you from end to end and back.

GETTING THERE

Transit: Take the SkyTrain or TransLink Bus 106, 112, 119, 133, 147 or 148 to Edmonds station.

Vehicle: From Highway 1, take Exit 33 (Kensington Avenue) to Canada Way, turn left and go east to turn right on Imperial Street. Turn left (south) on Griffiths. Or, from Highway 91A (Queensborough Connector), take the 20th Street exit and go north, staying with it as it becomes Griffiths. Park curbside on Southpoint Drive or Station Hill Drive near Edmonds station.

QUEENSBOROUGH RIVERFRONT

Distance: 4 km (2.5 mi)
Time: 1.5 hours
Surface: paved
Quality: ★★
Difficulty: ●

Season: all year
Car GPS entry: Ewen Ave & Boyd St New Westminster, BC
Trailhead: 49°11'41" N 122°55'38" W

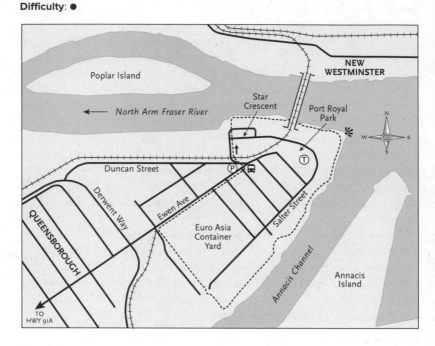

ONCE THE location of a sawmill owned by MacMillan Bloedel, the industrial-zoned land at the eastern tip of Queensborough/Lulu Island was transformed into the Port Royal residential development. Included in the development was the Riverfront Walk, with boardwalks, preserved natural sandy beaches and open views of the Fraser River.

If you arrived by vehicle, you start the walk by finding your way to the bus stop at Furness Street and Ewen Avenue. From there, proceed north on Furness Street and along a pathway to the riverfront boardwalk with its view of the North Arm of the Fraser River, from the Queensborough Bridge to Poplar Island and the New Westminster waterfront (Walk 73). Continue on the bricked path, passing the open sandy beach and onto the bridge that takes you under the train tracks before re-joining the path. Now the path widens and you arrive at a viewing platform at the tip of Lulu Island where

Looking upstream from Annacis Channel towards the SkyTrain and Patullo Bridges.

the river separates into the north and south arms. Looking upstream you see the Golden Ears peaks framed by the SkyTrain bridge, behind it the Pattullo Bridge and to your right the tip of Annacis Island across Annacis Channel.

As you proceed, notice the various activities that take place on the channel: log booms, barges and freighters loading and unloading, boats plowing by. And in the distance the fourth bridge of the day, the Alex Fraser. Eventually, the path leaves the river and turns 90 degrees to join the Stanley Street Greenway, which you follow to Ewen Avenue. There you turn right and follow Ewen back to your starting point.

To complement your walk, you may want to continue along Ewen to the green space at Port Royal Park, where there is an interesting terraced community garden and picnic tables.

GETTING THERE

Transit: Take TransLink Bus 104 (22nd St. Station/Annacis Island) to Furness Street and Ewen Avenue.

Vehicle: From Highway 91A, take the Howes Street exit and go south on Boyd until you reach Ewen Avenue. Turn left (east) and park on the street near the bus stop at Furness Street and Ewen Avenue.

BELCARRA REGIONAL PARK DUO

Distance: Burns Point 5.2 km (3.2 mi)

Time: 2 hours

Distance: Jug Island Beach 5.5 km (3.4 mi)

Time: 2 hours

Surface: rugged with rocks and roots
(Burns Point), trail (Jug Point)

Quality: ★★★★★

Difficulty: ● (Burns Point)/■ (Jug Island)

Season: all year

Car GPS entry: Ungless Way & Ioco Rd
Port Moody, BC

Trailhead (Burns Point): 49°18'44" N
122°55'32" W

Trailhead (Jug Island): 49°18'49" N
122°55'23" W

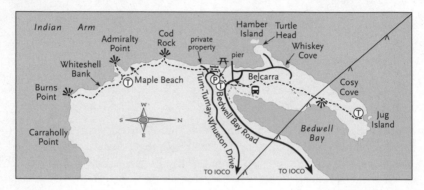

SITUATED ON a point of land between Indian Arm and Burrard Inlet, this popular park is a magnet for picnickers and water lovers. As well, there are two
attractive walks in distinctive settings: a woodland walk along the spine of the
peninsula to a delightful little beach at its north end, and a ramble south near
the shoreline at the mouth of Indian Arm. (Note that gates are closed when
the park is at capacity.)

For Jug Island Beach, you may start from the north (far) end of the parking
lot, cross Bedwell Bay Road and then walk a few paces left to find the trailhead, or you may start at the covered picnic tables on a signed trail leading
into the forest to meet the trailhead across the road. At a junction to Bedwell
Bay (a tidal flat, 35 minutes return), keep left on a gravel path working its way
north along the ridge. After some 25 to 30 minutes, your route bends right
onto a steeply rising, rocky path with stairs beside a mossy slab. A nearby
viewpoint overlooks Bedwell Bay. Now the track levels briefly before dropping steeply to the secluded little beach with Jug Island just across the water,
a pleasant spot to relax before you return.

For Burns Point, you start from below the concession stand on the south
side of the parking lot. Cross a footbridge and then a road leading to private

Jug Island, seen from the beach at the turnaround point. *Photo: Alice Purdey*

property before your forest trail begins to rise a little above the waters of Indian Arm's southern reach. Small cleared areas with flower gardens gone wild were home to squatters in the 1930s. Next comes Cod Rock, your first good viewpoint, followed by Periwinkle Notch, Maple Beach with its access trail and then a major junction at which the right fork takes you 100 m to Admiralty Point and expansive views.

Back at the junction, the trail becomes rougher, with ups and downs, until, after 1 km (0.6 mi), it reaches the rocky bluff of Burns Point, your destination, with its views up, down and across Burrard Inlet. At your leisure, you return the way you came.

GETTING THERE
Transit: Take TransLink Bus 182 (Moody Centre Station/Belcarra) to Belcarra Bay Road at Midden Road.
Vehicle: From Highway 7A, follow Ioco Road in Port Moody north and west along Burrard Inlet to First Avenue. Here, turn right and then, at a fork, left onto Bedwell Bay Road. Pass the White Pine Beach Road, stay left and leave Bedwell Bay Road, following the sign to Belcarra Picnic Area. After 1 km (0.6 mi), you fork right and pass through a gate to the parking area.

SASAMAT LAKE/
WOODHAVEN SWAMP

Distance: 8 km (5 mi)
Time: 3 hours
Surface: trail
Quality: ★★★
Difficulty: ●
Season: most of the year

Car GPS entry: Ungless Way & Ioco Rd
Port Moody, BC
Trailhead (White Pine Beach):
49°19'30.0" N 122°53'16.1" W
Trailhead (Woodhaven Swamp):
49°18'55.1" N 122°54'21.1" W

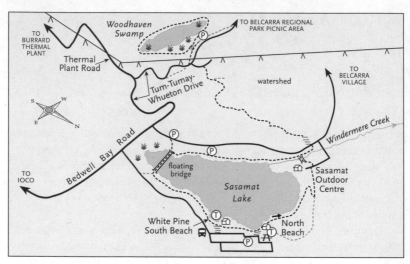

SASAMAT LAKE and its two sandy beaches are so popular that on bright summer days, only the early birds gain access through the capacity-control gates. Nearby Woodhaven Swamp also makes a good destination. Before and during the Great Depression of the 1930s, loggers and shake cutters toiled here and shipped their products to Hastings Mill (Walk 36) in Vancouver.

The Sasamat Lake Trail begins at water's edge at the north end of the beach. After hugging the lakeshore, it rises to an access road, where you turn left to meet the approach to the private Sasamat Outdoor Centre. Across this road, the trail resumes, dropping to and crossing the lake's outlet before coming to a T-junction. For the lake circuit, go left along the shore, paralleling Bedwell Bay Road above, until you come to the floating bridge with its swimming platforms, which cuts off the marshy southern end of the lake. Once across the bridge, the pleasant trail continues through woods near the water with little bridges over side streams and several old-growth trees. Soon, you arrive at South Beach and then North Beach and the completion of your walk.

Woodhaven Swamp can be reached by a connector trail (3.8 km/2.4 mi return) from Sasamat Lake or by driving to a parking lot adjacent to the swamp. From the lake circuit, turn right after crossing the outlet by the Sasamat Outdoor Centre, follow the creek downstream for about 200 m, then rise to road level at the Belcarra Village welcome sign, where a crosswalk leads to a flight of stairs. You now ascend between private properties, catch glimpses of the lake, cross a long bridge over a damp hollow and ascend on stairs around a rocky bluff, after which the trail undulates for about 1 km (0.6 mi) and comes to a power line access road. This, in turn, emerges on Tum-Tumay-Whueton Drive directly across from the swamp. təmtəmíxʷtən (Tum-tumay-whueton) is a Tsleil-Waututh ancestral village site located on the Belcarra Peninsula in present-day Belcarra Park.

Woodhaven Swamp was created by loggers but is now an important wetland habitat.

Cross the road, go through a gate and turn left immediately to descend to the Woodhaven Swamp trail. This trail (1.2 km/0.7 mi) encircles the margin of this charming wetland, a long boardwalk at its north end providing a place to pause. Finally, retrace your steps to Sasamat Lake to resume your circuit around its shore, perhaps finishing with a picnic or a swim.

SHORTER OPTION

For an hour-long walk of 3 km (1.9 mi), circle the lake by going left at the T-junction rather than heading to Woodhaven Swamp.

GETTING THERE

Transit: Take TransLink Bus 150 (Coquitlam Central Station/White Pine Beach) to White Pine Beach at Norton Court. Note that service on this route is seasonal—check www.translink.ca for details.

Vehicle: From Highway 7A, follow Ioco Road in Port Moody north and west alongside Burrard Inlet to First Avenue. Here, turn right and then, at a fork, left onto Bedwell Bay Road. At a well-signed junction, turn right to White Pine Beach to park, preferably at the farthest lot. To walk the swamp trail only, drive towards the Belcarra Picnic Area and watch for a well-signed parking lot at Woodhaven Swamp.

SHORELINE TRAIL

Distance: 6 km (3.7 mi)　　　　**Season**: all year
Time: 2 hours　　　　**Car GPS entry**: Saint Johns St & Moody St
Surface: trail, paved　　　　Port Moody, BC
Quality: ★★★★　　　　**Trailhead (at bridge)**: 49°16'48" N
Difficulty: ●　　　　122°50'52" W

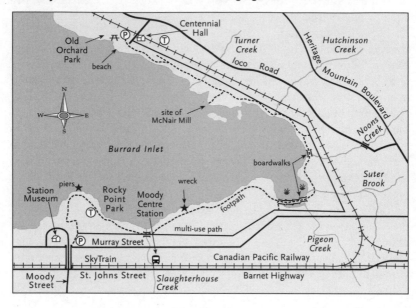

LYING MOSTLY secluded from busy roads and urban activities, this trail provides glimpses into shoreline activities in the late 19th century: remnants of sawmills and shingle mills, a steel mill and brickyards that fuelled the growth of Port Moody. Built to suit both those who prefer a natural footpath and those who require a smooth surface, the twinned trails between Rocky Point Park, off St. Johns Street in Port Moody, and Old Orchard Park, on the opposite shore off Ioco Road, form a rough horseshoe around the head of Burrard Inlet. (Alternatively, you could park at Old Orchard Park and hike the trail in the opposite direction.)

You might start your outing with a visit to the Port Moody Station Museum, which lies just west of your parking lot. Built as a railway station in 1908, it now displays interesting artifacts of First Nations origin and of local, early European activities. From the parking lot, the trailhead begins at a footbridge at the northeastern end of the grassy fields. The foot-trail

and hardtop paths diverge at the bridge over Slaughterhouse Creek, whose name evokes the days when a slaughterhouse operated here in the 1920s. As you head into the trees, fir and cedar being prominent, note the final remains of a long-ago shipwreck on the shore. Stop at Pigeon Cove to imagine thousands of band-tailed pigeons

Winding boardwalk protecting the intertidal marsh near Pigeon Creek. *Photo: Alice Purdey*

migrating in the spring and fall, an attraction for hunters until the 1970s. Winding boardwalks and bridges take you over the mud flats and sedges that mark the head of Burrard Inlet. Next, watch for a short detour to the water, where a grassy area and small platform with a bench offer fine views down the inlet and of shoreline birdlife.

Soon thereafter, at Noons Creek, another side trail rises to the Noons Creek Fish Hatchery, which is managed by the Port Moody Ecological Society. Continuing on your way, you may spot scraps from early industrial activity. At Old Mill Site Park, you might explore the remains of one of the cedar mills that once dotted this part of the coast: the cement foundations of a bee-hive lumber-waste burner and rotting stanchions that once supported busy wharves and mill buildings. Opposite, high in cottonwood trees, a heron rookery is active and entertaining in the spring months. Benches and information boards dot the trail. Finally, your trail ends at Old Orchard Park, an attractive picnic area with a beach, children's play area and toilets available in a hall across the tracks. To return, you could choose the more direct and evenly graded multi-use path that runs between the railway tracks and the footpath.

GETTING THERE

Transit: Take the SkyTrain or TransLink Bus 160 (Port Coquitlam Station/Kootenay Loop) or 180 (Moody Centre Station/Lougheed Station) to Moody Centre Station. From the bus loop, walk west through the parking lots to a flight of stairs that goes up to the Moody Street overpass (with a stroller, go south from the bus loop to Spring Street, walk west and then turn right on Moody Street). Cross the overpass on the east side and follow the ramp down to Rocky Point Park.

Vehicle: From Highway 7A (St. Johns Street), turn north at the Moody Street intersection, follow the curve around and turn left on Murray Street and then left into the parking lot east of the overpass.

COQUITLAM CRUNCH PLUS

Distance: 5.7 km (3.5 mi)
Time: 2 hours
Surface: gravel, stairs
Elevation gain: 242 m (794 ft)
Quality: ★★★

Difficulty: ■
Season: all year
Car GPS entry: Lansdowne Dr & Guildford Way Coquitlam, BC
Trailhead: 49°17'07" N 122°48'55" W

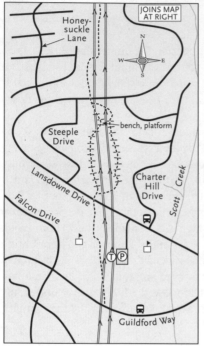
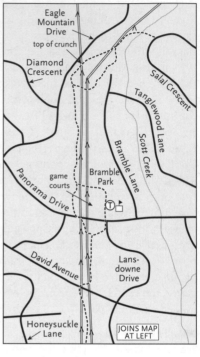

AS FORETOLD by its name, this hillside pathway provides an energetic walk with wide views on a clear day. The Crunch is south-facing and the entire corridor is without shade, so it is usually hot on a sunny summer's day.

The path begins opposite the community garden, where signs advise about safety precautions around power lines, since the route follows B.C. Hydro's transmission corridor. Within moments, you cross Lansdowne Drive for the first time and, choosing the left or right stairs, begin your climb. If you take the left, then just before the 0.5 km signpost you may pause for relief at a viewing platform with a bench. Onwards and upwards and, after 457 stairs, relief comes at your second crossing of Lansdowne Drive where the slope begins to lie back as you continue your crunch on the gravel trail.

Crunch this: 457 stairs!

North of David Avenue, the midway point, the path swings around a fenced off-leash area before arriving at a fork. Either way works. Going right leads to a crossing of Panorama Drive opposite Bramblewood Elementary School. You can then go straight ahead, past the sports facilities, and swing left at the tennis courts to rejoin the trail beyond. If you go left and up the stairs, stay right of the game courts, then go left on Panorama Drive (past a bus-stop bench), before crossing to Bramble Park. Within another 500 m you reach the top of the Crunch at Eagle Mountain Drive, about 242 m higher than your start. You can now reward yourself with a stroll through a strip of woods beside Scott Creek, the sound of nature in your ears and a soft path underfoot. Take a refreshing pause on the bridge over the creek before you exit onto Salal Crescent, your turnaround point.

Returning the way you came, you can extend your woodland moments by staying left at a junction until the gravelled trail reaches the transmission line clearing. Follow the path upwards to rejoin the Crunch, then head down to your starting point, enjoying the views en route. (Alternatively, you could choose to catch the #185 bus down Lansdowne Drive from Panorama Drive to Charter Hill Drive [your parking lot] or to Guildford Way and your bus.)

GETTING THERE

Transit: Take TransLink Bus 160 (Port Coquitlam Station/Kootenay Loop) to Guildford Way and Eagleridge Drive. Walk 200 m west on the north side of Guildford to reach your trail under the power line and proceed 200 m to the parking lot. Alternatively, take Bus 185 (Coquitlam Central Station/Lansdowne) to Guildford Way and Charter Hill Drive, then as below.
Vehicle: From Highway 7A (Barnet Highway), drive north on Lansdowne Drive, cross Guildford Way and then, 100 m past Scott Creek Middle School, turn left onto a dirt road under the power lines to the parking area.

COQUITLAM RIVER/
TOWN CENTRE PARK

Distance: 9 km (5.6 mi)
Time: 3 hours
Surface: trails, paved
Quality: ★★★
Difficulty: ●

Season: all year
Car GPS entry: BC-7 & Hastings St Port Coquitlam, BC
Trailhead: 49°16'36" N 122°46'43" W

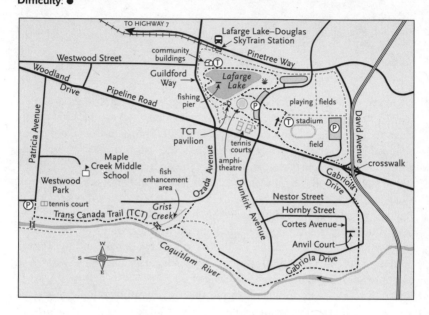

THIS WALK follows the Coquitlam River and skirts a residential area, then makes its way through a large urban park with all its seasonal amenities and culminates with a pleasant circuit of Lafarge Lake. The lake provides a nice place to rest before you must return. Most of the route follows the Trans Canada Trail (TCT), so the distinctive signs help keep you on track.

Your path begins near the tennis court on Patricia Avenue and almost immediately reaches a bridge over the Coquitlam River. Look, but do not cross (Walk 80 lies on the other side); instead, turn left on the TCT and continue through mostly deciduous, then mixed forest with some large conifers and cottonwoods. In spring, the cottonwoods' sweet smell (sometimes called Balm of Gilead) scents the air; there are a variety of plants in the undergrowth. After about 10 minutes, you cross the bridge over Grist Creek, which is a protected salmon habitat area (sorry pooch, no swimming). As you

Coquitlam means "red fish up the river" in the hən̓q̓əmin̓əm̓ language and inspired these leaping salmon in Town Centre Park.

proceed up the Coquitlam River, occasional side trails provide access to the water's edge.

After about 2 km (1.2 mi), leave the riverside and turn westwards beside power lines, cross a street and continue on a gravel path. You emerge on Gabriola Drive, where, a few paces to your left and opposite Nestor Street, a TCT sign beckons. A short track between houses leads to the busy intersection of David Avenue and Pipeline Road. Cross Pipeline Road at the light to a bench at the corner of Town Centre Park opposite. After resting and getting your bearings, follow a paved path in the trees parallel to Pipeline Road, passing expansive sports fields (with concessions and facilities) on your right, then continue past the playground, parking lots and amphitheatre to Lafarge Lake. This area, a former gravel quarry, was donated to the city when quarry operations ceased. Although the lake with its fountain is not suitable for swimming, it is popular with fisherfolk. Turn right to circumnavigate the lake, skirting the wetland environment at the north end and passing community facilities at the southwest side. Now, choose between the paved multi-use path or the Lakeside Nature Trail, which winds up and down close to the water and passes the fishing pier. Both will take you to the TCT pavilion (kiosk), from which you start your return walk.

Follow the TCT that rises to meet and cross Pipeline Road, turn left (north) to find the right-of-way near the intersection that leads you back to the Coquitlam River Trail and retrace your steps back to your vehicle.

GETTING THERE
Transit: Take the SkyTrain or TransLink Bus 160, 186 or 188 to Lafarge Lake-Douglas Station, then do the walk in reverse.
Vehicle: From Highway 7 (Lougheed Highway), go north on Hastings Street, 200 m west of Coquitlam River Bridge. Drive 700 m north to Patricia Avenue, turn right and park on the street at the end.

TRABOULAY POCO TRAIL/ COQUITLAM RIVER

Distance: 10.5 km (6.5 mi)
Time: 3 hours
Surface: paved, trail
Quality: ★★★
Difficulty: ●

Season: all year
Car GPS entry: Wilson Ave & Reeve St
Port Coquitlam, BC
Trailhead: 49°15'39" N 122°47'23" W

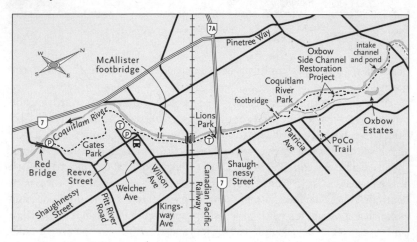

THE COQUITLAM River watershed is the traditional territory of the Kwikwetlem Nation, whose name means "red fish up the river" in the hәn̓q̓әmin̓әm̓ language and refers to the sockeye salmon. In the early 20th century, newcomers constructed the Coquitlam Dam and caused the near elimination of salmon from the Coquitlam River. By the late 20th century, additional water runoff into the river allowed restoration efforts to commence. The Oxbow Side Channel Restoration Project that you visit on this walk is one result of those efforts. Today, Kwikwetlem are leaders in stewardship to return salmon to the river. This walk begins along the Traboulay PoCo Trail between street and stream, then continues into the woods where fish and wildlife habitat has been extensively regenerated. It is but one section of a network of connecting trails that are yours to explore (see also Walks 79, 81 and 82).

From the parking lot, head northwest to join the wide, paved Traboulay PoCo Trail, where you go right. This is a popular area for people of all ages, many of whom spend a few minutes at the exercise stations along the route to Lions Park and the children's playground. Along the trail, a series of signs

The Coquitlam River is your companion for most of this walk.

notes historical highlights going either forward or back in time, depending on your direction of travel.

Beyond the Lougheed Highway Bridge, the path becomes narrower and changes to gravel as it enters a wooded environment with more opportunities to view and approach the river. About 1 km (0.6 mi) farther along, and just past the Patricia Avenue footbridge (which links to Walk 79), you enter Coquitlam River Park, where Fisheries and Oceans Canada, along with local groups, has reclaimed historic stream channels, ponds and wetlands. The area is an easily negotiable network of old roads and trails through mixed forest. Ignoring the PoCo Trail to the east, continue straight ahead. (On your way north, keep nearer to the river, taking left forks in the trail. On your return, keep nearer to Shaughnessy Street, taking left forks in the trail and discovering the many tranquil ponds.)

Soon, you'll pass a fenced-off stream of the wetlands restoration area, where you may see minnows in the summer or salmon fighting their way upstream to spawn in the fall. An information board describes the Oxbow Side Channel Restoration Project. Next, you pass Oxbow Lake, surrounded by private residences, then shortly thereafter the northern end of the restoration project at the intake channel flowing into a dyked pond. Your turnaround point lies a short distance beyond, at a residential cul-de-sac.

Returning, stay gently left after you pass the Oxbow Lake to see another part of the wetlands restoration works. And so back to Gates Park and its busy playing fields.

GETTING THERE

Transit: Take TransLink Bus 170 (Port Coquitlam Station/Port Coquitlam South) to Reeve Street at Wilson Avenue. Cross Reeve to the parking lot.
Vehicle: From Highway 1 or 7B, turn north onto Highway 7 and drive for 3 km (1.9 mi) to Pitt River Road. Turn right (east) to Reeve Street, where you go north. At Wilson Avenue, go west to the Gates Park parking lot.

DEBOVILLE SLOUGH/PITT RIVER

Distance: 12 km (7.5 mi)
Time: 3.5 hours
Surface: gravel
Quality: ★★★
Difficulty: ■

Season: all year
Car GPS entry: Victoria Dr & Cedar Dr
Port Coquitlam, BC
Trailhead: 49°17'9" N 122°44'2" W

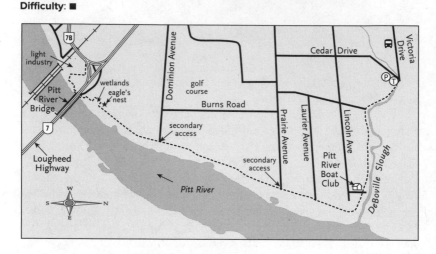

THIS PORTION of Port Coquitlam's 25 km (15.5 mi) Traboulay Trail (also part of the Trans Canada Trail [TCT]) begins along a tranquil slough, a freshwater tidal wetland, and then follows the banks of the Pitt River, with its views of mountains and river activities.

From Cedar Drive, the trail wanders for 2 km (1.2 mi) along the south bank of DeBoville Slough. Once an important hunting and harvesting area for the Katzie First Nation, the wetlands on either side of the slough were dyked by settlers over a century ago to protect the farmlands from tidal floodwaters in the Fraser backing up the Pitt River. Now the slough provides wetland habitat for fish, wildlife and birds, including kingfishers, great blue herons, mute swans and waterfowl. The graceful swans like to frequent the Pitt River Boat Club area in the slough.

Heading south along the Pitt, tall cottonwoods offer shade and occasional benches face the river for your enjoyment as you stop to take in the views, watch herons feeding in the intertidal zone or contemplate life itself. Across the river are the dykes of Chatham Reach (Walk 86). Near Laurier Avenue, you can see a large greenhouse complex; elsewhere are productive fields and pastureland. A tidal wetland area has been constructed about 700 m south

Looking across the Pitt River from the entrance to DeBoville Slough.

of Dominion Avenue to replace fish habitat that was lost to commercial and residential development nearby. Just before the viewing platform where your trail veers right to begin its way around this wetland, look for an eagle's nest high in a cottonwood tree on your right. On the far side of the wetland, the trail swings north, then bends back to parallel itself as it approaches the Pitt River Bridge underpass. Here, this section of the Traboulay Trail ends and the next section, the South Pitt River Trail, begins. (Other sections of the Traboulay Trail are included in Walks 80 and 84.)

Before you begin your return journey, however, you may give in to your curiosity and continue about 800 m farther, where you'll find yourself, surprisingly, amidst a hidden patch of industrial activity, once so commonly seen along waterways. Variously coloured piles of organic matter, woodchips and asphalt bits are bounded by the river, train tracks and highway. Where the trail descends into a tunnel under the train tracks is a good turnaround point.

GETTING THERE

Transit: Take TransLink Bus 173 (Coquitlam Central Station/Cedar) or 174 (Coquitlam Central Station/Rocklin) to Victoria Drive at Rocklin Drive. Walk east for 300 m on Victoria to reach the trail.

Vehicle: From Highway 7 (Lougheed Highway), go north on Coast Meridian Road, turn right on Victoria Drive and drive east to its end at Cedar Drive in northwest Port Coquitlam. Park in the nearby lot.

DEBOVILLE SLOUGH/ ADDINGTON MARSH

Distance: 8.2 km (5.1 mi)
Time: 2.5 hours
Surface: gravel
Quality: ★★★★
Difficulty: ●

Season: all year
Car GPS entry: Victoria Dr & Cedar Dr
Port Coquitlam, BC
Trailhead: 49°17'9" N 122°44'2" W

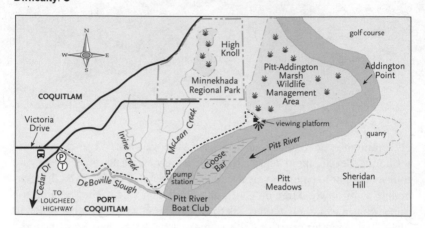

THIS SIBLING walk of Port Coquitlam's DeBoville Slough/Traboulay Trail (Walk 81) begins on the north bank of the DeBoville Slough, a tranquil fresh-water tidal wetland, and follows the bank of the Pitt River northwards to the Pitt-Addington Marsh Wildlife Management Area and a viewing platform with views of mountains and river activities. Prior to 1897 when dykes were built, Addington Marsh was part of the Pitt River floodplain and was sub-ject to the river's daily tidal fluctuation. In 1977 the Nature Trust of British Columbia purchased the marsh to protect its wildlife and habitats and turned the management of the area over to the Government of British Columbia.

From Cedar Drive, find the trail on the north bank of the slough where an information board describes the inhabitants of this important wetland habitat, including fish, wildlife and birds such as kingfishers, great blue her-ons, mute swans and waterfowl. The trail meanders for 2 km (1.2 mi) along the north bank of DeBoville Slough until it turns northeast where the slough meets the Pitt River.

Heading upstream along the Pitt, vast blueberry fields appear on your left and the Golden Ears peaks rise in front of you in the distance. Across the river is the quarry on Sheridan Hill, while Goose Bar occupies a mid-river position.

View of the High Knoll in Minnekhada Regional Park, from across Addington Marsh.

Occasional benches that face the river tempt you to stop, take in the views and watch herons feeding in the intertidal mud.

Just as you are opposite the tip of Goose Bar, the dyke turns inland and, in about 200 m, you find a trail on your right that leads to the viewing platform. Completed in 1985 and funded by a well-known beer company, this raised wooden platform affords views in all directions. Your return journey must begin—and with equal interest as your outbound one, as you now enjoy the panoramic views to the south while you head towards DeBoville Slough and, in the end, your starting point.

LONGER OPTION
When returning from the viewing platform, turn right and follow dyke for 500 m to its end and climb a rough path through forest to Addington Lookout in Minnekhada Regional Park.

GETTING THERE
Transit: Take TransLink Bus 173 (Coquitlam Central Station/Cedar) or 174 (Coquitlam Central Station/Rocklin) to Victoria Drive at Rocklin Drive. Walk east for 300 m on Victoria to reach the trail.
Vehicle: From Highway 7 (Lougheed Highway), go north on Coast Meridian Road, turn right on Victoria Drive and drive east to its end at Cedar Drive in northwest Port Coquitlam. Park in the nearby lot.

MUNDY PARK

Distance: 6 km (3.7 mi)
Time: 2.5 hours
Surface: gravel trails
Quality: ★★★★
Difficulty: ●

Season: all year
Car GPS entry: Hillcrest St & Austin Ave
Coquitlam, BC
Trailhead: 49°15'17" N 122°50'01" W

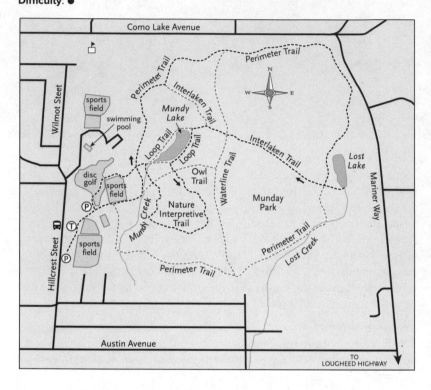

MUNDY PARK is Coquitlam's largest park, with over 178 ha (400 ac) of coastal rainforest, well laid-out forest trails and two tranquil lakes. Your route takes you to visit these lakes and tour a nature interpretive trail for an opportunity to practise shinrin-yoku.

Begin by making your way to the fieldhouse and, after taking an access road past a parking lot, follow the short Owl Trail. At the junction with the Perimeter Trail, go left to begin your clockwise perambulation. All intersections are well signed to keep you on your route as this wide, gravelled trail heads first north then east and south. At last, you are treated to tantalizing glimpses of water in the forest. Then, where the Interlaken Trail intersects

The snags in secluded and serene Mundy Lake attract birds and other wildlife.

the Perimeter Trail, you go left for a closer look at Lost Lake, which is now found.

Retrace your steps and stay on Interlaken Trail for some distance, crossing Waterline Trail as you do, until you find the left turn to Mundy Lake. Follow Lakeside Loop Trail clockwise around the lake. Near the end of the lake you cross a bridge over Mundy Creek, go left over a boardwalk and cross Owl Trail to find the Nature Interpretive Trail.

Here you begin a narrow winding trail that takes you through the heart of a temperate rainforest with fine second-growth trees (and old stumps, reminders of the ancient forest that was once here), vine maple and devil's club and its floor adorned with trilliums in spring. Turn off your phone, slow your pace and relax your breathing to experience the calming, rejuvenating and restorative benefits of the forest atmosphere.

You end this interlude near Mundy Lake, where you go left and find your way back to the sports fields and your starting point.

GETTING THERE
Transit: Take TransLink Bus 156 (Braid Station/Lougheed Station) to Hillcrest Street at Winslow Avenue.
Vehicle: From Highway 7 (Lougheed Hwy), take United Boulevard North to Mariner Way. Follow Mariner Way uphill to turn left onto Austin Avenue. Turn right onto Hillcrest Street and follow to the parking lot at the south end of the park.

COLONY FARM REGIONAL PARK

Distance: 8 km (5 mi)
Time: 2.5 hours
Surface: gravel, paved road
Quality: ★★★
Difficulty: ●

Season: all year
Car GPS entry: BC-7 & Colony Farm Rd
Coquitlam, BC
Trailhead (at first lot): 49°14'24" N
122°48'48" W

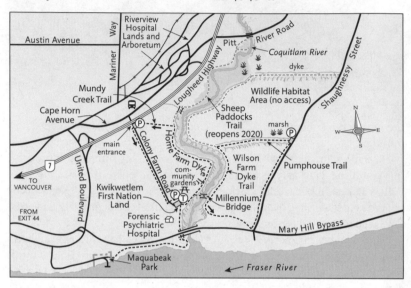

COLONY FARM Regional Park is a work in progress. For more than 70 years, from 1904, residents of the onsite mental health hospital operated it as a renowned produce and dairy farm. Straddling the lower Coquitlam River near its mouth with the Fraser, the fertile land is now restored with tidal flows and habitat enhancement to support an increasing variety of water-fowl, wildlife and birds. Walking the dykes in this oasis of tranquility provides opportunity for mental relaxation.

From the top parking lot, your trail parallels Colony Farm Road on its west side to another parking lot, a picnic area and community gardens. Birding enthusiasts may want to explore along the lush dyke that runs south between river and ditch to the meeting of the Coquitlam and Fraser Rivers 600 m from the second parking lot. Otherwise, pass to the east side of the gardens and follow the trail there north alongside a ditch to a small bridge. Cross this to the Home Farm Dyke, then go right to cross the Coquitlam River over the arching Millennium Bridge. Turn right again to make a counter-clockwise

Bees benefit from the wildflowers in the park and these sunflowers in the community garden.

circuit, beginning on an attractive section of the Traboulay PoCo Trail that winds westwards amongst trees with a wetland on one side and old farmlands on the other. When Shaughnessy Street looms ahead, turn left onto the verge for the least attractive part of your journey and know that a pleasant reward awaits you after about 20 minutes.

An information kiosk welcomes you back into the park on the Pumphouse Trail and immediately the variety of wetland life attracts your attention. Farther along, you arrive at a pumphouse that controls water levels in the ditches. Go left and head downstream to return over the Millennium Bridge to complete this loop.

Now you turn north along the meandering Home Farm Dyke Trail, with its views to distant mountains. At the next junction, you may proceed 200 m to a closed gate (the trail beyond, Sheep Paddocks, reopens in 2020) to read the information boards about land rehabilitation plans, but the route back to your transportation turns left onto Mundy Creek Trail.

You now have the option of visiting Western Canada's first arboretum, established in 1912, on the Riverview Hospital grounds across the highway from your parking lot. However, the provincial government is engaged in renewing the site and has limited the access. See the Riverview Horticultural Centre Society website (www.rhcs.org) for current information.

GETTING THERE

Transit: Take TransLink Bus 169 (Coquitlam Central Station/Braid Station) to Cape Horn Avenue at Colony Farm Road.

Vehicle: From Highway 7 (Lougheed Highway), turn south on Colony Farm Road (traffic lights) and park just across the tracks. Alternatively, drive 1 km (0.6 mi) farther to park.

GRANT NARROWS

Distance: 12 km (7.5 mi)
Time: 4.5 hours
Surface: trail
Quality: ★★★★
Difficulty: ■

Season: most of the year; Crane and Homilk'um Dykes closed during nesting season mid-March to mid-August
Car GPS entry: McNeil Rd & Rannie Rd Pitt Meadows, BC
Trailhead: 49°20'56" N 122°36'56" W

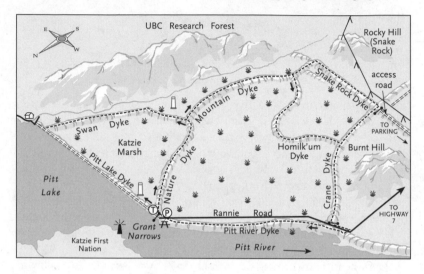

THE NETWORK of dykes at Grant Narrows was built to funnel Pitt Lake, one of the largest tidal lakes in the world, into the Pitt River, thus converting a natural floodplain into fertile agricultural fields. The dykes provide an ideal surface for walking and cycling against a backdrop of spectacular views of Pitt Lake and its surrounding mountains. Cool mountain winds, however, may flow down Pitt Lake, so carry extra clothing. (Since 2011, this area, formerly known as Grant Narrows Regional Park, is now the Pitt-Addington Recreation Area, managed by the Katzie First Nation.)

The Katzie Marsh Loop begins at the parking area, as does the eastbound Pitt Lake Dyke, but it diverges southeast onto the tree-clad, rooty Nature Dyke. Watch for wildlife, or at least signs of their presence. After some 30 minutes, you come to a viewing tower with lots of information about the birds and animals that are resident at different times of the year. More than 200 species of birds have been spotted. Ignoring the dyke that heads off to the south, continue north past a screen of trees and onto the open Swan Dyke,

View of Katzie Marsh towards Pitt Lake from Nature Dyke.

with the fine mountain vista ahead and lush pond plants on either side. This route brings you back to the east end of the Pitt Lake Dyke, along which you march to complete your circuit, observing the lake with pleasure craft on one hand and marsh life on the other.

The Long Loop circuit starts on Pitt Lake Dyke, then turns south on Swan Dyke to meet Nature Dyke, where you might also begin for a walk that is shorter by 1.9 km (1.2 mi). From this common point, continue south on Mountain Dyke to Homilk'um Dyke, which takes you westwards into the marsh and brings you to a T-junction, where you go right once again. Now on Crane Dyke, make your way to Rannie Road while observing the sandhill crane nesting area on your left. (Note that this area is closed during nesting season and becomes overgrown. Mown grass strews the trails after opening.) Turn left at the road for a short distance to a track leading onto the Pitt River Dyke on the far side of the ditch. Here, you go right on a multi-purpose trail with views across Pitt River to Widgeon Slough and surrounding ridges as you make your way back to the narrows and your car.

SHORTER OPTION
Walk just the Katzie Marsh Loop for a 6.5 km (4 mi) walk that takes 2.5 hours.

GETTING THERE
Vehicle: In Pitt Meadows, from Highway 7 (Lougheed Highway) turn north on Harris Road, east on McNeil Road and north on Rannie Road, then travel to a parking lot at Grant Narrows.

CHATHAM REACH

Distance: 11 km (6.8 mi)
Time: 3 hours
Surface: gravel
Quality: ★★★
Difficulty: ■

Season: all year
Car GPS entry: BC-7 & Harris Rd Pitt
Meadows, BC
Trailhead: 49°15'50" N 122°41'21" W

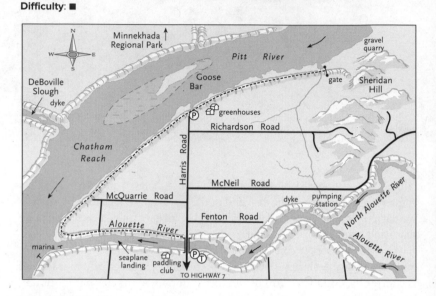

PITT RIVER, with its large dyke system, offers many fine outings; this one has particularly superb upriver views. You have a choice of distance as well: the full 11 km (6.8 mi) return along the waterside or a shorter version gained by returning along Harris Road, saving 1.5 km (0.9 mi). (Walk 87 heads east from the same parking lot.)

From Silver Bridge, your walk begins with crossing to the north bank prior to setting off westwards, downstream. A variety of boathouses and watercraft in various states of repair, as well as the Pitt River Paddling Club, make use of the Alouette River, while on the opposite side lie expanses of blueberry fields. Rounding the corner onto the banks of the Pitt River, you note the lines of rotting posts that once served as anchors for log booms and other river activities and the wide, marshy shoreline, home to many kinds of waterfowl as well as herons, raptors and land-based creatures. Now, on the right, the land is populated with large houses on mini-estates with equestrian facilities. But the view straight ahead is the most eye-catching: the Pitt-Addington Marsh (which you explore on Walk 85) occupies the inner elbow as the Pitt

View from the Harris Road bridge upstream along the Alouette River.

bends sharply, beyond that are the ridges and knolls surrounding Widgeon Slough and forming a beautiful backdrop are the snow-capped mountains at the head of Pitt Lake. Conveniently placed benches invite you to sit and enjoy.

Once again, the landscape changes a bit where Harris Road, your possible shortcut route, meets the dyke. Expansive greenhouses, and other evidence of industrial activities such as the construction of flood control systems, are screened from the dyke by a narrow band of trees, purposefully left in place as wildlife habitat. Just beyond the gate your turnabout is an active gravel pit on Sheridan Hill, the source of the dull noise that increases as you approach. If you've been curious about a very large building isolated amongst trees in the distance, it belongs to a golf resort.

Your return views are certainly no match for the outgoing landscape, but you can spot Simon Fraser University atop Burnaby Mountain and the towering pillars of the Port Mann Bridge in the distance. Your only decision on the return will be which route to take at the Harris Road exit.

GETTING THERE
Vehicle: From Highway 7 (Lougheed Highway), turn north onto Harris Road, drive 3.7 km (2.3 mi) to a bridge over the Alouette River and park in the lot on the south bank.

ALOUETTE RIVER DYKES

Distance: 14.8 km (9.2 mi)
Time: 4 hours
Surface: gravel
Quality: ★★★
Difficulty: ■

Season: all year
Car GPS entry: BC-7 & Harris Rd Pitt Meadows, BC
Trailhead: 49°15'50" N 122°41'21" W

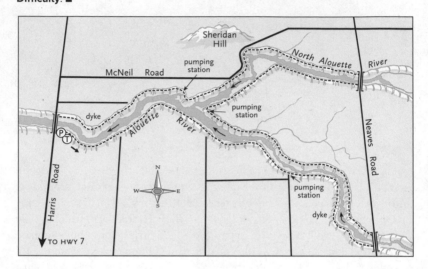

SITUATED IN the heartland of Pitt Meadows, this walk has much to offer: low-level, easy walking and magnificent mountain scenery (on a clear day) amidst rural peace and serenity. Your route essentially covers three stages of approximately equal length, with bridges marking the divisions along the multi-use paths. (Walk 86 heads west from the same parking lot.)

Head upstream (east) from the parking lot, sharing this busiest portion of the dyke with the Trans Canada Trail (TCT) for the first hour or so and passing several small sandy beaches loved by dogs that frolic in the water. Within 25 minutes, you arrive at the confluence of the North Alouette River and the Alouette proper; both are wide and slow moving as they traverse the flatlands. Now the dyke turns southeast and even due south on occasion, following the windings of the river until, at a bridge, you meet Neaves Road, which you have been paralleling for the last while.

Cross the bridge, turn left onto the grassy dyke along the north side of the river and embark on the most peaceful part of the trip, two sides of a triangle that is enclosed between the two branches of the Alouette River. Some of the original marsh remains, but dyking, draining and cultivating, begun

The confluence of the two branches of the Alouette River.

in the latter part of the 19th century, continue to reshape the landscape and alter the habitat of creatures dependent on marshlands, such as the great blue herons that nest in the vanishing cottonwood trees. Nowadays, extensive blueberry fields have taken their place. After about 30 minutes, you are back at the meeting of the waters, where one of several pumping stations controls water levels. Here, there is a bench, one of many dotted along the route, where you might rest and survey your surroundings. This spot—the crotch of the large, slightly contorted Y shape that is your route—is your halfway point.

Now you head northeast where the dyke runs straight, with a wide margin of marsh between you and the meanderings of the North Alouette and a full view of the peaks and ridges of the Golden Ears. Quite soon, your path bends eastwards, between river and drainage canal, towards Neaves Road and a clear view to Mount Baker. Over the bridge, turn left to resume your walk along the grassy north bank, looking ahead now to Sheridan Hill, whose base you eventually reach before you round a bend. The trail, now gravelled, leads you for the third time to the confluence of the two Alouettes before bending back on the last lap to Harris Road, your vehicle and the end of your excursion.

GETTING THERE
Vehicle: From Highway 7 (Lougheed Highway), turn north onto Harris Road, drive 3.7 km (2.3 mi) to a bridge over the Alouette River and park in the lot on the south bank.

UBC RESEARCH FOREST

Distance: 8 km (5 mi)
Time: 3.5 hours
Surface: trail
Elevation gain: 300 m (984 ft)
High point: 335 m (1100 ft)

Quality: ★★★★
Difficulty: ◆
Season: most of the year
Car GPS entry: 14500 Silver Valley Rd
Maple Ridge, BC
Trailhead: 49°15.856' N 122°34.380' W

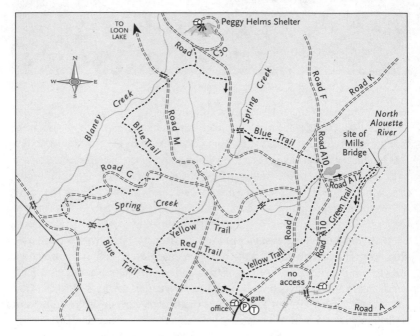

THE UNIVERSITY Demonstration Forest, with its arboretum and network of trails, lies within the much larger Malcolm Knapp Research Forest, maintained by the University of British Columbia's Faculty of Forestry as a research area for its students. Trail and other information is available at the office near the parking lot and at www.mkrf.forestry.ubc.ca. (Note gate closure hours. Also note that dogs are not permitted in this forest.)

The easy Red Trail takes about an hour and the Green Trail a little longer. Yellow provides the most detailed information about various aspects of forestry and requires about 2 hours. The Blue Trail, a longer and moderately strenuous trail, described here, adds a side trip to a knoll with a view and ends with an optional trek along the North Alouette River.

Low water along the North Alouette River in summer.

Walk left past the office and weather station by the arboretum and across an old road, then enter the forest. After crossing a creek in a gully, the Blue Trail ascends and then diverges left from Red and Yellow, descending to a T-junction where you go right. It then crosses Spring Creek and continues to a forest road (G), which it crosses several times as you ascend on the trail through a managed plantation. As you approach Blaney Creek, murmuring from the valley ahead, you turn right, rise and cross another road (M). Follow the blue markers northwards to a fork just as you start to veer east. Take the left fork up to meet a wide logging road, on which you jog right and then left onto a side road (C30), circling a forested knoll whose summit and shelter you finally attain from the north side. Views extend northwards to Golden Ears and westwards over Pitt Meadows and the Fraser Valley.

Retrace your steps to the wide logging road, go left and descend the road for some distance. Re-enter the forest at an opening on the left to a wide trail covered with wood chips, cross Spring Creek, continue over a rough up-and-down section of trail, cross two roads and finally meet the Yellow Trail beside a small pond. Now, go left on the road (A12 on map) beside the pond and onto a trail down to the Alouette River. You may return on the Green Trail to the right or, in dry weather, descend to the riverbank and pick up a narrow track that heads downstream. It leads to a shelter just short of the road bridge, where there are some spectacular rapids. Here, you must plod up Road A to join the main Road F and go left, back to your starting point, passing the restored steam donkey (stationary engine) as you do.

GETTING THERE
Transit: Take TransLink Bus 741 (Anderson Creek/Haney Place/Port Haney) to Silver Valley Road at 141st Avenue. Walk north on Silver Valley for 500 m to the trailhead.
Vehicle: In Maple Ridge, follow the signs for Golden Ears Park north from Highway 7 (Lougheed Highway), staying on 232nd Street when the park road turns right at the roundabout. Turn right onto Silver Valley Road and follow it to a parking area.

MIKE LAKE

Distance: 8 km (5 mi)
Time: 2.5 hours
Surface: trail
Elevation gain: 180 m (590 ft)
High point: 430 m (1410 ft)

Quality: ★★★★
Difficulty: ■
Season: March to November
Car GPS entry: Dewdney Trunk Rd & 232
St Maple Ridge, BC
Trailhead: 49°16'22" N 122°32'18" W

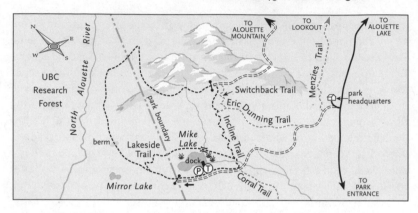

MIKE LAKE, with its substantial dock and forested, marshy surroundings, is popular with fisherfolk, whereas the Incline Trail, some 200 m before the parking area, sets hikers on their way into the backcountry towards Alouette Mountain and Blanshard Peak. This excursion is good for a leg stretch on a drizzly day, the most notable attraction being the peaceful surroundings of nature.

You have a choice of two trails or their combination: one, a 2 km (1.2 mi) circuit of the lake; the other, a longer loop within the forest, with the option of including the lake circuit at the end. Both begin by passing a gate at the west end of the parking lot onto a forest service road. Within 5 minutes the Lakeside Trail goes off to the right. (This drops to lake level in a series of switchbacks and over eroded roots to a boardwalk, beyond which is the best view of the lake.) Staying on the road, however, takes you into the Malcolm Knapp UBC Research Forest (Walk 88), where generations of students have conducted studies. Some 10 minutes later, your easy striding is suddenly halted at a berm; this marks the beginning of a decommissioned section where a narrow track bounces up and down across a steepish hillside, with sounds of the North Alouette River rising from below. This section lasts for about 30 minutes until the former roadbed resumes at a sharp bend south.

The dock at Mike Lake is a fine place to view the water and look for fish.

Now you see boundary markers for the research forest, then, at a 4.8 km marker, a gate. This is a junction for hikers and mountain bikers, and your route on the Incline Trail heads down here. You will be treading where, almost a century ago, old-growth logs were hauled down to Mike Lake using a cable system and railcars. Look for the rotting remains of the foundation of a steam donkey near the Lakeside Trail junction.

From this junction, you may continue to the road nearby and back to your vehicle, or you may jog right onto the eastern end of Lakeside Trail to circuit the lake, exiting on the road described earlier. Finally, take some time to visit the dock near the parking lot and read a bit of the area's history, trying to imagine a camp of 600 loggers bustling about in this now-peaceful setting.

SHORTER OPTION
A circuit of Mike Lake on its own is 2 km (1.3 mi) and takes about 45 minutes.

GETTING THERE
Vehicle: From Highway 7 (Lougheed Highway) in Maple Ridge, follow the Golden Ears Park signs to the park entrance, then drive 4.5 km (2.8 mi) to the park headquarters/Mike Lake turnoff and go left. Immediately branch left again. Continue 2 km (1.2 mi) to park at Mike Lake.

ALOUETTE NATURE LOOP

Distance: 6 km (3.7 mi)
Time 2.5 hours
Surface: trail
Elevation gain: 170 m (558 ft)
High point: 320 m (1050 ft)

Quality: ★★★★
Difficulty: ■
Season: March to November
Car GPS entry: Dewdney Trunk Rd & 232
St Maple Ridge, BC
Trailhead: 49°17'17" N 122°29'30" W

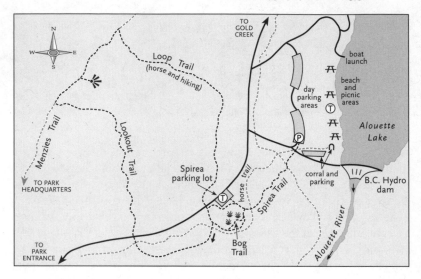

WHAT TITLE do you give a walk that embraces sections of four trails—Spirea, Lookout, Menzies and Loop—in Golden Ears Provincial Park? Our suggestion, as above, takes account of the fact that part of the loop is on the lower slopes of Alouette Mountain, that it provides a circuit and that a portion of it is a self-guided nature trail, the placards increasing your knowledge of forest lore as you walk along. Add interesting stretches of marsh with sphagnum moss and skunk cabbage, a second-growth forest of hemlock, a lookout over Alouette Lake and even a picnic table by its shore at the end of your outing.

Begin your walk on the Spirea Nature Trail, entering the forest off the south end of Lot 2. Almost immediately, you drop to a creek with a bridge. After crossing the bridge and a gravel access road to Alouette Dam, re-enter the trees and begin to rise in nice open forest, the bright green of the moss in the understory attesting to generous precipitation in the valley and the many large stumps recalling the grandeur of the original forest.

Water lilies blooming in the bog.

Cross the horse trail and ascend. Then, at a T-junction, go left, crossing horse trails, until you come to a fork where the trail from the Spirea parking lot joins and you are now on the universal-access trail that circumnavigates the bog, crossing muddy ground on boardwalks. Shortly thereafter, as the path begins to curve right towards the park road, go left on the signed Lookout Trail, cross the horse trail yet again, then cross the main park road and start ascending a rather rough trail in the forest. Eventually, your trail joins the Menzies Trail, where you turn right. Soon after, a clearing to your right provides a view over the lake and towards Mount Crickmer, which you may enjoy from a bench on a rock bluff.

Continuing on Menzies Trail for about 400 m, seek out a bridle trail on the right, signed Loop Trail, for your descent; it leads to the park road near the Spirea parking lot. Cross the road and go left on the horse trail, then jog left to the pedestrian path. This section takes you between road and bog until, within sight of the parking area, you swing away right to rejoin your outward route east of the boardwalk. Now, go left and retrace your steps downhill to your starting point.

Before the drive home, you may check out the popular beach at Alouette Lake for a final pause, perhaps a picnic or a plunge.

GETTING THERE
Vehicle: On 232nd Street in Maple Ridge, follow signs to Golden Ears Provincial Park. From the park gate, drive 7.2 km (4.5 mi) and then turn right into a day-use area, 1 km (0.6 mi) past the Spirea Trail parking lot. In Lot 2, park near the south end.

GOLD CREEK LOWER FALLS TRAIL

Distance: 5.4 km (3.4 mi)
Time: 2 hours
Surface: gravel
Quality: ★★★★
Difficulty: ●

Season: most of the year
Car GPS entry: Dewdney Trunk Rd & 232 St Maple Ridge, BC
Trailhead: 49°20'04" N 122°27'24" W

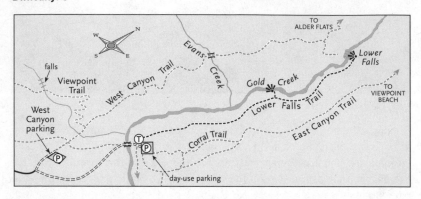

THIS TRAIL on the east side of Gold Creek is gentler and more popular than those on the west side; it features creekside beaches, close-up views of a seasonally changeable waterfall and backside views of the inspiring Golden Ears mountains.

For a family-friendly walk, you may follow the well-maintained Lower Falls Trail that runs more or less parallel to Gold Creek. A beach halfway to the falls provides access to the creek. After nearly an hour, the sound of the falls increases in volume, and you ascend a short steep section and arrive at the well-fenced viewpoint for the spray-enshrouded Lower Falls. Awe-inspiring in its power, the creek cascades 10 m over a ramp of rock into a deep, seasonally placid pool surrounded by massive boulders, before flowing onward to its ultimate destination, Pitt River.

As tempting as it may be, do not go higher on the rugged trail to the top of the falls. Even on a hot, dry day, the rocks are slippery and a fall will be fatal. Instead, just downstream of the viewing platform you can gain access to a safe pebble beach that makes a nice lunch spot before you head back.

On your return, you may pause at various viewpoints to take in the towering mountains of the Golden Ears group.

View across Gold Creek towards the Golden Ears peaks.

GETTING THERE

Transit: Better Environmentally Sound Transportation's Parkbus offers bus service on select summer weekends to Golden Ears Park from downtown Vancouver.

Vehicle: On 232nd Street in Maple Ridge, follow signs to Golden Ears Provincial Park. From the gated park entrance, drive 11.6 km (7.2 mi) to a fork. Go left, then right for the Gold Creek day-use area parking lot.

KANAKA CREEK TRAILS

Distance: Riverfront Trail 3 km (1.9 mi)
Time: 1 hour
Distance: Canyon Loop 3.3 km (2 mi)
Time: 1.5 hours
Surface: trail
Quality: ★★★★
Difficulty: ●

Season: all year
Car GPS entry: 23272 River Rd Maple Ridge, BC
Trailhead: 49°12'00" N 122°34'47" W
Car GPS entry: 116 Ave & 256 St Maple Ridge, BC
Trailhead: 49°12'40" N 122°30'34" W

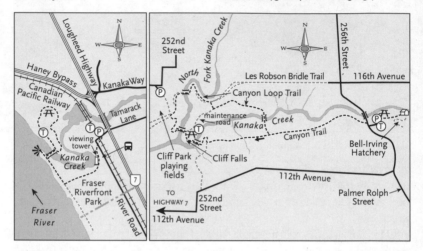

TWO PEARLS within the 12 km (7.5 mi) long Kanaka Creek Regional Park are the Riverfront Trail, where Kanaka Creek meets the Fraser River (described first), and the Canyon Loop–Cliff Falls trail farther inland. Other park attractions include a fish fence that operates in late autumn and a fish hatchery.

Within 5 minutes of setting out on the Riverfront Trail, you come to a tower that overlooks marshland caught within the last slow meander of Kanaka Creek before it joins the Fraser River. Farther along, turning right at the Fraser, you have occasional access to the sandy shore, or you may rest on a deck and read of historical activities and, on the arching bridge, of the Hawaiian origin of Kanaka Creek's name. Next, a narrow nature path leads through woodlands back to the trailhead. If you want more walking, continue upstream along the dyke for 1 km (0.6 mi) to the trail's end near a sawmill and other light industrial activity.

Canyon Loop Trail, where Kanaka Creek's north fork meets the main watercourse, has quite a different character. From the parking lot at the fish hatchery, which is certainly worth a visit, cross 256th Street to a yellow gate

Pools worn into the sandstone streambed by Kanaka Creek.

and begin your walk on Canyon Trail. This path gradually rises above creek level mainly amidst cottonwoods and moss-covered maples. Quite soon, you come to a fork; straight ahead and over a bridge leads to Cliff Falls, where you can watch the splashing rapids and falls in their ceaseless sandstone-eroding work. You next cross a bridge over the north fork and ascend to a junction, where you turn right towards 116th Street, only to soon recross the creek on a metal bridge. Enjoying views down to the creek, continue until, at a junction, a quick right then left to Pine Ridge Trail takes you back to meet the Canyon Trail and, soon thereafter, your vehicle.

Kanaka Creek has yet more to offer if you drive west on 112th Avenue from the Canyon Loop Trail and then south to the bridge on 240th Street. During October and November, a one-way fish fence is erected below the bridge; some of the trapped fish are taken for hatchery use and the rest are released to spawn upstream. From there, drive west on Kanaka Creek Road to a roadgate, park there, then walk less than 10 minutes to the Trans Canada Trail (TCT) and along it to the Rainbow Bridge for views of the creek and surrounding wetlands.

GETTING THERE
Transit (Riverfront Trail): Take TransLink Bus 748 (Thornhill/Haney Place) to the park entrance on River Road. Note that this bus runs on weekdays only.
Vehicle (Riverfront Trail): From Highway 7 (Lougheed Highway) just east of the Haney Bypass/Kanaka Way junction, turn west onto River Road and then immediately into the parking lot.
Transit (Canyon Loop): Take TransLink Bus 749 (Ruskin/Haney Place) to Dewdney Trunk Road at 256th Street (flagstop). Walk south on 256th for 800 m to the trailhead.
Vehicle (Canyon Loop): From Dewdney Trunk Road in Maple Ridge, travel south on 256th Street to the fish hatchery and parking lot.

MISSION TRAIL

Distance: 6.4 km (4 mi)
Time: 2.5 hours
Surface: paved, trail
Elevation gain: 150 m (492 ft)
High point: 200 m (655 ft)

Quality: ★★★
Difficulty: ■
Season: all year
Car GPS entry: 7494 Mary St Mission, BC
Trailhead: 49°08'16" N 122°17'16" W

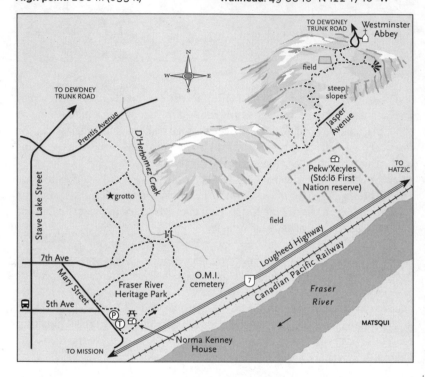

THE MISSION Trail begins at the Fraser River Heritage Park, where you gain a peek into the history of Stó:lō First Nation peoples, pioneer settlers and missionaries of not so long ago. The Heritage Park preserves the remains and expansive grounds of the former St. Mary's Mission and Residential School, which operated from 1862 to 1961. A steep trail east of the park climbs to Westminster Abbey and the Benedictine monks' seminary, which has occupied the hilltop 150 m above since 1954.

To begin, head towards Norma Kenney House, where a flat, groomed walkway leads east. Your route passes cement foundations that supported mission buildings for a century, offers an optional side loop to the Oblates of Mary

Wild tiger lilies emerging along the path to the viewpoint.

Immaculate cemetery, crosses a bridge spanning D'Herbomez Creek and stretches through open fields towards Stó:lō reserve land and buildings. This area, known as Pekw'Xe:yles, is used by 21 First Nation governments. Veer left into the forest towards the cul-de-sac on Jasper Avenue where there is a Heritage Park information board. Just before the trail reaches the cul-de-sac, watch for a footpath heading uphill and prepare for an invigorating ascent to the ridge and the abbey above.

Generally, ignore forks on the left as you head up and, for interest, note the religiously themed names such as Jacob's Ladder and Hail Mary attached to junctions. Be alert for mountain bikers, and in the fall, enjoy the bright colours of the bigleaf maples that populate the hillside. Eventually, as you approach the ridge, your route levels out at a small open junction of trails. From here, the path rolls up and down along the ridge for perhaps 15 minutes until it emerges into the open at the end of a wide field. Make your way to a gravel road going right, the abbey tower visible to your left behind rolling, grassy slopes. Soon you are rewarded with an expansive, bluff-top view over the Fraser River to gentle Sumas Mountain in the middle; mighty, snow-clad Mount Baker dominating the horizon to the right; and the jagged Cheam Range to the left. When you're ready to move on, stay right on the surfaced path to visit the abbey and seminary, then continue around to find your trail by the field.

Your best return is by the same route, though once descending south (left) from the ridge, you may opt to choose an alternate trail for variety. These exit at the groomed walkway from which you began your ascent. Turn right to return and, on crossing D'Herbomez Creek, you may opt to go right and find your way to The Lady of Lourdes Grotto before returning to your starting point.

GETTING THERE
Transit: Take Central Fraser Valley Transit Bus 34 (East Side) to Stave Lake Street and 5A Avenue. Walk 150 m east on 5A to the park.
Vehicle: On Highway 7 (Lougheed Highway), at the east end of Mission, turn north on Stave Lake Street, then east on 5th Avenue. Park near the park buildings.

HAYWARD LAKE: RAILWAY TRAIL

Distance: 12 km (7.5 mi)
Time: 3.5 hours (to Ruskin Dam and back)
Surface: gravel, trail
Quality: ★★★
Difficulty: ■

Season: most of the year
Car GPS entry: Wilson St & Dewdney Trunk Rd Mission, BC
Trailhead: 49°13'20" N 122°21'35" W

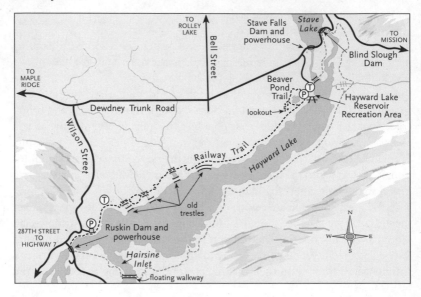

HAYWARD LAKE Reservoir was created in 1930, when the Ruskin Dam was built across a narrow granite gorge of the Stave River, approximately 6 km (3.7 mi) downstream from Stave Falls Dam. A railway along the lake's west side carried supplies from Ruskin to the dam and the company town at Stave Falls and returned loaded with cedar logs, shakes and shingles. That was long ago. All that remains today is the former railway right-of-way and support pilings where trestle bridges once carried the railway line across the mouth of inlets.

The Railway Trail walk starts from the Hayward Lake Recreation Area, where you should begin by orienting yourself at the information board. Combined with its sibling Reservoir Trail (Walk 95), a lengthy 18 km (11 mi) loop walk is possible. Additional to the longer Railway Trail walk, there is a short nature loop, Beaver Pond Trail, that gives you a chance to see the work of beavers—their skill in dam-building truly rivals that of their human counterparts.

The short walk around Beaver Pond provides glimpses of nature's dam-builder at work.

After walking south for some time on the level, gravelled Railway Trail, you encounter the first inlet and trestle; here, the trail makes the first of several detours over creeks and ravines once traversed by railway trestle bridges. It leaves the right-of-way, enters the forest and rounds the bay before rejoining the railbed trail. These detours, such as at Elbow Creek, take you up and over, with staircases, footbridges and walkways supplying the crossings in lieu of the derelict bridges. At one inlet detour, an alternative track, signed Tall Tree Loop, takes you past a solitary majestic Douglas-fir, enlivening your walk before you arrive at a beach and viewpoint for the Ruskin Dam intake. Your turnaround is ahead at the Ruskin Dam; for a longer return, complete the loop with Reservoir Trail (Walk 95), by crossing on the pedestrian walkway atop the dam. For more information about Ruskin Dam and B.C. Hydro recreation sites, see www.bchydro.com/community/recreation_areas.html.

GETTING THERE
Vehicle: From the east, drive west from Mission on Highway 7 (Lougheed Highway), turn right on 287th Street, then continue north on Wilson Street until it meets Dewdney Trunk Road, where you turn right. Drive east on Dewdney Trunk Road and turn right just west of Stave Falls Dam at the Hayward Lake Reservoir Recreation Area. From the west, drive east from Maple Ridge on the Dewdney Trunk Road, then proceed as above.

HAYWARD LAKE: RESERVOIR TRAIL

Distance: 8 km (5 mi)
Time: 3 hours (to Hairsine Inlet and back)
Surface: trail
Quality: ★★★★
Difficulty: ●

Season: most of the year
Car GPS entry: Wilson St & Dewdney Trunk Rd Mission, BC
Trailhead: 49°13'47" N 122°20'50" W

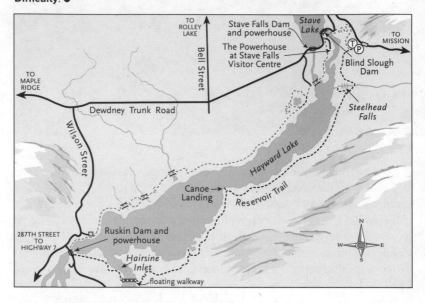

THE ONE-TIME railway track between Stave Falls and Ruskin gives us the Railway Trail walk along the west side of Hayward Lake (Walk 94). Its sibling Reservoir Trail, completed more recently (in 1999) with the joint efforts of Forest Renewal B.C., B.C. Hydro and the District of Mission, takes you along the east side of Hayward Lake through the second-growth cedar and Douglas-fir of the Mission Municipal Forest. Over the years, Reservoir Trail has aged gracefully into a welcoming woodland trail as both the construction scars left by its builders and the handrails fashioned from naturally curved branches have become carpeted with moss. The trails meet atop the Ruskin Dam to form a lengthy 18 km (11 mi) loop walk.

Begin by orienting yourself at the information boards, and then descend from the parking lot and go right then left at two T-junctions. Soon, your trail traverses a long walkway over gentle Brown Creek and later crosses

Steelhead Falls after a heavy rain.

boisterous Steelhead Creek before it arrives at a junction. The track dropping right takes you down stairs to a well-built platform and vantage point for the spellbinding Steelhead Falls as it issues from a chute before descending over a series of rock steps.

Continue your undulating forested route, noticing as you go the benches and chairs carved out of stumps and logs by the original trail builders. After a lengthy interlude, possibly some shinrin-yoku practice, and after crossing many bridged creeks, you arrive at a junction where you may go right to descend to the lakeshore at Canoe Landing. From here the trail climbs above the lake before descending from the forest to Hairsine Inlet, where you find a unique floating walkway built to avoid the steep and rocky terrain that surrounds the inlet. This provides a handy turnaround point for your return, or, for a longer return, complete a loop with Railway Trail (Walk 94) by continuing forward and crossing on the pedestrian walkway atop the dam. For more information about Ruskin Dam and B.C. Hydro recreation sites, see www .bchydro.com/community/recreation_areas.html.

GETTING THERE

Vehicle: From the east, drive west from Mission on Highway 7 (Lougheed Highway), turn right on 287th Street and continue north on Wilson Street until it meets Dewdney Trunk Road, where you turn right and drive east. Continue over the Stave Falls and Blind Slough Dams, staying on Dewdney Trunk Road until you reach the trailhead parking lot. From the west, drive east from Maple Ridge on the Dewdney Trunk Road, then proceed as above.

DERBY REACH REGIONAL PARK

Distance: 8.5 km (5.3 mi)
Time: 2.5 hours
Surface: gravel
Quality: ★★★
Difficulty: ●

Season: all year
Car GPS entry: 208 St & Allard Cres
Langley Twp, BC
Trailhead: 49°12'29" N 122°37'02" W

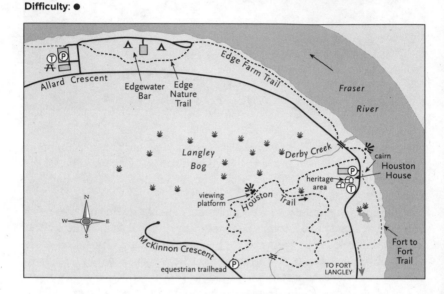

POPULAR WITH walkers, family cyclists and dog walkers, this well-groomed trail follows the inner bend of the Fraser River from Edgewater Bar to a cairn marking the location of the original Fort Langley. En route, you may be treated to magnificent views of the Golden Ears mountains, log-sorting activities across the water, hungry birds looking for lunch and perhaps a curious seal.

Begin your walk by approaching the river and going right at the campground onto the Edge Nature Trail. (It is named for the Edge family, who once farmed here. A member of the family was killed nearby, in January 1880, when a massive landslide into the Fraser on the Haney side inundated the river's south shore and caused severe destruction.) The Edge Trail winds through woodlands with imposing cottonwood trees and old stumps for 1 km (0.6 mi) until it nears the river again at the end of the campground. A few steps along, it then becomes Edge Farm Trail. The path stays close to the water's edge. Repeat visitors will notice the Fraser's changing moods: high

A tree hugger's view of a Sitka spruce along the Houston Loop.

water attacks and erodes the riverbanks; low water exposes muddy "beaches" to explore. After a short diversion beside the road, you reach the original Fort Langley heritage area, where you can learn about and imagine life at the time of the first settlers.

From here, you have two options: you may return the way you came or you may take the Houston Trail. The Fort to Fort Trail (Walk 97) also begins here. Houston Trail is a 4 km (2.5 mi) forest loop on a gravel path with many ups and downs. It starts across the grass from the parking area, goes left and meets the trail proper in about 10 minutes. If you then take the left fork, you will pass through a mixed forest with some fine cedars and bigleaf maples, the path rising and falling. Eventually you arrive at the horse-unloading lot off McKinnon Crescent.

The final lap of the Houston Trail begins across this parking area, winds towards Langley Bog, skirts right of the swampy ground, passes a bog-viewing platform and finishes at your original fork and the path back to the heritage area. Your return now lies downstream once more on the Edge Farm Trail.

SHORTER OPTION

For a walk of 4.5 km (2.8 mi) in 1.5 hours, from the original Fort Langley heritage site retrace your steps to your starting point.

GETTING THERE

Vehicle: From Highway 1, take Exit 58 (200 Street) north, go along the 201 Street diversion to 96 Avenue, turn east, continue to 208 Street, go left (north) and stay with 208 Street until it curves east onto Allard Crescent. Continue about 2 km (1.2 mi) to the entrance to Edgewater Bar on your left.

FORT TO FORT TRAIL

Distance: 8 km (5 mi)
Time: 2.5 hours
Surface: gravel
Quality: ★★★
Difficulty: ●

Season: all year
Car GPS entry: Allard Cres & 208 St
Langley Twp, BC
Trailhead: 49°12'01" N 122°35'41" W

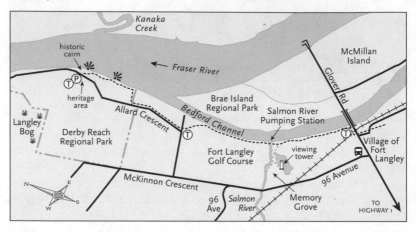

THIS OUTING transports you from the location of the original Fort Langley in
1827 to the present-day Village of Fort Langley and the historic site of the fort
established in 1840. Along your route are views of the Fraser River, mountains and diverse water-based activities.

Begin your walk at the cairn marking the site of the original fort, across the
road from the parking lot. After orienting yourself to the river and the Golden
Ears mountains at the fenced viewpoint behind the cairn, head east on the
gravel path (heading upstream) as it winds through fields and forest. Several
information signs describe the settlers' daily activities and their dependent
relationship with the Stó:lō First Nation. A grassy knoll near the heritage
pear tree affords an upriver view of Mount Baker towering over the valley.

Next, your route runs alongside Allard Crescent, protected from traffic
by a fence, until it leaves the road at a sharp right turn, enters the forest and
descends to river level. After passing a golf course and bridging the Salmon
River at the pumping station, the outflow of which is a favoured spot for fisherfolk, a junction presents you with the option of a side trip. By going right,
you visit a habitat-restoration area with a viewing tower over a beaver pond
and the commemorative Memory Grove with its Muskoka chairs, perfect for
a moment of relaxation.

Approaching the heritage area along the Fraser River.

Now the trail emerges from the trees to an unobstructed view of Bedford Channel. On any given day, you may witness a wide range of non-mechanized pursuits on the water: paddleboarding, kayaking, rowing and dragonboating practices. On hot summer days, many people enjoy a plunge at the beach on Brae Island. Continue to follow the Fort to Fort Trail to its terminus in present-day Village of Fort Langley before retracing your steps to your starting point.

LONGER OPTION
Turn right onto Glover Road and walk up Mavis Street to visit the Fort Langley National Historic Site located 600 m farther on.

GETTING THERE
Transit: Take TransLink Bus 562 (Langley Centre/Walnut Grove) to Glover Road at 96 Avenue. Walk northeast on Glover to intersect the trail, and do the walk in reverse.
Vehicle: From Highway 1, take Exit 58 (200 Street) and travel north to 96 Avenue. Turn right and then left at 208 Street. Follow 208 to Allard Crescent and turn right. Continue past the entrance to Derby Reach parking and watch for heritage area parking on your right.

BRAE ISLAND

Distance: 4.2 km (2.6 mi)
Time: 1.5 hours
Surface: gravel
Quality: ★★★★
Difficulty: ●

Season: most of the year, subject to flooding and mosquitoes in June & July
Car GPS entry: Glover Rd & Billy Brown Rd Langley Twp, BC
Trailhead: 49°10'23" N 122°34'32" W

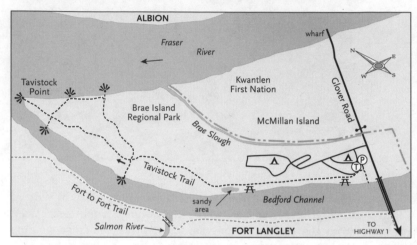

BRAE ISLAND—as the western end of McMillan Island is known—was once a separate body of land, but the channel between them has filled in over time. McMillan Island, which lies across the 70 m wide Bedford Channel opposite Fort Langley, is composed primarily of settled silt and debris from the Fraser River and has been shaped and reshaped by the Fraser's forces. When the river's waters are high in the spring, they may flood parts of the trails, making them impassable. The Stó:lō people of the Kwantlen First Nation occupy much of McMillan Island where their ancestors lived for possibly 10 millennia. And McMillan? In 1824, he was chief trader for the Hudson's Bay Company and led the preliminary survey party for the establishment of Fort Langley.

Begin your walk on the Tavistock Trail at the map board near the parking lot. The gravel path runs between the campsite and water until, at the end of the campsite, you come to an open picnic area that overlooks Bedford Channel. Continue along the wooded trail until you arrive at a four-way junction. Go left for a short walk to the first viewpoint of Bedford Channel on the west side of the island; the Fort Langley Golf Course lies opposite. Return to the

Stalwart cottonwoods guarding the approach to Tavistock Point.

trail and go left towards Tavistock Point. After about 500 m, you encounter another junction with a short trail on your left to the second viewpoint. After returning to the main trail, turn left and walk a short distance through a corridor of cottonwoods to Tavistock Point, noting as you do the Tavistock Loop Trail junction on your right. Tavistock Point marks the northern tip of Brae Island and on a clear day provides scenic views of the Fraser River and both shorelines.

Once you've absorbed the view and the variety of activities on the river, walk back to the Tavistock Loop Trail junction. Go left for an alternate return route. Not far along, you come to a viewpoint from which you look north across the Fraser River to the distant Coast Mountains, including the Golden Ears group. Continue along the trail as it weaves through the forest and across small wooden bridges over freshwater marshes before re-joining the main trail. Go left at the junction to return to your starting point, passing the picnic tables and campsite en route.

GETTING THERE

Transit: Take TransLink Bus 562 (Langley Centre/Walnut Grove) to Glover Road at 96 Avenue. Walk northeast on Glover, cross the bridge and then turn left into the parking lot.

Vehicle: From Highway 1, take Exit 66 (232 Street) north to Glover Road. Turn north and continue on Glover Road through the Village of Fort Langley, cross the bridge and turn left into the parking lot for Brae Island Regional Park.

NICOMEKL FLOODPLAIN TRAIL

Distance: 6 km (3.7 mi)
Time: 2 hours
Surface: paved, gravel
Quality: ★★
Difficulty: ●

Season: all year
Car GPS entry: 204 St & 53 Ave
Langley, BC
Trailhead: 49°05'48" N 122°39'27" W

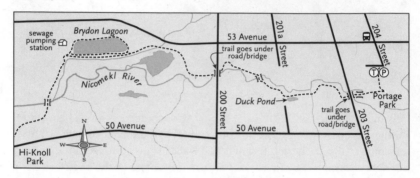

YOUR OUTING begins at Portage Park, where in 1824, Hudson's Bay Company chief trader James McMillan, having travelled up the Nicomekl River from Mud Bay, began a 7 km (4.3 mi) portage overland to the Salmon River on his way to the Fraser River to choose a site for Fort Langley. John Work, a clerk with the party, described the river as thick with willows and having low banks "well wooded with pine, cedar, alder and some other trees." Compare his description with what you find on your walk today.

From your starting point, walk through the playground and turn right on the paved floodplain walkway. Soon, you encounter the first of several bridge crossings over the Nicomekl River, after which you walk towards and then under 203 Street. Emerging from under the street and after a slight uphill section, you come to the Duck Pond, a favourite stopping place for people of all ages and ducks alike. Next, take the right turn at the T-junction and then soon thereafter turn right again to cross the bridge over the Nicomekl River to its north side. Once across the bridge, you leave the pavement and continue on a gravel trail towards and then under 200 Street. Here, you may want to leave the trail momentarily and wander over the grassy meadow to the riverbank. The trail swings right as the floodplain widens, and soon the entrance to Brydon Lagoon nature trail appears. The lagoon, a settling pond for sewage treatment until 1973, now provides an opportunity for a quiet walk with glimpses of wildlife, such as songbirds, bullfrogs, turtles, rabbits and waterfowl. Go right on the lagoon perimeter trail.

The entrance to Brydon Lagoon.

At the west end of Brydon Lagoon, turn south where the trail heads onto the floodplain. Soon, you come to your third and final bridge on this walk, where you may decide to pause, contemplate the steady flow of the Nicomekl and compare your view with the one described by John Work. During Work's time, this area lay within an extensive intertidal zone, which farmers began to reclaim for agricultural purposes half a century later. Sea dams were built on the Nicomekl and Serpentine Rivers and the City of Surrey began an ambitious program of flood control in 1997, but seasonal flooding persists in some areas.

The bridge makes a good turnaround spot, or, for a longer walk, you may continue 250 m to Hi-Knoll Park and explore its woodland trails.

GETTING THERE

Transit: Take TransLink Bus 560 (Murrayville/Langley Centre) or 564 (Willowbrook/Langley Centre) to 53 Avenue at 204 Street or 563 (Langley Centre/Fernridge) to 53 Avenue at 203 Street. Walk 250 m south on 204 Street to Portage Park.

Vehicle: From Highway 1, take Exit 58 (200 Street) and go south to Highway 1A (Fraser Highway). Turn left and go east to 204 Street. Turn south on 204 to Portage Park.

CAMPBELL VALLEY REGIONAL PARK

Distance: 11 km (6.8 mi)
Time: 4 hours
Surface: trail
Quality: ★★★★
Difficulty: ■

Season: all year
Car GPS entry: 16 Ave & 200 St Langley Twp, BC
Trailhead: 49°01'46" N 122°39'38" W

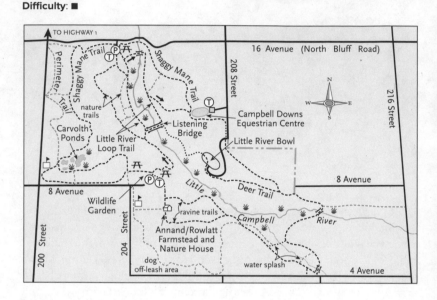

THIS NATURE park, bisected as it is by the Little Campbell River, takes full advantage of the surrounding countryside. The 28 km (17.4 mi) of trails range from a valley floor walk near the river's banks on Little River Loop Trail to a half-day circuit of the whole park on the multi-use (watch for horses!) Shaggy Mane Trail.

The Little River Loop Trail begins near the southeast corner of the parking area and passes through trees to a boardwalk over wet meadows bordering the river. On the far side, it turns south, parallels the verge of the marsh to the Listening Bridge, which it crosses, then meets a T-junction on the west side. Here, you turn north, heading back on the loop trail and crossing a wide meadow. For variety, consider taking one of several detours through woodland routes on its west side.

If you opt for the Shaggy Mane Trail, walk towards the parking lot entrance and then, just before 16 Avenue, turn east and cross the river before rising to level ground. More attractive, however, is to follow Little River Loop

A tranquil pond in the Wildlife Garden.

Trail across the boardwalk and south to a fork where a minor trail rises to the left out of the valley and joins Shaggy Mane Trail, passing south of an equestrian centre. Alternatively, stay with the loop trail to the Listening Bridge junction where you join the Deer Trail. This goes straight ahead across a meadow and enters the trees beyond. After traversing the Little River Bowl, the route takes you through a forest of mature Douglas-fir and finally joins Shaggy Mane as it descends to the valley floor.

Next comes a turn to the right at a major fork where you cross the watercourse. A stretch of open country follows as you wind circuitously until, after an uphill section, you turn onto Ravine Trail on your right. This descends stairs into a picturesque forested valley, where, just across a small creek, you come to a junction. Right takes you past a lookout over the marsh and past many mature cedars; left emerges in a meadow near a heritage farmstead, with the one-time schoolhouse a little beyond. Leaving the farm, the trail heads north across an open field to a picnic area and the park's 8th Avenue Wildlife Garden.

To return to your vehicle, you may drop into the valley and take the Little River Loop Trail's west leg—its scenic meadow is particularly attractive in fall. Or you may stay above, on the rim of the valley, using Shaggy Mane Trail to round the western perimeter before dropping to your starting point.

SHORTER OPTION
For an easy 2.3 km (1.4 mi) stroller-friendly outing of about 1 hour, stay on the Little River Loop Trail rather than taking Shaggy Mane.

GETTING THERE
Vehicle: From Highway 1, take Exit 58 (200 Street) and drive 15 km (9.3 mi) south to 16 Avenue (North Bluff Road). Turn east and go 600 m to a parking lot on your right.

ALDERGROVE REGIONAL PARK

Distance: 7 km (4.3 mi)
Time: 2 hours
Surface: trail
Quality: ★★★★
Difficulty: ●

Season: all year
Car GPS entry: 272 St & 8 Ave Langley Twp, BC
Trailhead: 49°00'43" N 122°27'56" W

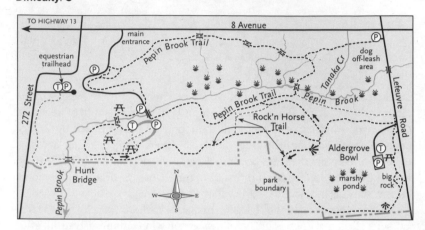

THIS PARK features many highlights for you to discover. Expansive views? Check. Forested trails? Yes. An enormous glacial erratic? It's got that too. And wetland habitat? In spades. It's home to frogs, salamanders, beavers and even two endangered fish species: the Nooksack dace and Salish sucker fish—rare minnow-sized survivors of the ice age.

Pepin Brook Trail begins, at the east end of the parking lot, as a pleasantly winding trail beside the watercourse before climbing to stay above the marsh. After 700 m, you pass two trails to the right that connect with the Rock'n Horse bridle trail. Ignore these and descend gently into the peaceful Pepin Brook valley. As you cross the long arching bridge over the brook, pause to view the adjacent marsh, an area often flooded thanks to the activity of beavers. Soon after leaving the bridge, a side trail leads to a fenced off-leash area. From this junction, the Pepin Brook Trail takes you alongside the watercourse and over three bridges. As you near the third bridge with its delightful waterfall, the trail begins a steady ascent up the valley wall past large cedars and hemlocks to treetop level, where you traverse a short ridge section with the ground dropping away on either side. Finally, you pass through a meadow and then descend through forest until you reach the road, which you follow back to your start.

A boardwalk and bridge along the Pepin Brook Trail.

For a longer circuit, walk west from your parking spot and circle the sand and grass play area to join the Rock'n Horse Trail. This multi-use route heads east and then south, where it leaves the comfort of the trees to emerge on the edge of the Aldergrove Bowl, a one-time gravel pit now green with grass, trees and a picnic site. Keep right, skirting the hollow, and gradually work your way around to the east, into a treed valley and out again, eventually arriving at a viewpoint. Here, broad berry fields stretch south and east with Mount Baker and other great peaks of the Cascade Range providing the backdrop.

Resuming your walk, you turn north into the trees on an undulating trail, pass an enormous boulder deposited by a long-ago receding glacier and emerge onto a park road. Cross the road and continue west on the Rock'n Horse Trail above the marshy valley before finally descending to a junction. Go left for a quick return to your vehicle, or right, as described previously, for the Pepin Brook Trail.

SHORTER OPTION

The Pepin Brook Trail (4 km/2.5 mi), which begins at the east end of the parking lot, is an easy 1-hour loop around the wetland habitat.

GETTING THERE

Vehicle: From Highway 1 in Langley, take Exit 73 (Highway 13) and follow 264 Street south. Turn left (east) onto 8 Avenue. Continue across 272 Street to the park entrance 200 m beyond. Turn right into the park, descend into the valley, perhaps taking a few minutes to look at the information board at a pullout, then park on the far side of the brook.

DISCOVERY TRAIL/ FISHTRAP CREEK

Distance: 7.2 km (4.5 mi)
Time: 3 hours
Surface: paved
Quality: ★★★
Difficulty: ●

Season: all year
Car GPS entry: Livingstone Ave & Peardonville Rd Abbotsford, BC
Trailhead: 49°03'04" N 122°21'48" W

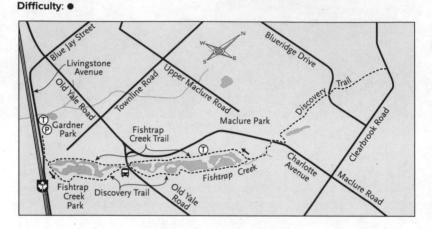

THE DISCOVERY Trail, which is nearing completion, is a 30+ km (18+ mi) all-season recreation corridor that crosses Abbotsford from Gardner Park in the west to McKay Creek in the east. This walk includes part of the trail as it passes through Fishtrap Creek Park. Over the years, the land has been inhabited by the Sumas First Nation, logged by pioneers and occupied by the Abbotsford Lumber Company. Most recently, the area has been modified to help manage stormwater and the park encircling the creek includes a paved loop that wanders around wetlands that provide habitat for wildlife and green space for human recreation.

From the east end of the parking lot, follow Discovery Trail east and over a wooden bridge to a junction at the southern tip of Fishtrap Creek Nature Park. From the junction, go right to stay on Discovery Trail, noting that you will return to this junction on the other trail, the Fishtrap Creek Trail, which traverses the west side of the creek.

Catch glimpses of the southern basin of the Fishtrap Creek wetlands on your left as you walk north on the gently undulating trail. Eventually, the trail leaves the forest temporarily at Dehavilland Drive. Turn right and walk to Mitchell Street, where you turn left to Old Yale Road. Cross Old Yale Road

Mallards are a common sight in this park.

at the pedestrian crossing and turn right to the entrance for Discovery Trail, where you re-enter Fishtrap Creek Nature Park at its northern basin. Along the trail, notice the gnawed stumps of fallen trees, sure signs of beavers at work. On the water, look for aquatic birds such as mergansers, mallards, Canada geese and great blue herons. Amongst the variety of trees, see if you can spot Sitka spruce and redwood. Allow time to pause at a bench or on a bridge to absorb the details of this natural but human-built landscape.

Eventually you leave the wetlands and encounter the T-junction with Fishtrap Creek Trail. For a short loop walk, go left to return to your vehicle on the west side of the creek. To stretch your legs with a longer walk, stay on Discovery Trail, cross Charlotte Avenue and continue to Maclure Road. Cross Maclure at the pedestrian-controlled light, then turn right to rejoin Discovery Trail as it enters the forested Fishtrap Creek area of Maclure Park.

A curving boardwalk takes you over a widening of the creek before the trail begins a gradual ascent towards Blueridge Drive. Cross at the pedestrian-controlled light and continue on Discovery Trail until you reach Clearbrook Road, your turnaround point. Retrace your steps to your starting point.

SHORTER OPTION

For a 1.5-hour circuit of 3.5 km (2.2 mi) around the Fishtrap Creek wetlands, go left at the T-junction instead of taking the Discovery Trail onward to Charlotte Avenue.

GETTING THERE

Transit: Take Central Fraser Valley Transit Bus 2 (Bluejay–Huntingdon GoLine) to Old Yale Road at Mitchell Street. Enter the park on the north side of Old Yale Road.

Vehicle: From Highway 1, take Exit 83 (Fraser Highway/Highway 1A) north and then east to Livingstone Avenue, then turn right and continue to Gardner Park. Park in the lot on the north side of Livingstone.

MATSQUI DUO

Distance each section: 14 km (8.7 mi)
Time each section: 4 hours
Surface: gravel dyke, trail
Quality: ★★★
Difficulty: ■

Season: all year; possible closures during spring freshet
Car GPS entry: Tall Rd & Riverside St Abbotsford, BC
Trailhead: 49°07'18" N.122°18'06" W

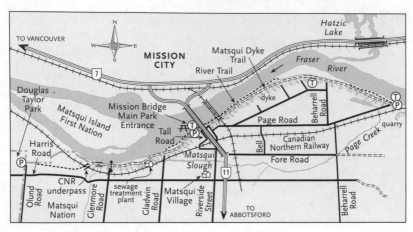

MOUNTAIN VIEWS, river watching, woodlands and farmers' fields—these are attractions along this trail between Page Road in the east and Douglas Taylor Park (Olund Trailhead) in the west. Travelling end to end makes a long return trip, though you could arrange a car shuttle for a one-way walk. However, by starting at the Mission Bridge, you may go in either direction. Begin by orienting yourself at the information boards near the Mission Bridge parking and picnic facilities for historical and trail information.

Heading east, the more picturesque of the two walks, you may either stay on the dyke or drop to the water's edge on the River Trail, which threads through tall cottonwoods that gradually mute the sounds of traffic. Just shy of your midpoint, the Fraser River makes a dogleg bend, the River Trail rejoins the dyke and you find a conveniently located bench and outhouse. Look to the hilltop across the river to see the tower of Westminster Abbey (see Walk 93) above the town of Mission. Soon, an intervening ridge to the north gradually recedes to reveal the stunning peaks of Mounts Judge Howay and Robie Reid in Golden Ears Park; the Cheam Range dominates the eastern view and Mount Baker the southern. At one point, a trail drops to the water's edge to provide you with an alternate path to your turnabout at Page Road Trailhead.

Many parts of the walk skirt horse farms and farmer's fields.

As you stroll the trails, you might reflect on how different your surroundings are today from a century ago, before the dykes were built, when the Fraser River was a major transportation artery and when footpaths provided peaceful inland routes. Heading west from Mission Bridge towards the Olund Trailhead at Douglas Taylor Park, you have an immediate choice of staying on the dyke or taking a path along the river's edge unless inundated as it usually is in late May, early June. These trails unite at Gladwin Road to skirt the J.A.M.E.S. sewage treatment plant. From Gladwin Road, where you enter the Matsqui First Nation Reserve, the trail begins with a loose gravel surface as it passes through marshland. It then becomes earthen and climbs steeply to the bench above the river, where it passes through forest and field, until it arrives at the Olund Trailhead at Douglas Taylor Park, your turnabout. Retrace your steps to your starting point.

GETTING THERE

Vehicle: From north or south of the Fraser River, make your way to Highway 11 (Abbotsford-Mission Highway) and the south end of the Mission Bridge. Travelling from the north, immediately south of the bridge, take the Riverside Street exit northbound. From the south, take the Matsqui Village exit and travel north on Riverside Street. Watch for park entrance signs and park in the lot.

WILLBAND CREEK PARK

Distance: 2.5 km (1.6 mi)
Time: 1 hour
Surface: gravel
Quality: ★★★
Difficulty: ●

Season: all year
Car GPS entry: Bateman Rd & Abbotsford-Mission Hwy Abbotsford, BC
Trailhead: 49°4'28" N 122°16'48" W

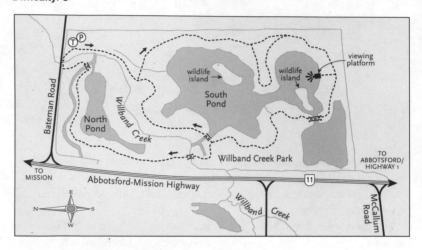

TO HELP with flood management for the Willband Creek catchment area, most of which is within Abbotsford's urban core, two large ponds and surrounding marshes in Sumas Flats hold back stormwater. As a bonus, these lands protect diverse populations of waterfowl, various species of migratory birds and other wildlife. For humans, the park offers easy year-round walking on wide, level paths and an opportunity to experience a wetland habitat and its inhabitants as they change throughout the seasons.

Begin your walk by heading south from the parking lot along the edge of Willband Creek to a junction. To take a clockwise route around the south pond, go left and at the next junction veer right onto the mini-peninsula to view the ponds and the first of two wildlife islands. Farther on at the south end of the park, a spacious viewing platform is an ideal place to watch mallards, Canada geese, American wigeons, northern shovelers and green-winged teal in migration. The water level here varies throughout the year, alternately revealing and submerging the waterfowl's favourite feeding grounds. Often a few fisherfolk are here too, looking to try their luck. On the northern horizon, you might spot the broad southwest face and summit of Mount Robie Reid and the jagged twin peaks of Mount Judge Howay.

The large south pond is home to many birds in its wetlands and on its wildlife islands.

Cross the gracefully arched bridge spanning a narrow channel, where just a trickle of water flows in the fall and it swells with seasonal floodwater in the spring. Continuing north, you find a junction where, by going left, you may extend your walk around the smaller north retention pond. The alternative completes the loop of the south pond, where a bench on a rise beside the trail beckons you to slow down, breathe deeply and absorb more of the natural ambience before returning to your transport.

GETTING THERE

Transit: Take Central Fraser Valley Transit Bus 31 (Abbotsford-Mission Connector) to Highway 11 at McCallum Road. Walk 800 m north on the highway to Bateman Road and 300 m east to park.

Vehicle: Take Highway 11 to Bateman Road. Turn east and drive 300 m to the park.

ARNOLD DYKE TRAIL

Distance: 12 km (7.5 mi)
Time: 3.5 hours
Surface: gravel dyke
Quality: ★★★
Difficulty: ■

Season: all year
Car GPS entry: Campbell Rd & Cole Rd
Abbotsford, BC
Trailhead: 49°02'47" N 122°10'59" W

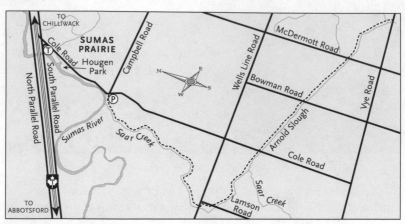

TODAY THE rich agricultural land around Abbotsford supports farms and pastures, but this area between Sumas Mountain and Vedder Mountain was once occupied by Sumas Lake. The Sumas First Nation relied on the lake and its surroundings for salmon, sturgeon, waterfowl, elk and deer and the Stó:lō maintained berry picking and root harvesting areas around the lake through selective burning. Many newcomers, however, considered the wetlands a nuisance and so, by 1924, the Sumas River was dyked and the lake was drained into the Fraser River. The Arnold Dyke Trail follows one of these raised dykes, which is used to irrigate farmland and control floods. While your walk offers a panoramic view of the Fraser Valley, you are exposed to the elements, so come prepared for wind, sun and rain.

Exit the parking lot onto the dyke and set off as it follows Saar Creek, a tributary of the Sumas River. To your left, on a clear day, the peaks of the Lucky Four Group (Foley, Welch, Stewart and Knight Peaks) are in view, and Vedder Mountain is in front of you. At the junction with Wells Line Road, jog left then right onto Lamson Road. Before you cross the bridge, go left to rejoin the dyke, which also serves for a short distance as the access road to a farmhouse and barns. At a forested area, Saar Creek turns south and the dyke follows an artificial channel known as Arnold Slough. As you continue, you

Arnold Slough, near its confluence with Saar Creek.

cross, in succession, Cole, Bowman and McDermott Roads until the end of the dyke—announced by the large white letters A R N O L D mounted on the train trestle—comes into view. Soon you arrive at your turnaround point where the dyke meets Vye Road. From here, retrace your steps to your vehicle.

And the name Arnold? South of Vye Road, between the tracks and the U.S.-Canadian border, is the largely Mennonite community of Arnold, named for the local slough and tram stop on the B.C. Electric Railway's interurban Fraser Valley Line.

SHORTER OPTION
For a walk of about 4 km (2.4 mi), retrace your steps at the junction with Wells Line Road.

GETTING THERE
Vehicle: From the west on Highway 1, take Exit 99 (South Parallel Road). From the east on Highway 1, take exit 104 (No. 3 Road) and go east, crossing the highway onto South Parallel Road. From South Parallel, turn south onto Cole Road and continue past the rest area and Hougen Park to the small parking lot at the junction with Campbell Road.

HERON NATURE RESERVE/
ROTARY TRAIL

Distance: 14 km (8.7 mi)
Time: 4 hours
Surface: gravel dyke, trail
Quality: ★★★
Difficulty: ● (Heron Nature Reserve)/
■ (Rotary Trail)

Season: all year
Car GPS entry: 5200 Sumas Prairie Rd
Chilliwack, BC
Trailhead: 49°05'46" N 122°02'44" W

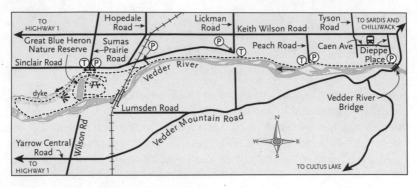

THE GREAT Blue Heron Nature Reserve is a 130 ha (325 ac) site located on undyked floodplain of the Vedder River in the territory of the Ts'elxwéyeqw Tribe, a Stó:lō First Nation. It protects restored wetland habitat required for the survival of the at-risk, non-migratory great blue herons that live here. Between March and July, the most interesting season to visit, the colony broods in more than 150 nests. During this time, the Heron Colony Loop Trail is closed and the best viewpoint is on the dyke, west of the parking area. This walk begins near the reserve and follows a gravel dyke trail upstream for 7 km (4.3 mi) along the Vedder River, which provides points of interest in all seasons. (For a shorter one-way walk, you can arrange a car shuttle.)

Walk south from the interpretive centre past the iron truss structure left by military engineers from the 1940s and '50s, cross the bridge between the north and south lagoons and continue to a T-junction where you turn left onto Rotary Trail East. The trail meanders through forest before emerging at the banks of the river atop a gravelled dyke. The many benches along the trail invite you to stop from time to time to absorb the sights and sounds of the river.

The Vedder Bridge marks a name change in the river: above, where it collects water from the North Cascades watershed and fills Chilliwack Lake

Peach Creek, east of Lickman Road, has been restored to provide more habitat for salmon to spawn.

before running through the valley, it is the Chilliwack River; below, where it crosses the floodplain and is harnessed into the Vedder Canal, it is known as the Vedder River. If you have organized two cars, this is the end of your outing; if not, this is your turnaround point for the walk back to the Nature Reserve and to your vehicle.

SHORTER OPTION
Explore only the Heron Nature Reserve loop trails (3.6 km/2.2 mi). If you are visiting between March and July, allow time at the dyke viewpoint to watch the herons in their colony. Trail information, available at the interpretive centre kiosk, provides a map of the various loops in and around the lagoons and describes highlights along the way to enrich your experience. (See chilliwackblueheron.com for more information.)

GETTING THERE
Transit (Rotary Trail): Take Chilliwack Transit System Bus 1 (Vedder) to the last stop, on Caen Avenue. Walk 900 m to trailhead: go east to Sicily Road, turn right and walk to Petawawa Road, where you turn left. At Vedder Road, turn right and walk to Rotary Trail at the Vedder Bridge.

Vehicle (Heron Nature Reserve): From the west on Highway 1, take Exit 104 (Dixon Road) and go east on No. 3 Road. Turn left on Boundary Road and then right over the bridge to Keith Wilson Road. Drive east to Sumas Prairie Road, turn right (south) and follow signs to the Great Blue Heron Nature Reserve. From the east on Highway 1, take Exit 116 (Lickman Road) south, turn west onto Keith Wilson Road, then turn south onto Sumas Prairie Road to the Nature Reserve.

Vehicle (Rotary Trail): From Highway 1, take Exit 119 (Vedder Road) south and continue through Sardis and Vedder Crossing. Turn right into the trailhead parking lot just before the Vedder Bridge.

CHILLIWACK COMMUNITY FOREST

Distance: 5 km (3.1 mi)

Time: 2 hours

Surface: trail

Elevation: 120 m (394 ft)

Quality: ★★★★

Difficulty: ■

Season: most of the year ·

Car GPS entry: 51642 Allan Rd

Chilliwack, BC

Trailhead: 49°8'56" N 121°47'31" W

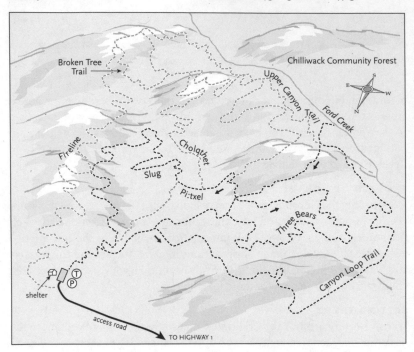

VOLUNTEERS FROM the Chilliwack Park Society, in partnership with the City of Chilliwack and the Fraser Valley Mountain Bike Association, have recently created a community nature park on 52 ha (130 ac) of forest on the lower north-facing slopes of Mount Thurston. The trail system also serves hikers, runners and mountain bikers, so always stay alert for other users—and for bears, which are often spotted in the area.

Begin at the kiosk by the parking lot, heading southwest. At the T-junction, go right on Pi:txel (Salamander) Trail and, soon thereafter, veer right and downhill on Canyon Loop Trail. Meander gently down through the open second-growth cedar canopy and its understory of sword ferns, and practise shinrin-yoku as you relax into a state of quietude. Switchbacks take you

Young devil's club emerging in spring.

deeper into the forest before the trail levels and contours towards the Ford Creek ravine. To counterbalance your recent descent you now climb uphill, accompanied by the susurration of the creek, to the junction with Upper Canyon Trail. A short side trail here allows you to take a moment to dabble in Ford Creek before continuing your route on Canyon Loop Trail.

Upon reaching the junction with Pi:txel Trail, you may go right on Pi:txel and a possible option on the more difficult Slug Trail or left on the easier Three Bears Trail. Either way adds about 1 km (0.6 mi) to your outing. On choosing to go right, you first pass a junction with Cholqthet Trail (hənq̓əmiṅəm for "dropping in, as in a bird falling out of the nest for the first time") and, being up for the challenge, go right on Slug Trail at the next junction. This trail loops uphill before returning to Pi:txel Trail, where you go right to your vehicle. Three Bears Trail, with its winding course and moderate ups and downs, is a family trail to enjoy. It returns you to Pi:txel Trail, where you go left to return to your vehicle.

GETTING THERE

Vehicle: From Highway 1 east of Chilliwack, take Exit 129 (Annis Road) to the south side of the highway. Turn onto the Highway 1 eastbound onramp and then immediately right onto Hack-Brown Road. Veer right onto Nixon Road. Turn left (east) onto Allan Road and follow it to a signed access road approximately 1 km (0.6 mi) farther on your right. Drive to the Community Forest parking lot.

EAST SECTOR LANDS

Distance: 4.5 km (2.8 mi)
Time: 2 hours
Surface: trail
Quality: ★★★★★
Difficulty: ●

Season: most of the year, except during spring flood
Car GPS entry: McPherson Rd & McCombs Dr Kent, BC
Trailhead: 49°17'05" N 121°46'39" W

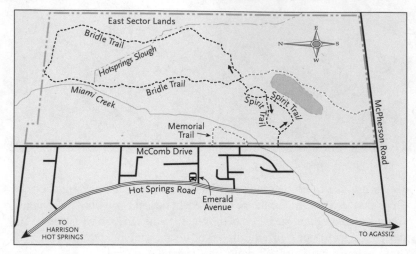

DESPITE THEIR rather mundane name, the East Sector Lands offer a diverse landscape of mixed coniferous and deciduous forest and wetlands that enclose the Miami Slough in the territory of the Sts'ailes, a Coast Salish First Nation. Although the paths are undeveloped and rough in places, ceramic masks by Ernie Eaves, a local artist, are mounted on many trees along the Spirit Trail and promise an uplifting experience!

From the parking area, you begin on the Spirit Trail where, as you walk, you may spot some of the dozens of faces amongst the trees. Stay right at both forks (these are loop trails and you will walk the other side on your return). A boardwalk, which you cross, marks the transition from the Spirit Trail to the Bridal Trail.

At the next junction, go right to head towards the eastern boundary, where the floodplain rises abruptly to forested mountainside. At this point, the trail turns north and winds past small verdant ponds on either side—sections of the Miami Slough—and through drier glades of Douglas-fir and hemlock. Swinging west, the track becomes enclosed, as in a tunnel, by vine maple and alder. Later, as the trail heads south, you travel parallel to the Miami Creek

Ceramic masks, by artist Ernie Eaves, keep watch over walkers on the Spirit Trail.

through groves of second-growth cedar and nurse stumps, remains of the ancient forest.

Cross the boardwalk where you began the Bridle Trail and then go right to find a bench and, amongst the surrounding trees, a gallery of faces, serene and unconcerned by your presence. Complete your outing by staying right to complete the Spirit Trail loop and return to your vehicle.

GETTING THERE

Vehicle: From Highway 1 east of Chilliwack, take Exit 135 (Highway 9, Agassiz/ Harrison Hot Springs) and make your way north towards Harrison Hot Springs. As you approach the town on Highway 9 (Hot Springs Road), turn right onto McPherson Road and left onto McCombs Drive. Look for the parking lot on your right.

HICKS LAKE/SASQUATCH PARK

Distance: 6.5 km (4 mi)
Time: 2.5 hours
Surface: gravel road, trail
Quality: ★★★★
Difficulty: ●

Season: most of the year
Car GPS entry: Rockwell Dr & Lillooet Rd
Harrison Hot Springs, BC
Trailhead: 49°20'58" N 121°42'18" W

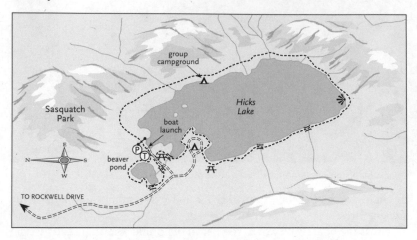

POPULAR WITH campers and fisherfolk, Sasquatch Provincial Park also provides a fine outing for walkers around one of its lakes. Keep an eye out for the legendary Bigfoot after which the park is named, or extend the lake circuit by adding a loop around Beaver Pond to look for beavers and their lodges.

Begin your outing on the road behind a locked gate where you find the Hicks Lake Trail sign, a few steps past the boat-launching ramp. Once on your way, pass the entrance to the group campground after which the road continues as a pleasant trail with the usual suspects: cottonwood, hemlock and cedar intermixed with sword ferns and devil's club on either side.

As your route bends to the west, the trail descends to lake level and, just past a defunct outhouse, a short detour to the lakeside brings you to an attractive sandy beach with a view of the lake and surrounding hills. Resuming your walk, you ascend and soon come to a junction where you leave the road and take the right fork on a usable woodland footpath that heads north along the west side of the lake, with creeks and gullies bridged by sturdy new boardwalks. Along the way, notice enormous stumps, the remains of an ancient forest. The trail emerges from the forest at a small bay with sandy beach and picnic tables and where, in May or June, you may see rather tame Canada

Hicks Lake from the sandy beach at its south end.

geese and their goslings as they forage on the grass. Your route continues around a peninsula between campsites and shore, mainly in trees, but with viewpoints here and there. Finally, you come to another open bay, the lake outlet and its fish ladder a little beyond. A metal bridge takes you over the creek, through a picnic area and back to original approach road.

To extend your outing, find your way to the Beaver Pond Loop Trail, going clockwise around it to save the lodge-viewing platform until the end.

GETTING THERE

Vehicle: From Highway 1 east of Chilliwack, take Exit 135 (Highway 9, Agassiz/Harrison Hot Springs) and make your way north towards Harrison Hot Springs. As you approach the town on Highway 9 (Hot Springs Road), follow the park signs onto Lillooet Road and turn north along the east side of Harrison Lake on Rockwell Drive for approximately 6 km (3.7 mi) to a marked right turn onto a gravel road. At a T-junction, you turn right for Hicks Lake and soon a left takes you to the boat launch and parking.

WEBSITES

BUS AND SKYTRAIN INFORMATION
www.translink.ca
www.bctransit.com/central-fraser-valley/home
www.bctransit.com/chilliwack/home
www.bctransit.com/squamish/home
www.parkbus.ca

NATURAL HISTORY
www.bcnature.ca
www.natureguidesbc.com

REGIONAL PARKS
www.env.gov.bc.ca/bcparks
www.fvrd.ca (see Parks & Recreation > Parks)
www.metrovancouver.org (Services > Regional Parks, Greenways & Reserves)

WALKING GROUPS
www.meetup.com
www.outsetters.org
www.surreytrekkers.com
Search online for groups in your area, including through community centres.

TRAIL INFORMATION
www.clubtread.com
www.vancouvertrails.com
thegreattrail.ca
Search also for "greenways" in your area.

REGIONAL LINKS

SQUAMISH
squamish.ca/recreation/nature-and-outdoors/trails/

WEST VANCOUVER
www.westvancouver.ca/parks-recreation

CITY OF NORTH VANCOUVER
www.cnv.org/parks-recreation-and-culture/parks-and-greenways

DISTRICT OF NORTH VANCOUVER
www.dnv.org/recreation-and-leisure

LOWER SEYMOUR CONSERVATION RESERVE TRAILS MAP
www.metrovancouver.org/services/parks/parks-greenways-reserves/
lower-seymour-conservation-reserve

CITY OF VANCOUVER
vancouver.ca/parks-recreation-culture/parks-and-recreation

RICHMOND
www.richmond.ca/parks/overview.htm

DELTA
www.delta.ca/parks-recreation/parks-trails/overview

SURREY
www.surrey.ca (Home > Culture & Recreation > Parks)

BURNABY
www.burnaby.ca (Home > Things To Do > Explore Outdoors)

NEW WESTMINSTER
www.newwestpcr.ca (Home > Parks and Recreation > Parks)

COQUITLAM
www.coquitlam.ca (Home > Recreation Parks & Culture > Parks & Trails)

PORT COQUITLAM
www.portcoquitlam.ca (Home > Recreation > Parks, Sports Fields & Trails)

PORT MOODY
www.portmoody.ca (Home > Parks and Recreation > Parks > Trails & Paths)

PITT MEADOWS
www.pittmeadows.ca

MAPLE RIDGE
www.mapleridge.ca (Home > Your Government > Departments >
Parks, Recreation & Culture > Parks & Facilities > Parks & Trails)

DISTRICT OF MISSION
www.mission.ca (Discover > Parks & Trails)

CITY OF LANGLEY
city.langley.bc.ca (Parks & Recreation)

TOWNSHIP OF LANGLEY
www.tol.ca/recreation-culture/trails-cycling-equestrian-pedestrian/

ABBOTSFORD
www.abbotsford.ca/leisure/parks/trails.htm

CHILLIWACK
www.chilliwack.com (Parks, Recreation & Culture > Parks & Trails)

HARRISON
www.tourismharrison.com

ACKNOWLEDGEMENTS

WE ARE indebted to the late David and Mary Macaree for the enormous amount of enthusiasm and work they put into exploring Lower Mainland trails for the first six editions of this guide. Their legacy continues to inspire others who have assisted with the revision of the current edition, for whose help we are most grateful. Most notably, Amanda, Ellen and Mary Halliday, who walked several of the walks retained from the seventh edition. As well, the British Columbia Mountaineering Club (BCMC), whose involvement began with the first edition of this book, has continued its valued support. Finally, a special thank you to our editor, Lucy Kenward.

INDEX

ABOUT THE BCMC

THE BRITISH Columbia Mountaineering Club is a group of like-minded individuals who participate in outdoor activities. The club was established in 1907 and currently has more than 800 members. The club organizes mountaineering, rock-climbing and backcountry skiing trips throughout the year. The BCMC holds monthly socials, offers courses to members and represents the interests of mountaineers and backcountry skiers in British Columbia. The club dedicates royalties received from sales of this book to conservation efforts. See bcmc.ca for more information.